Fostering Unaccompanied Asylum-Seeking Young People

Fostering Unaccompanied Asylum-Seeking Young People
Creating a family life across a 'world of difference'

Jim Wade, Ala Sirriyeh,
Ravi Kohli and
John Simmonds

University of
Bedfordshire

LOTTERY FUNDED

ADOPTION
& FOSTERING

Published by British Association
for Adoption & Fostering
(BAAF)
Saffron House
3rd Floor, 6–10 Kirby Street
London EC1N 8TS
www.baaf.org.uk

Charity registration 275689 (England and Wales)
and SC039337 (Scotland)

British Library Cataloguing in Publication Data
A catalogue record for this book is available
from the British Library

ISBN 978 1 907585 55 5

Editorial project management by Shaila Shah,
BAAF Publications
Designed by Helen Joubert Associates
Typeset by Avon DataSet Ltd, Bidford on Avon
Printed in Great Britain by T J International
Trade distribution by Turnaround Publisher Services,
Unit 3, Olympia Trading Estate, Coburg Road,
London N22 6TZ

BAAF is the leading UK-wide membership
organisation for all those concerned with
adoption, fostering and child care issues.

Contents

List of tables

Acknowledgements

All research projects rely upon teamwork and a great many people have helped to make this study possible. First, we would like to thank the Big Lottery Fund which sponsored the study and whose personnel provided helpful advice and support throughout.

The study could not have taken place without the commitment, energy and support of managers, social workers and administrators working within our four participating local authorities. Their co-operation was grounded in a strong desire to see services for unaccompanied asylum-seeking young people strengthened and, in particular, to understand how their experiences of fostering could be improved. For this, we thank them. They responded to our persistent requests for information and made time to talk to us with patience and good humour. Thanks also to the Refugee Council's Children's Team for helping to organise our focus group discussions with young people.

Special thanks go to the members of our advisory group who provided helpful advice, support and encouragement throughout the life of the project and provided insightful comments on earlier drafts of these chapters. Many thanks then go to Mohammed Bashir, Elaine Chase, Judith Dennis, Paul Dennis, Karen Goodman, Tracey Maegusuku-Hewitt, Judy Walsh and Andrea Warman.

We would also like to recognise the important role played by members of our research team. Jennifer Cousins and Margaret Grant, both of BAAF, undertook many of the research interviews with young people and their foster carers and did so with a very high level of expertise and sensitivity. Our thanks also go to Danielle Sawyer (BAAF) and Dawn Rowley (SPRU) who provided us with excellent administrative and editorial support throughout the project. This book would not have attained the high standard it has without the expert, determined and focussed eye of Shaila Shah, BAAF's Director of Publications.

Most of all we are indebted to the foster carers and young people who participated in our study. Without their willingness to complete questionnaires and to spend time talking to us openly about their experiences, this book could not have been written. We hope we have been able to represent their views and experiences adequately and that their commitment to help us will, in some small way at least, contribute to improvement of the services that matter to them.

Notes about the authors

Jim Wade is a qualified social worker with a background in youth and community work and social work with teenagers. He is a Senior Research Fellow in the Social Policy Research Unit, University of York. For more than 20 years he has researched and published widely in the area of social work and related services for vulnerable groups of children and young people, including looked after children, care leavers, young runaways and asylum-seeking and refugee children. His recent research interests have centred on the use of special guardianship for children, the reunification of maltreated children and the fostering experiences of unaccompanied asylum-seeking children.

Dr Ala Sirriyeh is a Lecturer in Sociology in the School of Social and International Studies at the University of Bradford. She was previously a Research Fellow in the Social Policy Research Unit, University of York. Her research interests centre on migration, asylum, gender and young people. She completed her PhD in 2010 at the University of Leeds. In this she explored young refugee women's narratives of home in the context of their migration to the UK and transitions to adulthood. A book, titled *Inhabiting Borders, Routes Home*, which is based on this study, is forthcoming in 2013.

Ravi KS Kohli is Professor of Child Welfare at the University of Bedfordshire. He qualified as a social worker in 1984. He has a longstanding interest in the lives of children seeking asylum, and the ways in which they are assisted in finding a "home" after forced migration. He is the author of *Social Work with Unaccompanied Asylum-Seeking Children*, and *Working with Unaccompanied Asylum-Seeking Children: Issues for policy and practice*, both published by Palgrave Macmillan. Ravi's own journey as a migrant continues to inform his teaching, writing and research.

Dr John Simmonds is Director of Policy, Research and Development at the British Association for Adoption and Fostering. Before coming to BAAF, he was head of the social work programmes at Goldsmiths College, University of London. He is a qualified social worker and has substantial experience in child protection, family placement and residential care settings. He has published widely, including *The Role of Special Guardianship: Best practice in permanency planning for children*, and *The Child Placement Handbook*, co-edited with Gillian Schofield, both published by BAAF.

1 Introduction

Over many generations, the population of forced migrants has included children and young people who have been forced to leave their homelands by themselves to seek asylum in countries distant from their own families and communities. In earlier historical periods, some groups of children were able to find sanctuary from wars and conflicts in quite organised ways, as part of major resettlement initiatives. These groups have included the Basque and Kindertransport children during the 1930s, children displaced by wars in Vietnam, Cambodia and Korea and, in more recent decades, smaller groups of children from Africa, Eastern Europe and Asia (Ressler *et al*, 1988; Luster *et al*, 2009). This is less often the case today.

Most unaccompanied young people who now reach the United Kingdom, tend to do so by taking more individualised and uncertain pathways. Their experiences are diverse. Initial flight may occur very quickly, in response to crises that leave little time for planning, while others may have lived for some time in internal or external exile before making their final journey to the UK. Some arrive by plane, while others undertake long and arduous journeys by road; journeys that may leave them open to further exploitation during transit. The exercise of choice in relation to final destination may also be limited, with control frequently resting in the hands of agents who organise their transit arrangements (Crawley, 2010).

Irrespective of how and why these young people come to the UK, they share common experiences of transition that are complex and multi-layered. First, enforced migration uproots young people from everything that has been familiar and places them in a strange social landscape, lacking clear signposts, and often without the language skills to be able to communicate with new people they meet. Second, they transition from family rootedness (for most) to being alone in this new world and carrying a burden of worries about what may have befallen members of their families at home and/or about why they, as an individual, were selected to travel. Third, they transition from having a status as citizens in their home countries to seeking new rights of citizenship and (for many young people) from dislocation (in countries often marked by war, conflict or civic breakdown) to a new structured location as young people who will be placed in the care of strangers. Finally, alongside these changes, young people are also negotiating the well-travelled pathway from childhood to emerging adulthood, but in a context where the future for them in the UK is always uncertain. The extent to which most young people are able to meet these challenges and lead purposeful lives speaks well of their resilience and fortitude.

Once young people arrive in the UK, they are confronted by a bewildering array of professionals, from immigration officials, solicitors and social workers through to those foster carers, residential social workers or support workers who will endeavour to meet their everyday needs. It is understandable that anxiety and confusion should predominate in these early encounters, which are generally brokered by interpreters, and in which young people attempt to weigh the aspects of their lives and histories that can be safely shared with authority figures without jeopardising the safety of their families or their asylum claim. The primary needs of young people at this stage are for resettlement. Resettlement is a complex process that involves meeting a range of practical, psychosocial and cultural needs. These include finding a safe and supportive place to live; gaining access to education; being able to retain continuity with past relationships, customs and cultures whilst simultaneously finding opportunities to make new ones; and being able to move forward from troubling experiences to find new purpose in the routines and activities of everyday life (Wade *et al*, 2005; Kohli, 2007).

This book describes the experiences of a sample of unaccompanied young people as they attempt to take these transitional steps. Its primary focus is on a sub-section of the population; those who experience foster care. It charts the fostering experiences of these young people and examines how, from uncertain beginnings, the often remarkable relationships that are formed between young people, their foster carers and social workers can help them to negotiate the layers of transition and to discover pathways towards successful resettlement. In doing so, we hope that the findings and the messages from this study will have considerable relevance to the wider fostering experience.

Of course, not all unaccompanied young people gain access to foster care. Some move straight to supported or independent accommodation at the point of referral to local authorities. We also therefore endeavour to situate foster care in the context of all the placements that are available to local authorities and examine how care and placement pathways for unaccompanied young people have been changing in recent years.

Definition and numbers

An unaccompanied asylum-seeking child, according to the United Kingdom Border Agency (UKBA), is someone below the age of 18 years (or who appears to be so if proof is not available) who is claiming asylum in their own right and who has no adult relative or guardian in this country to care for them (Home Office, 2002). This definition is important, since meeting these criteria provides the basis for local authorities to claim for the costs of providing care and support through the Home Office Special Grant.

The numbers of unaccompanied children and young people seeking asylum in the UK vary from year to year, ranging from a high point of 6,200 in 2002 to 4,285 in 2008 and 3,175 in 2009, the majority (72% in 2009) being aged 14-17 years (Home Office, 2010). This represents a tiny fraction of the seven or more million forcibly displaced minors identified at the end of 2008 across the world, the vast majority of whom sought sanctuary in developing countries (UNHCR, 2009). Very few young people are granted refugee status in the UK (just 11% in 2009) and the majority (72% in 2009) are granted discretionary leave to remain for three years or until they reach 17.5 years of age (whichever arrives soonest) or receive an outright refusal (17%). After this they may apply to extend this leave or appeal a negative decision.

Government statistics on children looked after by local authorities in England show a slight increase in the number of unaccompanied young people in their care over recent years, from 2,200 in 2001/2 to 3,880 in 2008/9, although the numbers fell again quite sharply in 2010/11 to 2,680. Most likely this fall reflects the decline in the overall number of asylum applications. Most of these young people are male (89 per cent in 2010/11) and are located in London or the South East of England. Reflecting this regional pattern, the data suggest that unaccompanied young people currently constitute around four per cent of the 65,000 young people in public care nationally, but around 10 per cent of young people looked after in the London area.

The legislative context

Where a young person claims to be a minor but UKBA does not accept them as such, they are treated as an adult asylum seeker until evidence is produced to substantiate their claimed age. Age disputes are not uncommon. Official figures point to 1,130 cases in 2009 alone, and the accuracy of procedures for assessing age are a matter of considerable concern to local authority practitioners and non-governmental organisations (Crawley, 2007). Age also affects local authority funding for services, since levels of payment under the Special Grant are significantly lower for those aged 16 or 17 when first applying for asylum – an age group that accounts for nearly one half of all asylum applications made by unaccompanied minors (45 per cent in 2009). Earlier studies identified this distinction as an influential driver of differentiated services for unaccompanied young people, with local authorities having made extensive use of the community based accommodation (usually private sector shared housing) for older teenagers in the community, while reserving placements in more highly supported settings, such as foster or residential care, for those who were younger or otherwise considered more vulnerable (Audit Commission, 2000; Stone, 2000; Stanley, 2001; Wade *et al*, 2005). Chapter 3 considers the extent to which these placement patterns may have changed in recent years.

Once an unaccompanied asylum-seeking young person's age has

been accepted, they have the same rights and entitlements to welfare services as other citizen children. Lacking the presence of their parents or customary caregivers, they should be treated by local authority children's services as children "in need" under the provisions of the Children Act 1989, receive a full assessment of their needs and, unless clear contrary evidence is revealed at that time, should be accommodated and looked after by the local authority under these provisions (Department of Health, 2003).

Being granted the status of a looked after child not only gives young people the protection of statutory regulations while they are looked after, but also access to the provisions of the Children (Leaving Care) Act 2000 (CLCA 2000) to assist them through transition to adulthood. These developments, reinforced by government guidance and emerging case law, have been important in providing a strengthened regulatory framework for the support of unaccompanied young people. Whereas many (mainly older) young people in the past had lacked this protection and were supported in the community as children "in need" under Section 17 of the Children Act 1989, this no longer appears to be the case.

Local authorities have clear duties in relation to looked after children that do not apply to those supported in the community. These include, amongst other things, requirements for child care planning and review, allocated social work support and contact, and for promoting the health, education and training of young people. Furthermore, those looked after are also eligible to receive leaving care services up to the age of 25 (if they continue in education or training). The CLCA 2000 includes duties to prepare young people for adult life, to assess and meet their needs, to provide pathway plans and ensure ongoing support from personal advisors (Department of Health, 2001). Where a young person's asylum application is undecided as they approach the age of majority, these services may continue until all asylum appeal rights have been exhausted and they are classified as being "unlawfully present in the UK" under Schedule 3 of the Nationality, Immigration and Asylum Act 2002. Even at this point local authorities need to be mindful about whether a withdrawal of services would breach a young person's rights under the European Convention on Human Rights (Dorling, 2009).

The research context

It is only in recent years that studies have emerged that have begun to detail the lives and circumstances of unaccompanied asylum-seeking children in the UK, to describe their resettlement experiences and to explore how social workers, foster carers and others assist their efforts to refashion their lives in a new and unfamiliar world (Mitchell, 2003). The evidence base to support work with this group of young people has therefore been relatively weak.

Research material on unaccompanied young people has generally combined policy reports, service inspections and relatively small-scale research studies. Reports on refugee and asylum-seeking children, mainly emanating from non-governmental organisations, have often been policy focused and quite prescriptive, concerned with interpreting domestic and international legislation and guidance and outlining principles of good practice based on these (see, for example, Rutter, 2003; Save the Children, 2003; Separated Children in Europe Programme, 2004). This work has been helpful in benchmarking positive practice and in reinforcing rights and entitlements, but has not helped us to understand very much about young people's experiences, how services are provided in practice, how and why they vary as they do, and about the characteristics of support that appear most helpful to young people. A number of mostly small-scale research studies have emerged over the years that have tended to focus on different aspects of the refugee experience, including: their educational needs and experiences (Rutter and Jones, 1998; Candappa, 2000); issues associated with the physical, mental and emotional well-being and social adjustment of refugee children (Blackwell, 1997; Ahearn, 2000; Kohli and Mather, 2003; Bean *et al*, 2007b; Chase *et al*, 2008; Hodes *et al*, 2008); on different aspects of young people's support needs throughout the asylum process (Ayotte, 1999; Russell, 1999; Crawley, 2004, 2007) and on models of social work practice with unaccompanied minors (Wade *et al*, 2005; Kohli, 2007). This body of research has provided a deeper understanding of the experiences of refugee children, has alerted us to the diversity that exists amongst unaccompanied young people, the complexity of the transitions that are made by them, and to the range of issues that service providers need to take account of when planning and delivering support services.

Although transitions and adaptations are central features of the refugee experience, there have been relatively few studies in the international literature that have connected young people's ordinary lives in their homelands to their experiences of flight and resettlement (Gifford et al, 2007). Most UK research has started at the point of young people's arrival in the UK and may, in consequence, tend to overemphasise the rupture of separation and underestimate the continuities that may exist for young people between the past, present and future (Kohli and Connolly, 2009). Where young people have been asked to reflect back on their lives, positive memories of home and family life often (though not always) coexist with those of fractured or decaying civic structures or of sudden dangers arising from ongoing wars and conflicts (Hopkins and Hill, 2008). Thomas and colleagues' (2004) study of the pre-flight experiences of 100 unaccompanied young people in London found that actual or perceived threats to themselves or their families figured prominently amongst their reasons for flight. The vast majority of young people had experienced violence (86) or had witnessed the death of family members (13), suffered sexual violence (32) or lived in hiding (16). The high number of trauma events here is consistent with findings from other studies and the potential effects of these, combined with post-settlement difficulties, as risk factors for anxiety and depression has been highlighted in the literature (Bean et al, 2007a; Hodes et al, 2008). However, the same literature also gives emphasis to the resilience of many unaccompanied young people when confronting these adversities and it is with this combination of confusion, difficulty and capability that young people first approach children's services for help (Kohli and Mather, 2003; Wade et al, 2005).

Not enough is yet known about the forms of care and protection that work best for unaccompanied young people who seek asylum in industrialised societies (Tolfree, 2004). In a UK context, there is also a lack of research evidence about how these young people get on while they are looked after by local authorities or about how their experiences compare to those of other looked after children. Reports from social workers tend to suggest that, despite the adverse events encountered by these young people, many are able to approach the challenges of resettlement with a strong sense of purpose, are quite resilient and resourceful and appear determined to make the most of the personal and educational opportunities available to them (Kohli, 2007; Chase *et al*, 2008).

There is some evidence from research on looked after children and young people that tends to support this perspective and which suggests that unaccompanied young people may fare relatively well in the care system. Sinclair and colleagues' (2007) study of the 7,399 children in the English care system found evidence that, in comparison to other looked after children, unaccompanied young people tended to experience greater placement stability and, according to social workers, were more likely to do well at school and manifest fewer emotional and behavioural problems. This is consistent with findings from a small study of 106 young people leaving care (Dixon *et al*, 2006). Although small in number, unaccompanied young people were less likely than others to have displayed troublesome behaviours while looked after, were more likely to be participating in education after leaving care and were less likely to commit offences. More recent research tends to confirm these findings and also provides evidence of higher levels of participation in higher education (Brownlees and Finch, 2010). However, there is a need to understand more about the particular contexts that may foster success for unaccompanied young people and about the ways in which foster carers together with other professionals can help young people to harness and develop their talents.

An exploration of foster care for unaccompanied young people is therefore timely. There is now a growing evidence base to support fostering policy and practice for the wider population of looked after young people. Recent studies have explored factors associated with the recruitment, retention and training of foster carers, successful placement making, contact with birth families and the range of factors that help foster placements to work well for children (Quinton *et al*, 1998; Cleaver, 2000; Beek and Schofield, 2004; Farmer *et al*, 2004; Sinclair *et al*, 2004a; Sinclair *et al*, 2004b; Wilson *et al*, 2004; Biehal *et al*, 2010). However, the needs and experiences of unaccompanied children and young people have been largely absent from this mainstream body of work.

Foster carers will need both generic fostering and specialist skills to help young people to settle, adjust to new environments, develop new attachments, resume a pattern of education, to monitor and support their claims for asylum and to help them acquire the skills they will need for adulthood, whether that be in the UK or in their countries of origin. In addition to these practical tasks, there is a need to help young people to make sense of and reconnect the threads of their past and present lives that have been disrupted by migration. This may involve promoting continuities with the past (through food, language, culture and religion), by listening to young people's stories about the past as they seek to heal emotional wounds, by promoting new connections with family members (where these exist), with their communities of origin and through involvement in mainstream youth and leisure activities. This is obviously challenging work that takes foster carers into territories beyond those normally experienced in foster care. As such, caring for unaccompanied young people incorporates humanitarian activity in the practical domains of life, therapeutic care to address psychosocial needs and reliable companionship as young people reorient their lives (see Kohli, 2007). On balance, existing evidence, though very limited, suggests that good foster placements try to address children's needs at these levels (Hek, 2007). However, our knowledge of how this is done is at best partial.

From a research perspective, we also only have a limited understanding of what it is that unaccompanied young people want from foster care. International research informs us that that children and young people may come with different culturally specific notions of what fostering means and may worry about being exploited (Tolfree, 2004). Where studies have sought out the views of young people, their responses are not dissimilar to those of looked after citizen children – a need to feel safe, secure and included within the family; to have their experiences, origins, cultural and religious needs respected; and to be listened to and supported in ways that meet their needs (Sinclair, 2005; Hek, 2007; Chase *et al*, 2008). Young people's perceptions of placement are also likely to be influenced by their socio-economic backgrounds, their past experiences of family life and by their determination to prioritise English language acquisition over other considerations (Hek, 2007).

It is in all of these areas that this study seeks to make a substantial contribution and, in doing so, provide a range of messages to support fostering policies and practices with this group of young people. The chapters that follow will explore a number of important and inter-related themes and issues, including:

- young people's views of foster care and their perspectives on the issues that living with foster families raise for them;
- their progress, both within and outside the placement, and how their foster families help them to be successful;
- how foster carers come to foster unaccompanied young people and how their past experiences, training and support influence their fostering role;
- the specific features of the fostering task and how these intersect with what we know about fostering more generally;
- finally, the key challenges for local authorities that affect placement-making and provision of the support and resources necessary for the successful resettlement of young people.

However, before we consider these findings, we first need to describe how the study was conducted and this forms the substance of our next chapter.

2   Study design and methods

Local authorities place the majority of looked after children in foster care. This has also been the case for younger asylum-seeking and refugee children (those aged below 16 at referral). In recent years, as we have seen, there has been a substantial increase in research evidence to support fostering practice and a stream of research has explored factors associated with the recruitment, retention and training of foster carers, the making of successful placements, contact with birth families and the range of factors that help foster placements work well for children and young people in general (see Sinclair, 2005 for an overview of this research). Hitherto, however, there has been no UK research that has focused on the specific fostering needs and experiences of unaccompanied young people and their foster carers. This study attempts to redress this imbalance.

Research aims

The study focused on a sample of unaccompanied asylum-seeking and refugee young people and their foster carers. It had a number of specific aims:

- to describe the fostering experiences of the young people and their foster carers
- to identify specific features of the fostering task, taking account of the broad resettlement needs of children and young people
- to assess the support provided to young people and issues arising from the preparation, training and support of foster carers
- to identify factors that facilitated or constrained the range of placement choices available, how placements were made and the support that was provided to placements.

The research study represented a first phase of the overall project. Once these findings became known, Phase 2 involved the preparation of best practice guidance in an attempt to further the development of fostering policy and practice with this group of children and young people. In these respects, the project proposed to fill current gaps in mainstream fostering research – a body of research that has been largely silent on the specific needs and experiences of children and young people who have settled in the UK as a result of forced migration and who form a sizeable minority of the looked after population in some local authorities.

Research design

The study took place in four local authority areas in England chosen to provide diversity by region and type of area. The areas included a county, a London borough, a metropolitan borough and a city. They were also geographically spread, ranging from London and the "home" counties to the north of England. Finally, each authority was responsible for different numbers of unaccompanied asylum-seeking and refugee young people. Although we cannot claim that the findings presented in this study provide a nationally representative picture of fostering services for unaccompanied minors, they are based on a reasonably good cross-section of young people referred to local authorities.

The project adopted a descriptive analytic design and incorporated a number of discrete phases:

- **A census study** drew on local authority information systems to provide a basic profile of all 2,113 unaccompanied young people identified as being supported by these local authorities on 31 March 2009, including those supported as care leavers, and a description of all placements that were being used to accommodate them.
- **A postal survey** of 133 foster carers who were providing a placement to an unaccompanied child on 31 December 2009 to gather information on:
  - the history and progress of this index child
  - the type of support provided to the child and the placement
  - the characteristics and fostering experience of carers

   – carers' perceptions of the fostering task and of the preparation, training and support they had received during their fostering careers.

- **Semi-structured interviews** with 23 foster carers and 21 young people in their care to provide a detailed understanding of histories, experiences and support arrangements. These were supplemented by three focus-group discussions with older unaccompanied young people who had left care.
- **A policy and practice study** to provide an understanding of the policy, practice and resource contexts that underpinned fostering services for unaccompanied young people. This included document analysis, four focus groups with social workers and telephone interviews with asylum team managers.

Sampling

The census and survey phases of the study were conducted anonymously, using only the child identifier codes held by the local authorities. As we will see below, this may have had implications for survey response rates, since all materials designed to promote participation had to be routed through the relevant social work teams or their administrators. No direct approach to foster carers could be made by members of the research team.

Census sample

The census study was intended to capture information on all unaccompanied young people being supported by these local authorities on 31 March 2009, whether as looked after children, as children in need or as care leavers. This proved not to be possible, at least within the timescale of the study. In particular, two areas were unable to provide any information for care leavers aged 18 or over and information on the types of placement being used was patchy. Further discussion of these issues is provided in Chapter 3.

The final sample achieved is presented in Table 2.1. While a couple of our local authorities were supporting large numbers of unaccompanied young people, the populations in other areas were smaller. For reasons suggested above, however, this table almost certainly under-estimates the total population in these areas. Returns from Areas 1 and 4 included all young people looked after (up to age 18 or beyond) and all those supported under s23 of the Children (Leaving Care) Act 2000 (up to age 24). Area 2 was only able to provide information for those below the age of 18 and Area 3 only included information on 13 young people aged 18 or over.

Table 2.1
Numbers of young people in the census sample by local authority

Local authority	Number
Area 1	842
Area 2	61
Area 3	176
Area 4	1,034
Total	**2,113**

Returns would vary in any case according to the size and location of these local authorities. An unaccompanied asylum-seeking child will become the responsibility of the local authority in which s/he first arrives in the UK or otherwise first comes to the attention of agencies as being in need of support. Three of the local authorities were therefore supporting larger populations due (at least in part) to the presence of a port of entry (Area 1) or of UK Border Agency public enquiry centres (Areas 3 and 4). For young people who first reported to these offices, therefore, this represented an important referral route to local children's social care services. Only our northern authority (Area 2) had none of these characteristics and was therefore supporting a relatively small population of unaccompanied young people.

Survey sample and response rates

The survey focused on foster care. The sample was drawn from all foster carers who were identified as caring for an unaccompanied child or young person on 31 December 2009. A list of these carers (and their social workers) was provided by administrative teams in each local authority. A total of 402 carers were initially identified (see Table 2.2). However, there were some inaccuracies in these data, including duplicate entries, young people who were no longer resident on census day and foster carers who were no longer working for the fostering agency concerned. Once these issues were resolved, questionnaires were sent to all remaining foster carers in Areas 1, 2 and 3. Area 4 had identified a larger number of foster carers. Our original objective was to survey 130–150 foster carers. We therefore randomly selected two-thirds of the carers in Area 4 for inclusion, taking account of the sex of young people. The number of unaccompanied girls and young women included in the sample was boosted by selecting all foster carers looking after females. Males are known to greatly outweigh females in populations of unaccompanied minors and we wanted to reduce the risk of achieving an all-male sample.

Table 2.2
Survey sample frame and final sample achieved by local authority (numbers)

	Foster carers identified by local authorities	Foster carers approached	Final sample
Area 1	92	90	39
Area 2	6	5	1
Area 3	76	71	40
Area 4	228	150	53
Total	**402**	**316**	**133**

As Table 2.2 shows, questionnaires were completed and returned by

133 foster carers, making an overall survey response rate of 42 per cent. Unfortunately, it has not been possible for us to analyse the effects of non-participation by foster carers on the nature of the final sample, even though it would be helpful to know whether those who did not participate shared certain characteristics or experiences. The initial information provided by local authorities was only sufficient to enable us to identify a survey sample frame. Since non-response had to be understood as a signal that consent may not have been provided, it would have been unethical to go back to social workers to seek additional information about non-respondents.

The survey response rate has introduced some bias into the survey sample when compared to (a) our census sample and (b) government statistics on unaccompanied minors looked after by local authorities. The information upon which comparisons can be made is very basic (age, sex, countries of origin). Our census sample very closely mirrored the national data with respect to age and sex.[1] However, there was some variance between the census and survey samples in these respects and in relation to countries of origin. The survey sample was slightly younger (37% under 16 compared to 32%), contained a higher proportion of males (93% compared to 88%) and contained more young people who had originated from Afghanistan (69% compared to 49%).

In addition, country of origin proved to have some significant effects on the progress of young people in the survey sample. Although the numbers of young people arriving from countries other than Afghanistan were relatively small, young people from Afghanistan were found to be faring worse in relation to one of our key "overall progress" measures in the survey. In comparison to young people from other regions (Africa or "other"), they were less likely to be perceived by foster carers as making "good" progress in key domains

---

1 The census and national snapshots of looked after unaccompanied minors pertain to 31 March 2009. There was very little difference with respect to age (32% compared to 33% were aged under 16) or sex (88% and 87% respectively were male). The government does not release data on countries of origin. Statistical First Release data available: http://www.education.gov.uk/rsgateway/DB/SFR/s000878/index.shtml

of their lives (education, emotional and behavioural development, emotional ties and self-confidence) than were young people from any other region.[2] These findings are considered further in Chapter 10.

It is important to be mindful of these differences when considering the overall findings from the study. In general the findings are optimistic. It is therefore likely that the over-representation of young people from Afghanistan would, if anything, mean that the findings tend to over-emphasise the resettlement difficulties of unaccompanied minors and the challenges of caring for them. Had the sample drawn more heavily on young people from other countries, therefore, the findings may have been still more optimistic. We also tried to compensate for this over-representation by ensuring (as best we could) that young people in the interview sample originated from a range of countries.

Interview sample

A number of case studies were undertaken to provide a depth understanding of the experiences of young people and their foster carers. The sample was drawn from the larger survey sample and selected according to certain criteria. We hoped to obtain roughly equal numbers from each area. This was not achieved. No interviews were possible in Area 2 and additional interviewees were selected in other areas to compensate for this. In order to facilitate discussions with young people, we imposed an age restriction of 12 years or over. The age range of the final sample was between 13 and 18 years. We also wanted young people to have been resident in the UK for at least 12 months to allow time for them to have settled into foster care and to be able to reflect on their experiences – the final range was between ten months and five years. The interview sample was all-male. Unfortunately, no young women had agreed to participate. Altogether, 32 foster carers and young people had been approached for interview and 23 case studies were finally completed, comprising 23 foster carers

---

2   Ninety-one young people were from Afghanistan, 21 from African countries and 20 from "Other" regions (including other Asian countries, the Middle East and Europe). Our overall progress measure is discussed in Chapter 10.

and 21 young people.[3] The young people originated from seven different countries, with 14 coming from Afghanistan.

Data collection

The census study

The purpose of the census study was to provide a snapshot description of all unaccompanied young people being supported by our local authorities on census day and to provide an overview of the range of placements being used to accommodate them. This has enabled us to situate fostering in the context of all the placement resources available to local authorities. It has also enabled us to provide updated answers to two important questions. First, to what extent are unaccompanied young people now being formally looked after? Second, where this care status has changed, to what extent has this led to the use of different placement resources? The two questions are distinct. For example, it is perfectly possible to be formally looked after (under Section 20 of the Children Act 1989) and still to be accommodated in unsupported shared housing in the private sector. It is important to understand how these patterns may have changed in comparison to those uncovered during earlier research studies (Stanley, 2001; Wade, et al, 2005). The answers to these questions are provided in Chapter 3.

The census utilised the central information system in each local authority area. The information we could request was therefore limited and included:

- the characteristics of young people (identifier code, age, sex and, where possible, country of origin and asylum status)
- the type of placement young people were living in on that date (including different categories of foster care, residential care, semi-independent and independent accommodation), where it was located and who provided it
- the name and location of their current or most recent social worker.

---

3   Six case studies were completed in Area 1, eight in Area 3 and nine in Area 4.

Negotiations were undertaken with data processors in each area to assess whether this information was readily available and, if not, what level of data could be provided. Some areas had difficulty and the implications of this are discussed in Chapter 3. The data were provided through anonymous data transfer in Excel format and subsequently checked, cleaned and transferred to the software package SPSS-19 for analysis.

The survey

Survey data from foster carers were collected via postal questionnaires during 2010 and early 2011. The survey was conducted anonymously and foster carers were identified and recruited through our links with children's services and placement commissioning managers in our participating areas. Representatives in each local authority approached these carers with an agreed letter on our behalf. The letter was accompanied by information leaflets (for foster carer and young person) and a questionnaire. The information pack explained the nature and purpose of the research and what their involvement would entail. It asked carers to indicate their agreement to participate in the study by completing the questionnaire or, if they were unwilling to participate, to return the questionnaire uncompleted. Freepost envelopes were provided for this purpose. Consent to participate in a subsequent interview was sought at the end of the questionnaire. Only at this point would we be provided with personal contact details. If that consent was not given, the questionnaire was returned to us anonymously. In recognition of the time taken to help us, each foster carer received a £10 gift voucher for returning a completed questionnaire.

In an effort to maximise response rates, a reminder letter was posted to foster carers by our local authority representatives after six weeks. If this failed to provide a response, we spent time telephoning social workers of non-respondents asking them to follow up and encourage participation. If these strategies failed, we had to assume that consent had been withheld.

The survey sought information on an index child or young person currently in placement and on the foster carer and the carer's household. Where more than one young person was accommodated, the eldest child was designated as the index child. In outline, the questionnaires included information on:

The young person:
- personal characteristics (age, sex, religion, country of origin, health status and disability)
- features of care career (age at arrival in UK, length of time looked after, past placements, length of time in current placement, reason for placement, immigration status)
- current placement (type of placement, relationship of carer to young person, anticipated duration of placement, placement provider and placement location)
- carer assessment of how the young person is faring in placement, at school, with respect to emotional and behavioural development, and their overall health and well-being.

The foster carer:
- personal characteristics (age, sex, religion, ethnic origin, country of origin of carer/carer's partner)
- composition of household (including presence of other birth/foster children)
- past experience of fostering (how they came to foster, length of time, numbers of children, types of fostering undertaken, employing agencies)
- preparation and training received for (a) general fostering, and (b) fostering unaccompanied children; carer assessment of quality of this preparation and training
- support provided by children's services/fostering agency (contact with supervising social worker and child's social worker; assessment of quality of this contact and support and of support provided at times of specific crises; other sources of practical and emotional support – family members, support groups, other foster carers, and so on)
- practical impact of fostering (remuneration, family finances, leisure, employment, effects on other individuals in the household)

- perceptions on the rewards and challenges of fostering unaccompanied children; overall assessment of satisfaction with fostering.

The case studies

Covering similar territory to the content in questionnaires, the purpose of the case studies was to provide a depth understanding, from the perspectives of both foster carers and young people, of young people's journeys from arrival in the UK to the present. Semi-structured schedules were developed to guide the interviews. They traced how the current foster placement came to be made, how young people experienced life in the foster family, how they had been helped to rebuild their lives in the UK (by foster carers, social workers and others), how they were faring in relation to important aspects of the resettlement process (in school, in the community, with friends and in relation to their physical, spiritual and emotional health) and how they were being prepared for adult life in the context of uncertainties created by the asylum decision-making process. In this context of uncertainty, interviews with foster carers also explored what it was they tried to do to help young people to settle, find peace, stability and the contours of an ordinary life; what sources of support were at their disposal to help them; and how the wider policy, resource and organisational environment affecting foster placements helped or hindered them in this task.

A sub-sample of cases was chosen from those respondents who indicated on their postal questionnaires a willingness to meet for interview. Interviews were carried out by researchers in the carers' homes. All young people were offered the opportunity to have the interview conducted in their first language, although only one young person took up this option. The interviews were digitally recorded and subsequently transcribed. In recognition of the time spent to help us, young people were given £20 gift vouchers as a way of expressing our thanks.

The young people's focus groups

There is always a risk that young people living in a foster placement (and interviewed there) might find it difficult to express criticism. Where this had been the only placement experienced by a young person, they may also lack alternatives against which it could be compared, although some young people referred to experiences among their peers. In order to protect against these risks, three focus-group discussions were held with groups of young people (two all-male groups and one all-female group) who had previously lived in foster (and other types of) placements and were now in the process of leaving care. Two groups were organised through the auspices of the Refugee Council and the third was organised in Area 4. A total of 19 young people participated in these groups (15 males and four females). Each young person was given a £20 gift voucher to thank them for their participation.

The purpose of the groups was to enable young people to reflect on their experiences of living in foster care and to compare these experiences with those of other kinds of placement. A loose schedule was constructed to guide the discussion. In brief, this covered:

- expectations of foster care (to explore ideas of family and foster care in their countries of origin, how UK foster care was described to them and what they expected to find)
- good and bad things about being in foster care (feelings of trust and inclusion, language and communication, food, religious and cultural practice, location of placements and how these compared to other kinds of placement)
- leaving foster care (how plans were drawn up, how involved they were in decision-making, contact and support arrangements after leaving)
- messages for foster carers and social workers (what they were doing well, what they could do better).

Young people were also encouraged to take control of the agenda by bringing up issues that were important to them, that might otherwise be overlooked in discussion and to share their ideas about the relative merits of different kinds of placement and how their experience might have been improved.

Policy and practice study

The policy and practice study was intended to provide a resource, policy and practice context through which findings from the survey and interviews could be better understood. The policy study included two main elements.

First, four focus-group discussions were held, one in each local authority, involving a total of 31 social workers from children's asylum and fostering teams. These took place relatively early in the study to help us focus the research. The purpose was to explore practitioner perspectives on the organisation and delivery of fostering services to unaccompanied young people, to highlight key practice issues and dilemmas, and to understand the pathways of young people from referral through to leaving care.

The discussions were divided broadly into two sections. The first explored referral, assessment and planning processes. It explored what practitioners first took account of when confronted by young people, how assessments were conducted (and the knowledge, skills and judgements upon which workers relied), the pathways (outcomes) to which this process gave rise and how factors such as organisational cultures, team practices and resources affected decision-making. The second section explored fostering experiences. This discussion considered what young people want from foster care, what makes a good foster placement, what core skills foster carers rely upon (what it is they do), and what support and resources help or hinder them in carrying out these tasks.

Second, an analysis of relevant policy documents was supplemented by a telephone interview with the manager of each children's asylum team (four in total). The interviews covered very similar ground to that covered in the focus groups. They focused on assessment, placement pathways, placement matching, the characteristics of good foster carers, variations in the quality of placements and factors associated with this, similarities and differences between the needs of unaccompanied minors and those of other looked after children, the training and support needs of foster carers, what kinds of support helped foster placements to prosper, how the local authority supports young people's transitions to adulthood and what else would help to improve the fostering experience of unaccompanied minors. Taken together with policy-related data from the focus groups, foster carer survey and interviews, these aspects of the study provided a basis for understanding the resource, policy and practice environments and how these helped to shape the fostering experiences of young people.

Data analysis

The study was exploratory and descriptive-analytic in approach. Its intention was to describe and explore the fostering experiences of a sample of unaccompanied young people and their foster carers, to elucidate important aspects of the fostering task (and factors that facilitated or constrained it), to assess the progress that was being made by young people on their journey towards (an often imperm-anent) resettlement and to understand how professionals, carers, friends and other significant adults may successfully act as supports, guides and companions on this journey.

Statistical data arising from the census study and the survey of foster carers were analysed using the software package SPSS-19. Wherever possible we have used non-parametric tests for bivariate analyses, since these make fewer assumptions (for example, about the distribution of the data), but some parametric tests have been used where these seemed appropriate and there was no suitable non-para-metric equivalent. A test result of $p = 0.05$ was considered statistically significant (that is, at a 95% confidence level). Factor analysis and reliability tests (Cronbach's alpha) were used to assess the coherence and internal consistency of scales. Multivariate analyses (including logistic and linear regression) were employed to assess factors con-nected to young people's progress and integration. All p values, coefficients and sample size indicators for test results are included in the text to enable the reader to reach their own judgements about the relative importance of particular findings.

Qualitative data from interviews and focus groups were digitally recorded, transcribed and analysed using the software package MAXQDA. Information from document analysis and key informant interviews was added to enhance data triangulation. The principal focus of our analysis of the interviews with young people and their foster carers was an exploration of the narratives used to describe and make sense of: (a) what had happened in the young person's life; (b) what tasks the young person and foster carer undertook to develop their own relationship and also relationships with others in and outside the household; (c) what sense they made of the support and resources that were available to help them; and, (d) how each viewed the quality of these relationships and the progress young people were able to make in discrete spheres of their lives. The focus groups drew in reflective material from young people on past placement journeys and experiences and from social workers on the policy and practice issues that predominate in their work with unaccompanied young people and foster carers.

The interview data were coded thematically using a range of descriptive and conceptual coding categories. Some were initially developed *a priori* (adapted from the survey categories to which the interview data needed to relate) and others emerged through the analytic process (through a process of identifying, counting and grouping different types of experiences). This enabled us to conduct analyses within and across cases to draw out the range of experiences and respective viewpoints of young people and foster carers in relation to each theme. Brief pen pictures were created for each case, using information from the interviews and survey, so that this analysis could be set within the context of the whole "story" for each young person and to prevent the thematic data becoming too de-contextualised. This approach permitted each theme to be analysed in the context of the whole complex set of issues for each young person. Once completed, the collated data for all cases (including lengthy textual quotations) were printed out on a theme-by-theme basis for final analysis and write-up.

Ethical considerations

The study was funded by the Big Lottery. Formal ethical approval was secured from the Humanities and Social Sciences Ethics Committee at the University of York and from the Association of Directors of Children's Services. The ethical framework for the study was developed in line with the Social Policy Research Unit's (SPRU, University of York) code of practice, which has been informed by the Social Research Association's Ethical Guidelines 2003, the Data Protection Act 1998 and guidance on research governance provided by government. An advisory group was established for the study to advise on, among other things, ethical issues that might arise during the course of the study.

All participants (carers and young people) were sent leaflets explaining the purpose of the research, what their involvement would entail and what would happen to the information they provided. Guarantees were also provided with respect to the handling, storage and subsequent use of data in line with data protection legislation. At the time of interview, this information was reiterated and it was made clear that interviewees could withdraw consent at any stage and that, if any questions caused discomfort, they were at perfect liberty not to answer or to take a break from the interview. A guarantee of confidentiality was provided to all participants and it was made clear that no agencies, professionals, carers or young people would be identified in any products of the research. In this light, some case study material has been altered to protect identities and any names used in the text are entirely fictitious. The only exception to the confidentiality guarantee would be in circumstances where a young person (or another child) was reported to be at significant risk of harm. This was made clear at the outset of interviews and in the advance information sent to participants. Fortunately, this situation did not arise during the course of the fieldwork.

Summary

The study began in 2009 and included four local authorities chosen to provide a spread by type and region. The purpose of the study was to provide new evidence on the fostering experiences of unaccompanied asylum-seeking young people and their foster carers, to identify key features of the fostering task for this group, to assess the support being provided to young people and their placements from all possible sources, and to identify factors that facilitated or constrained the making and sustenance of placements.

The study design comprised a multi-method approach, including:

- a census study (using local administrative data) on all 2,113 unaccompanied young people supported by these authorities on 31 March 2009
- a postal survey of 133 foster carers who were caring for an unaccompanied child on 31 December 2009
- semi-structured interviews with 21 young people and 23 foster carers
- three focus groups with young people formerly in foster care
- a policy study involving document analysis, four focus groups with social workers from children's asylum teams and four key informant interviews with asylum team managers.

The postal survey of foster carers yielded a 42 per cent response rate. Although these represent quite a good cross-section of cases, an over-representation of Afghan young people in this sample (compared to the census sample) introduced some bias, since these young people were found to be faring rather less well than young people from other regions in some respects. Young people included in the interview sample were drawn from the survey sample, taking account (as far as possible) of age, sex and region of origin.

3   The census study: a profile of care arrangements and placement pathways

Detailed information about unaccompanied asylum-seeking and refugee young people being supported by local authorities is scarce. The census study was therefore designed to provide a basic profile of all 2,113 unaccompanied young people who were either looked after or being supported as care leavers by our four local authorities on 31 March 2009. It was intended to provide a snapshot of current arrangements for the support of these young people and of the range of placements that were being provided as a context for the more detailed findings on fostering that follow. Profiles of this kind are not otherwise currently available.

Local authority information

The information was provided by data processors drawing on data held in the local authority information systems and in response to questions that we posed to them. In order not to overburden the data processors, the anonymous information we requested was limited, so far as possible, to that which is generally submitted to central government as part of the annual returns on looked after children. Our retrospective date for the profile was chosen with these issues in mind, since it also coincided with the collation of these aggregated data.

Negotiations were undertaken with each local authority in an effort to ensure that the information we needed could be provided. Some authorities recognised that it would present difficulties, but all agreed to do the best they could. The information on young people that was requested included:

- official date of birth, and dates of arrival and referral to the local authority
- sex, country of origin, care status and immigration status

- type of placement, whether it was located in or outside the local authority, and the placement provider.

It was surprising for us to find that, in some areas, not all this information had been entered onto the local authority's central information system. Our data processors were therefore trying to draw together information from two or more databases or, in some instances, by trawling through paper files. The information that we finally received is therefore subject to limitations and not all of it could be provided within the project timeframe.

- Only two local authorities (Area 1 and Area 4) were able to provide us with complete information on the leaving care population (those aged 18 or over). In the other areas, no accurate information was provided on this older age range. This affects the presentation of other variables – for example, legal care status, immigration status and the description of placements.
- The information available on placements also varied considerably between local authorities. Not all were able to distinguish between different forms of accommodation – for example, between use of hostels, supported lodgings, semi-independent and independent housing.

Account will be taken of these differences between local authorities in the presentation that follows. In particular, information will sometimes only be presented on sub-sections of the sample where it is considered to be reasonably accurate. Although these limitations exist, the information we provide is nonetheless important, as descriptive data on the overall support arrangements for this group of young people is not generally available. However, the challenges that have been presented to local authorities in providing us with this inform-ation point to the need for greater consistency in the recording and aggregation of data on unaccompanied refugee and asylum-seeking young people in the future. There have been important legal and policy changes in recent years affecting the duties and responsibilities of local authorities in relation to this group of young people. Without accurate information of this kind, it will be difficult to identify the nature and extent of local authority compliance with these duties or for local authorities to allocate resources and plan services appropriately.

Characteristics of young people

The administrative data provided by our local authorities enable us to describe the population according to age, sex and country of origin. No information could be provided on physical, sensory or learning impairments.

Age

The age distribution of young people across the four local authorities on our census date is presented in Table 3.1.

In recent years, central government and the courts have clarified and strengthened the duties of local authorities in relation to un-accompanied asylum-seeking young people.[4] As a result of these developments, it is to be expected that a greater proportion of older young people would continue to be supported into early adulthood than was found in earlier research studies (see, for example, Stanley, 2001; Dennis, 2005; Wade *et al*, 2005). At the time that those studies reported, the majority of unaccompanied young people (especially those aged 16 or over at referral) were neither formally looked after nor eligible for leaving care services. In the majority of cases, all services ended on reaching 18 years of age. The findings presented in Table 3.1 highlight the extent to which these patterns may be changing. In the two local authorities for which full information was provided,

---

4   In particular, government clarification in 2003 of the appropriate use of Section 17 and Section 20 of the Children Act 1989 for lone children (Department of Health, LAC (2003)13), including asylum seekers, and the findings of the Hillingdon Judicial Review in 2003 have been influential in increasing the numbers of unaccompanied minors looked after and therefore entitled to receive leaving care services (*R. (Beher and others) v Hillingdon Borough Council (2003) EWHC 2075 (Admin)*).

care leavers aged 18 or over accounted for 54 per cent (Area 1) and 30 per cent (Area 4) of all unaccompanied young people in the care of those authorities.

Sex and country of origin

The proportion of males and females seeking asylum in the UK tends to ebb and flow according to the weighting of arrivals from different countries of origin. In our sample, 88 per cent of young people were male. Although young people originated from a total of 55 different countries, around one-half of the sample had arrived from Afghanistan (49%) and a further 15 per cent from Iran and Iraq. All but five of these young people were male. This pattern of distribution is broadly consistent with national statistics for asylum applications by unaccompanied asylum-seeking children in 2009, as Table 3.2 shows.[5] Around one-quarter of young people had arrived from African countries, with Eritrea and Ethiopia most strongly represented (10% of the sample).

Table 3.1
Age of young people at 31 March 2009 by local authority (number)

Age	Area 1	Area 2	Area 3	Area 4	Total
12 or under	7	4	0	20	**31**
13–15	87	13	54	239	**393**
16–17	278	44	109	468	**899**
18–20	369	0	13	239	**621**
21 or older	101	0	0	68	**169**
Total	**842**	**61**	**176**	**1,034**	**2,113**

---

5   Home Office statistics can be found at: http://webarchive.nationalarchives.gov. uk/20110218135832/http://rds.homeoffice.gov.uk/rds/asylum.html

Table 3.2

Region of origin of sample compared to national asylum statistics for 2009 (per cent)

Regions of origin	Census sample (31.3.2009)	All unaccompanied asylum-seeking children applicants (2009)
Asia (all)	55	62
(Afghanistan)	(49)	(51)
Africa	24	21
Middle East	15	13
Europe	4	3
Americas	0	0.3
Missing	2	–

Immigration status

Only one local authority (Area 1) was able to provide detailed information on young people's immigration status at the census date. The other areas had not updated information that had previously been entered onto their information systems. As a result, a number of problems were evident. In Area 3, the immigration status of one-half of the sample was listed as "unknown" and in Areas 2 and 4 virtually every young person was entered as an "unaccompanied asylum-seeking child", irrespective of how their status may have changed over time.

Given these difficulties, it is only possible to present information on immigration status for Area 1. Table 3.3 shows this distribution, sub-divided by whether young people were aged under or over 18 years at the time of data collection.

Table 3.3
Immigration status of young people by age group in Area 1 (per cent – n = 842)

Immigration status at 31.03.2009	Under 18	18 or over	All
Seeking asylum	51.5	16.5	32
Discretionary leave to remain	30	49	40.5
Refugee	1	8	5
Humanitarian protection	1	0.5	0.5
Applying to extend leave	13	21	18
Appealing a negative decision	1	3	2
Refused asylum (no further appeal rights)	2	1.5	1.5
No status (no record of any asylum application)	0.5	0.5	0.5

Immigration and pathway planning to assist young people into adulthood are integrally related for this group of young people. Where unaccompanied young people are still awaiting a final decision on their asylum applications, the approach of adulthood can be a time of great uncertainty. It is evident that very few young people had been granted a long-term right to remain in the UK at this stage. Among those aged 18 or over at census, around two-fifths were still seeking asylum or were awaiting the outcome of an extension application or an appeal against a negative decision. Although the Home Office attempts to give priority to asylum applications from unaccompanied young people, waiting times for a final decision may still be lengthy. With respect to young people who were still seeking an initial asylum decision when aged 18 or over (16.5%), the average length of time since they had first entered the looked after system was 25 months and 16 per cent had been resident in the UK for four or more years.

Across all ages, around two-fifths of the sample had been granted discretionary leave to remain and, in almost two-thirds of these cases (62%), this had been extended beyond the 18th birthday. This pattern of extended leave appears to be in some tension with recent changes in Home Office policy, accepted by the Department for Education, with respect to the granting of discretionary leave. Revised policy has the intention to grant leave for three years or until age 17.5 years (whichever is sooner) to give time for a final decision to be made (including appeals) before young people reach 18 years of age (Department for Education, 2010). In this sample, however, those aged 18 or over with discretionary leave had been looked after for a significantly longer period of time than had those under 18.[6] Over two-thirds of those aged 18 plus (69%) had been looked after for more than three years compared to just nine per cent of those aged under 18. Most of the older age group would therefore have entered the looked after system no later than 2005/06 and their extended leave may therefore reflect (at least in part) the legacy of earlier immigration policies. In any event, policies relating to the granting of leave are likely to become more rather than less constricted in the future.

Care pathways

As discussed above, government clarification of guidance concerning the care and support of lone children has been bringing about a steady increase in the proportion of unaccompanied young people formally looked after (Department of Health, 2003; Dennis, 2005). Our census findings, some six years later, highlight the progress that has been made in relation to the legal care pathways of unaccompanied young people. Previous studies found that only a relatively small minority of unaccompanied children had been afforded the security of a looked after status and that the majority of 16–17-year-olds had been supported in the community under s17 of the Children Act 1989 (Stanley, 2001; Wade *et al*, 2005). This is not the case for the current sample.

If we consider only young people aged under 18 years (to include data from all four local authorities), only 28 young people (2% of the

---

6   Mann Whitney U exact test (p<0.001, n = 291)

total of 1,321) were being supported under s17 arrangements, 93 per cent were looked after under s20 of the Children Act 1989 on our census date and a further five per cent (65 young people) were being supported through s23 of the Children (Leaving Care) Act 2000 as young people leaving care. The change in legal profile is important, since the regulatory framework for support under s17 arrangements is considerably weaker than is the case for young people formally looked after (s20). Young people who are supported as "children in need" have no legal entitlement to allocated social work support, to care planning and review procedures nor, as they age, to pathway planning and aftercare support. For most young people who took a s17 pathway in the past, all social work support ended when they reached 18 years of age (Dixon and Wade, 2007).

The entitlement to leaving care services associated with a s20 pathway is evident when we look at those in the census sample aged 18 or over (n = 790). This analysis is restricted to the two local authorities that could provide this information. Among this group, 97 per cent were being supported through s23 provisions, 17 young people through s20 and just six young people through s17 of the Children Act 1989. Obviously we cannot know what numbers of young people may have ceased to receive any social work support from these authorities on turning 18, since all young people in our sample were being supported on census day. However, as discussed earlier, these care leavers represent a substantial slice of the total caseload of asylum teams in these authorities (54% and 30% respectively). In combination the findings do therefore point to a substantial change having taken place in the legal throughcare pathways of unaccompanied young people.

Placement patterns and pathways

An important purpose of the census study was to provide a picture of the overall use made of placements for unaccompanied young people by our local authorities. The picture, however, is not a complete one due to the quality of information our local authorities were able to provide. As we have seen, not all were able to provide information on young people aged 18 or over (at least within the project timeframe) and not all were able to disaggregate information on the use made of different forms of supported and independent accommodation. Despite these difficulties, the description we provide is the most detailed yet for a large sample of unaccompanied young people.

Table 3.4 shows that almost one-third of young people were living in foster care on census day. A very small number of young people were living with relatives – six were fostered with relatives or family friends and 16 were living with relatives outside the care system, reflecting more generally the efforts of children's asylum teams to identify, approve and reunify young people with relatives in the UK where this proves possible (see, for example, Kearney, 2007 for a discussion of this kinship work). Residential care was being used for a relatively small minority of young people and another small group was living in "other" types of accommodation. This included young people in young offender institutions (7), young people who were recorded as being homeless or held in immigration detention (8), in residential employment (1) or as missing from placement (2).

Table 3.4
Placement of young people at 31 March 2009

	Number	*Per cent*
Foster care (unrelated)	659	31
Foster care (family and friends)	6	0.5
Residential care	247	11.5
Kinship care (not fostered)	16	1
Aftercare accommodation (supported or independent housing)	1,161	55
Other	18	1
Total	**2,107**	**100**

Supported and independent accommodation

A majority of young people (55%), however, were living in supported or unsupported accommodation on census day. They had either been placed in these forms of accommodation from referral (or soon after) or were in the process of moving on from care. The range of provision available varied from area to area. Where local authorities were able to provide us with detail about the numbers of young people in supported accommodation (n = 800), it was evident that the vast majority were living in shared housing with floating support (around 90% of the total). Most of this accommodation was provided by the private sector, although some use was made of housing projects provided by voluntary sector organisations. Support was delivered either through the managing agents themselves or directly through support workers or social workers within the children's asylum teams.

Other forms of supported accommodation were much less common. Areas 1 and 3 operated small supported lodgings schemes, accounting for around three per cent of all those reported to be in supported accommodation. In addition, a small number of young people in Area 3 were living in supported hostels (n = 14) or in shared houses with on-site support operational during office hours (n = 11). Across all local authorities, therefore, the continuum of supported placement options for young people moving on from care was very restricted. Apart from floating support arrangements, the availability of supported lodgings, hostels and supported housing with a daily staff presence was scarce.

In two local authority areas, access to independent housing in the form of council and housing association tenancies was also scarce. With respect to asylum-seeking young people, access to these types of permanent tenancies is, in any case, often difficult. Councils are often reluctant to offer tenancies where young people do not have an extended right to remain. In the other two areas, however, team managers reported that there was less pressure on the social housing stock and access to these tenancies was quite good. Where access was denied, there was a heavy reliance on private sector shared housing which, as we know from previous research on asylum-seeking young people, tends to be of highly variable quality (Audit Commission, 2000; Stone, 2000; Stanley, 2001; Wade *et al*, 2005).

Foster care

Age has been identified in the literature as a key determinant of the subsequent placement pathways of unaccompanied asylum-seeking children and young people, with younger children entering foster or residential care and older young people (aged 16–17), in the main, moving to independent or semi-independent accommodation. These pathways have been reinforced by variations in the level of Home Office Special Grant for those aged under or over 16, the grant local authorities rely upon to provide services (Audit Commission, 2000; Stone, 2000; Stanley, 2001; Wade *et al*, 2005). Evidence from our census study suggests that these distinctive pathways continue to be played out today. They may also become more divergent, as the Home Office has, at the time of writing, recently made cuts to these local authority grants that, as one team manger made clear, might have serious implications for placement choices and pathways:[7]

> *It's going to be straitened circumstances, and one of the issues will be whether we can sustain 16- and 17-year-olds in foster care, given the money that UKBA's going to give us ... You know, for a 16-year-old they're only giving us £500 a week and that's got to cover everything, so there's not much scope there really.* (Team manager, Area 3)

Foster care is known to be the preferred placement option for younger unaccompanied children (Hek, 2007; Wade, 2009). In our study, almost all the young people (94%) who were in foster care on census day had been younger than 16 years of age when they had first entered care. In contrast, those who were in supported or unsupported accommodation at census had been significantly older on entry, with

---

7   See also Pemberton, C., 'Protests against the cuts', *Community Care*, 8 April 2011.

82 per cent aged 15–17 years.[8] Unless the initial assessment process revealed young people to have particular vulnerabilities, evidence of the standardised nature of these (primarily resource-driven) pathways was provided in interviews conducted with asylum team managers:

> *If they're under 16 then they will be going into foster place-ments . . . [However] if it is believed the young person is 16 or over then those young people will go straight into the community. So they will still be looked after children but they will be in the community.* (Team manager, Area 1)

> *One of the main issues is their age, unfortunately. If they are under 16, they are placed in foster care or in residential care. If they are over 16 . . . they move into independent living, unless they have some specific need, but even then they wouldn't necessarily go into foster care, they might go into more a . . . supported lodgings placement, rather than foster care.* (Team manager, Area 2)

Furthermore, in the two areas for which we had reliable information about those who were aged 18 or over on census day, almost all of those in foster care (99%) were still aged below 18 years of age. Only five young people were aged 18 at this point and none were older than that. The literature on leaving care has long advocated the perceived benefits that may accrue to young people from staying on with foster carers until they are ready to leave (see Stein, 2010, for a review of this literature). Strategies to delay young people's transitions, including the potential for "staying on", have formed an important strand of government policies towards care leavers in recent years; policies that currently include the Right2BCared4 and Staying Put pilot initiatives in this area (see Stein, 2010). Although two of our areas were now attempting to provide some "staying put" arrangements for unaccompanied young people in full-time education, at the time of the census

---

8   Mann Whitney U test comparing age on entry for young people fostered or in aftercare accommodation at census ($p < 0.001$, n = 1487)

(in 2009) there was very little sign of young people being afforded this opportunity. In our other areas, moving on at age 18 was expected, and these expectations were linked to local authority policies and an overall shortage of fostering resources. Even where arrangements for staying on existed, the current resource climate meant that these opportunities were being squeezed:

> They tend to move on when they're 18. Some have stayed in their placement, but not many, they tend to move on after they're 18 because that's ... the arrangements ... It's more about policies and resources. (Team manager, Area 4)

> Yes ... we have got some staying on arrangements ... But I think the reality is that there aren't enough foster placements to go round anyway ... The realities are that we need to try and find ... attractive alternatives to that because the resources simply aren't there. (Team manager, Area 3)

Shortages in the supply of foster placements, especially in areas with high numbers of unaccompanied young people, have led to a heavy reliance on independent fostering agencies (IFAs) and on out-of-authority placements. In relation to the provision of placements on census day, 80 per cent of foster placements were being provided through IFAs. This contrasts greatly with the national picture for that year (Department for Children, Schools and Families, 2009). As a percentage of all those fostered by unrelated carers, just 29 per cent were being provided through IFAs. Reliance on out-of-authority placements was, however, less marked. While 54 per cent of placements were provided within the boundaries of the local authorities involved in the research, this was the case for 64 per cent of foster placements nationally.

Residential care

Earlier research has suggested that unaccompanied children and young people are not frequently placed in residential settings and that, where they are, such placements are most likely to be used for relatively short periods of assessment and adjustment soon after arrival (Williamson *et al*, 1998; Stanley, 2001). Our census study would suggest that this is still largely the case. As Table 3.4 suggested, around one in eight young people were placed in a residential setting at census. At the point these young people entered the care system they tended to be older than young people in foster care and younger than those in supported/independent accommodation.[9] Three-quarters of those in residential care (76%) were aged 15–17 at entry compared to less than one-third of young people in foster care (32%). In contrast, 62 per cent of young people in more independent accommodation had been aged 16 or 17 on entry compared to just over two-fifths (43%) of those in residential care.

Not only was residential care being used for young people who were older at entry compared to those in foster care, these young people had also been looked after for a shorter length of time at census.[10] Furthermore, the use of residential care also varied by local authority.[11] According to our census data, Area 3 had no young people at all in residential care and Area 2 was only accommodating four young people in this way. In contrast, Area 1 had nine per cent and Area 4 had 28 per cent of its young people (under age 18) living in residential placements. In these two areas, close to two-thirds (60%) of young people in residential care had been in the UK for six months or less. For the majority, therefore, residential placements were being used primarily for young people on the cusp of 16 or 17 years as spaces for reception, assessment and adjustment to life in the UK before young people moved on once again, often to semi-independent living. Information provided by team managers in policy interviews tended to confirm this picture:

---

9 Kruskal-Wallis test for placement at census by age at entry ($p<0.001$, n = 1962). Paired tests showed differences in age at entry for foster/residential care (Mann Whitney U test: $p<0.001$, n = 900) and for residential/independent ($p<0.001$, n = 653).

10 Mann Whitney U test for length of time in care by foster or residential care ($p = 0.003$, n = 912)

11 Chi square test ($p<0.001$, n = 2107)

Obviously, if someone comes in and says they're 15 but they look clearly older, we want to be making sure that . . . we place the right people in foster care. So we place . . . them in; we've got a provision in our local area for small run temporary accommodation that facilitates about eight or ten young people. (Team manager, Area 4)

Now if they were, say, 16 and a bit [and] they were a little bit, you know, vulnerable, for whatever the reason . . . They really are finding it very difficult to acclimatise, they're not mixing with other young people, they're reticent and so on, and we want to draw them out of their shell . . . We may say, OK, we need to place them in one of our residential units. (Team Manager, Area 1)

These two authorities tended to provide specialist residential resources for unaccompanied young people where time was needed to prepare them for greater independence. Views on the potential of generic residential units for accommodating this group were decidedly more mixed. The experiences, attitudes and behaviour of citizen young people in residential care could be confusing and uncomfortable for young people newly arrived in the UK. In these circumstances, placement was viewed as very much a last resort:

We've piloted residential. It doesn't generally work well because we find that the other young people who are in residential care have their own needs. Unaccompanied children really struggle with why these young people would act in a certain way, why they'd be disrespectful to staff, these are all the things that we've had. We've had difficulties where unaccompanied minors have been placed with girls. Well, there's been a residential home with girls who have sexualised behaviour and, again, they just don't know how to handle that. So residential care is, you know, almost like the last resort. (Team manager, Area 2)

Research on mainstream children's homes has pointed to the importance of considering the mix of young residents and the implications of this for the culture of homes and the quality of life within them (Berridge and Brodie, 1998; Sinclair and Gibbs, 1998). Tensions may also arise where unaccompanied young people are placed together in specialist children's homes or shared housing projects. While these placements can allow for the particular needs of these young people to be addressed and provide an important resource of support and solidarity during transition, this needs to be set against the known heterogeneity of this population and the socio-political tensions that can result (Khan, 2000; Stanley, 2001).

Summary

During the past ten years, the legal and policy framework affecting services for looked after children and young people leaving care, including unaccompanied young people, has undergone substantial change. The purpose of the census study was to provide a profile of a large sample of unaccompanied young people and to examine the extent to which these changes have been reflected in changes to the legal and placement pathways of unaccompanied children and young people. Despite limitations in the quality of information provided by our local authorities, the findings are important, since profiles of this kind are not generally available.

Previous research, conducted in the early 2000s, had highlighted the disadvantages faced by unaccompanied children supported by local authorities in comparison to their citizen peers (Stone, 2000; Stanley, 2001; Wade *et al*, 2005). Only a small minority of younger children had been formally looked after (s20) and accommodated in foster or residential care by local authorities while the majority of older young people (aged 15–17) had been supported in the community as children "in need". For this group, services were highly variable and generally ended at age 18.

Our findings show substantial changes in these *legal* pathways. The vast majority of young people are now afforded the protection of a looked after status and benefit from the statutory duties associated with the care system, including an extended entitlement to leaving care services. These changes are to be welcomed. However, the findings also suggest that changes to the *placement* pathways of these young people have been much less robust. Indeed, the patterns are broadly similar to those uncovered in earlier studies. Age is still the key determinant of whether young people are able to access foster or residential care or whether they move straight to some form of semi-independent or independent living. Although there is some flexibility where young people exhibit particular vulnerabilities, these pathways are broadly procedural and resource led.

The range of accommodation options for those who are supported in the community also remains restricted, with a heavy reliance on private sector shared housing (see Wade *et al*, 2005). Leaving care services in general have proved to be successful in developing supported accommodation for care leavers – including trainer flats, supported lodgings, hostels and floating support schemes – and in promoting multi-agency partnerships to co-ordinate access to housing (Wade, 2006; Stein, 2010). Further developments of this kind will be needed to help expand the placement options available to unaccompanied young people.

We also know that there are economic and emotional benefits attached to young people staying on in foster care until they are ready to leave (Courtney *et al*, 2005; Dixon *et al*, 2006). At the time of writing, the government is exploring the potential of "staying on" through a number of funded pilot initiatives. However, its potential for supporting unaccompanied young people appears to have been relatively untapped and, in the resource climate of today, such progress as has been made appears vulnerable. In all of these respects, therefore, there is work to be done. Children's asylum teams could also be helped in their placement decision-making if the Special Grant provided by government took greater account of the actual cost of providing these services and if it was based on the particular needs of individual young people, irrespective of whether they happen to be under or over 16 years of age.

4 The young people and their foster carers

Our survey provides information on 133 foster carers and on the "index" unaccompanied young person in their care. Where they were caring for more than one young person on 31 December 2009, the index child was the eldest. The postal survey was conducted during 2010 and early 2011. This chapter introduces the young people and foster carers in order to provide context for the detailed chapters that follow. It provides a short demographic profile of the young people and their foster carers. It describes the backgrounds of foster carers, their past fostering experiences, the composition of fostering households and the type of placement being provided for our index young people.

The characteristics of the young people

Age
Most unaccompanied asylum-seeking young people enter the UK in their mid-teen years. For example, official statistics for 2009 show that 45 per cent of unaccompanied young people who made an application for asylum in that year were aged 16 or 17 and a further 27 per cent were aged 14 or 15. Only nine per cent of children were known to have been below 14 years of age.[12]

In Chapter 3, we saw that the majority of unaccompanied young people who enter foster care do so before the age of 16. Since all the young people in our survey sample were in foster care, it is not surprising to find that they were younger than the national profile of unaccompanied young people. Table 4.1 shows that almost all had entered the UK before the age of 16 and almost one-half had arrived before the age of 14. At the point of data collection, almost all were still below 18 years of age.

---

12 Home Office (2010) *Control of Immigration: Statistics United Kingdom 2009*. Available: http://www.homeoffice.gov.uk/rds. For one-fifth of young people (19%) age was not known.

Table 4.1
Age of young people at data collection – per cent (n = 133)

	Age at arrival	*Age at data collection*
Under 12 years	8	–
12–13 years	39	2
14 years	28	9
15 years	14	24
16 years	3	32
17 years	–	24
18 years	–	4
Missing	9	5

Where a young person claims to be a minor but the UK Border Agency (UKBA) does not accept them as such, they are treated as an adult asylum seeker until evidence is produced to substantiate their claimed age. Age disputes are not uncommon. Official figures point to 1,130 cases in 2009 alone (Home Office, 2010) and procedures for assessing age have been a matter of major concern to local authority practitioners and non-governmental organisations (Crawley, 2007).

Among young people in the survey sample, there was not always agreement about the young person's official age. This uncertainty was expressed by foster carers in around one-fifth of cases (21%; n = 26). In at least two instances, age disputation by UKBA had been official. In other cases, the reasons for this uncertainty about age were quite evenly split between the foster carers or other professionals (mostly social workers or teachers) thinking the young person was older than their official age (7), the child claiming a younger age (9) or being uncertain about their date of birth and current age (6). Only in one case did a foster carer think that a young person might be younger than officially stated and, in another case, a foster carer reported that from their young person's perspective all the fuss about age largely seemed an irrelevance: '[My] child seems to treat the concept of birth date as a triviality and does not understand the need for it.' However, as will see further in Chapter 7, continuing concerns about age had some corrosive implications for the quality of relationships that developed between foster carers and young people over time.

Sex, siblings and countries of origin

Only ten young people were female (8%), which may reflect the countries from which this sample of young people originated. Although the young people came from 17 different countries, the overwhelming majority (69%) had originated in Afghanistan. Of the other countries, only young people who had arrived from Eritrea reached double figures (n = 11). Most young people in the sample were therefore Muslim (89%), with just 13 young people reported to be Christian, one Hindu and five as belonging to no faith.

Only nine young people had come to the UK as part of a sibling group, although two others had older siblings living independently who had arrived at a different time. Five of these young people had arrived with a single sibling, the others having arrived in sibling groups of three or four. Four index young people each had a sibling living in the same foster placement at the time of data collection. A further six siblings (aged 17 or over) had moved on to semi-independent or independent living while, in one instance, the whereabouts of a 17-year-old brother was unknown to the foster carer.

Health and disability

Very few disabled young people were included in the sample. No young people were reported by foster carers to have physical impairments or chronic physical health problems and only two young people were considered to have a learning disability. Five young people were reported to be experiencing mental health problems. One young person was reported to have attempted suicide and another had engaged in self-harming behaviour. Other symptoms of emotional distress included depression, post-traumatic stress disorder and distress arising from loss and bereavement. Most of these young people appeared to be receiving or waiting for counselling from the local Child and Adolescent Mental Health Service (CAMHS). Broader issues affecting the health and well-being of young people, including issues that emerged from the interviews with young people and foster carers, will be explored in Chapter 10.

No young people were reported to have a statement of special educational needs. Although, as we will see in Chapter 9, many young people were receiving additional support to improve their spoken and written English, a number of foster carers emphasised the need for some young people in their care to receive greater support than was currently being provided.

Immigration status

At the time of data collection, while one-quarter of young people were still awaiting an initial decision on their asylum application, over one-half had been granted discretionary leave to remain in the UK (see Table 4.2). A small proportion had been granted refugee status, although this is identical to the proportion of unaccompanied minors nationally who had received this initial decision during 2009 (11%).[13] "Other" included one young person who had been granted Humanitarian Protection, one who was appealing a negative asylum decision and another who had not applied for asylum but had arrived on a student visa and subsequently entered foster care.

Table 4.2
Young people's asylum status at data collection

Immigration status	Per cent (n = 131)
Seeking asylum	25 (33)
Discretionary leave to remain	57 (75)
Refugee status	11 (14)
Application refused	4.5 (6)
Other status	2.5 (3)

13 Home Office (2010) *Control of Immigration: Statistics United Kingdom 2009.* Available: http://www.homeoffice.gov.uk/rds.

The characteristics of foster families

We asked foster carers to provide information about themselves, their partners or other adults living with them and also about other birth, fostered or adopted children living in the household.

The characteristics of foster carers and their partners

The ages of foster carers ranged from 33 to 72 years with a mean age of 49.7 years. The median age was also 50 years. In other words, roughly half of the sample was aged below 50 and one-half was older. This age pattern is slightly higher than the average age of 45–47 years found in previous research on the profiles of foster carers (Dando and Minty, 1987; Bebbington and Miles, 1990; Triseliotis *et al*, 2000; Sinclair *et al*, 2004).

The vast majority of foster carers (85%) who completed the quest-ionnaires were female. Thirty-nine foster carers (29% of the sample) reported that there were no other adults living in the home and at least eighty-one (61%) that they were living with a partner.[14] In a small number of cases, a third (8) or fourth (1) adult was also living in the family home. These findings differ slightly from those reported in Sinclair and colleagues' (2004) survey of 944 foster carers, which found that one-quarter (24%) were lone carers and that 74 per cent reported living with a partner.[15]

Foster carers were asked to report both their and their partner's ethnic origin (where appropriate). The breakdown for this sample is presented in Table 4.3.

---

14 The total number of lone carers is uncertain, since ten carers did not complete this question. The remaining three carers were living with a parent, a sibling and an unrelated adult.

15 The proportion of couples engaged in fostering has tended to vary slightly in different samples, ranging from 69–79 per cent in past studies (Bebbington and Miles, 1990; Triseliotis *et al*, 2000; Farmer *et al*, 2004).

Table 4.3
Ethnic origin of foster carers and their partners – per cent (n)

Ethnic origin	Foster carer	Partner
White	37 (49)	28 (37)
Black or black British (Caribbean/African any other Asian background)	33 (44)	18 (24)
Asian (Indian/Pakistani/Bangladeshi/ any other Asian background	26 (35)	20 (27)
Mixed white and black Caribbean	2 (2)	1 (1)
Any other ethnic group	1 (1)	2 (2)
No partner	–	29 (39)
Missing data	1 (2)	2 (3)

The proportion of foster carers from minority ethnic backgrounds appears high. This may reflect, at least in part, the determined attempts of social work teams to provide an ethnically diverse range of foster carers for unaccompanied young people. It may also reflect location and the availability of foster carers. As others have found (see Sinclair *et al*, 2004), the differences between our local authorities were highly significant ($p<0.001$; $n = 129$). In one area, for example, the vast majority of carers were white (92%), while in another this was the case for just four per cent of carers. Whatever the primary reason for these variations, it does highlight the potential that may exist for recruiting foster carers from minority ethnic groups where these communities are of substantial size.

This pattern was also reflected in the countries of origin of foster carers. While 52 per cent had been born in the United Kingdom, almost one-half had been born overseas. Our foster carers had come to the UK from 17 different countries. Furthermore, while two-thirds (67%) reported that they belonged to the Christian faith, significant minorities were Muslim (26 carers), Sikh (5), Hindu (4) or Buddhist (1). In addition, a sizeable minority of foster carers (17%) reported that they did not practise any faith.

Relationships with other people living in the family home

The placement of an unaccompanied young person also involved them in a network of relationships with birth children (young and adult) and other fostered, related or unrelated children and adults who lived in or orbited around their foster home. Only just over one-quarter of foster carers (26%) reported not having birth children of their own connected to the family home. Almost one-third (30%) reported the presence of one birth child, 29 per cent reported two children, ten per cent reported three children and one carer reported as many as five birth children.

Relationships also needed to be established with a range of other children, including other fostered, adopted or non-related children living in the foster home. Most foster carers reported the presence of one (35%) or two (30%) or three (1.5%) of these children and young people.[16]

Our young people, therefore, needed to find their place within a broad network of pre-existing social relationships. Most foster carers felt they had done so rather well, with over two-thirds (69%) thought to be getting on 'very well' with the carers' birth children and a further 31 per cent doing as well as the foster carer might have expected. The figures for relationships with other children and young people in the family setting were equally impressive, being 70 per cent and 30 per cent respectively. The nature, quality and importance of these relationships will be considered further in Chapter 7.

Background experience of foster carers

Most foster carers had had considerable experience of fostering by the time they completed our questionnaires. Only nine per cent had fostered for one year or less, 31 per cent for 1–3 years, 17 per cent for 3–5 years and over two-fifths (43%) had been fostering for more than five years.[17]

---

16 For one-third of carers (33%) there was no evidence of any other children associated with the placement.
17 Mean duration for fostering was 66.84 months; the median was 60 months.

It was not surprising to find, therefore, that many foster carers had fostered a number of children in the past. The median number of young people fostered in the past was five; ten carers reported having previously fostered 30 or more children. Only four foster carers reported that our index young person was the first they had fostered, even though some others had only fostered for a few days on an emergency basis.

Most (71%) had also fostered a wider range of young people than just unaccompanied minors. All forms of fostering were well represented, from short-break placements, through emergency and short-term to long-term placements for teenagers preparing for independence. Once young people had aged out of care, some foster carers continued to provide them with supported lodgings placements during the process of transition. Many foster carers had also cared for children with a wide range of therapeutic and behavioural needs, while others had tended to specialise in particular groups, such as children from minority ethnic backgrounds, children with physical or learning disabilities or young mothers with babies. The brief comments provided by foster carers in the survey attempt to capture this range of experience:

We cared for a sibling group of two children of Indian descent due to concerns about their parents' ability to protect them from harm.

I have fostered children who come from dysfunctional and broken families, children whose mothers were unable to take care of them.

I have provided emergency placements, short term, respite, medium term, long term, preparation for adoption and supported lodgings.

Mainly short term, they have stayed from three months to three years, and mainly Black British-born boys and girls in their teenage years.

I have mostly fostered teenagers with behavioural problems and children with learning disabilities.

Most foster carers were working for independent fostering providers (83%), only 14 per cent for the local authority directly and a small number for voluntary agencies (3%). This reliance on IFPs appears disproportionate, given that this sector accounts for less than one-third of placements nationally (29%).[18] Our interviews with team managers highlighted the difficulties they had experienced in finding appropriate placements and, in particular, in-house foster placements using local authority foster carers. In Area 1, reliance on IFPs was total – 'within the service we only use independent foster carers' – and the team was unable to access any local authority placements. In other areas, team managers pointed to difficulties in accessing internal foster placements for teenagers (a factor not only affecting unaccompanied minors) and also to a tendency for increased pressure on placement supply resulting from increasing admissions to the looked after system in recent years. The emergency circumstances in which placements were often needed only increased these pressures.

I think something like 75 per cent of our placements are with external independent fostering agencies . . . Within the region, certainly in the two years, sort of, post Baby Peter there's also been . . . more kids in the system. (Team manager, Area 3)

Well . . . the times that I've had young people arriving here [and] they've been sat in the office all day waiting for a placement to be found and there's just a complete lack of in-house foster carers to the point, obviously, we have to go out of authority and pay for private foster care. (Team manager, Area 2)

Although local authorities were making heavy use of IFPs, most of

---

18 Department for Education (2010) *Children Looked After by Local Authorities in England (including adoption and care leavers) – year ending 31 March 2010* (see Table A9). Available: http://www.education.gov.uk/rsgateway/DB/SFR/s000960/index.shtml

these placements were located inside the local authority boundary (65%). The use of out-of-authority placements (35%) is broadly consistent with the national picture. In 2010, 37 per cent of all placements nationally were located outside authority boundaries (Department for Education, 2010). Where foster carers had specified the distance to the local authority, around three-quarters were at a distance of ten miles or less. The largest distance specified was 40 miles.

About the current placement

All of the young people had been placed with unrelated foster carers. However, when asked in the survey to comment on the nature of the relationship between themselves and the young person in their care, it was not uncommon for carers to express the close nature of these relationships in family-like terms, as the extracts below suggest:

> I am an unrelated foster carer for this child. This child was placed with us via a fostering agency, but he now feels like part of our family.

> I describe this child as my son.

> I am his foster carer but I see my relationship to him as an aunt.

> She is like a daughter. I got a phone call from the local authority at 6:30pm and was asked if I was happy to look after a 15-year-old Muslim girl. I said yes and picked her up and we get along so well. At first she was very difficult and challenging, but after giving her love and security here she gradually became good. Now she is much better and needs me so much, as I do her as well.

> Our foster young person calls me Dad, which I believe relates to how he fits in within our family. It makes me feel rather special.

Most foster carers had anticipated providing their young person with a longer-term placement of one year or more (83%). In keeping with this expectation, only just over one-third of young people (37%) had been living in the placement for 12 months or less and one-fifth (21%) had been in placement for two years or more. It was not surprising to find that there was a correlation between the length of time young people had been in placement and the likelihood that they would feel integrated into the family.[19]

At the point of data collection, the vast majority of young people (88%) were still resident with the foster carers who completed the questionnaires. Only 16 young people had left and all but one of these had left within the previous four months. Around one-half of these young people had moved on to semi-independent or independent living and the remainder had moved to alternative placements. Two placements had ended after allegations had been made against the foster carers and another because a young person would not adhere to boundaries set by the foster carer.

Where young people had left the placement, two-thirds of foster carers (n = 11) were still in touch with their young people, although contact varied from weekly (6), monthly (2) to less often (2).[20] While it is therefore reasonable to assume that they had current knowledge about how young people were faring, an important consideration for our study findings, it does suggest that these ties were gradually being loosened. This would be consistent with wider research on leaving care, which has pointed to a weakening of ties with past caregivers in the period after leaving care (Biehal et al, 1995; Stein, 2004; Wade, 2008). Preparation and planning for leaving care, set within the context of young people's immigration claims, will form the substance of Chapter 12.

Summary

This chapter has briefly introduced the 133 foster carers and young people who were included in our survey sample. In so doing, it has

---

19 Those who had been in placement longer were more likely to score highly on our family integration measure – described more fully in Chapter 7 (Kendall's tau b test: $p < 0.001$, 0.243, n = 117).

20 One foster carer failed to provide an answer to this question.

helped to set the scene for the substantive chapters that follow.

Foster care is generally used for younger unaccompanied children. In keeping with this trend, most young people had arrived in the UK before the age of 16 and almost one-half before age 14. Almost all were still below age 18 at data collection. There was uncertainty about young people's official age for one-fifth of the sample.

Only ten young people were female; most young people had originated from Afghanistan and most were therefore Muslim, although not all were practising. Only nine young people had arrived as part of a sibling group and just four were living with a sibling in placement. Very few young people were reported by foster carers to have physical, sensory or learning impairments or chronic physical or mental health problems. At data collection, most young people had either been granted discretionary leave to remain (57%) or were still seeking asylum (25%). Only six young people had been refused asylum outright.

Our foster carers were slightly older than those found in general fostering samples, were much more likely to come from minority ethnic communities and to have been born overseas. Most foster homes contained partners or other adults and a number of other birth, fostered or adopted children. As such, our index young people were generally being introduced into a complex web of pre-existing relationships and most were considered to have managed this transition quite successfully.

Most foster carers had considerable experience of fostering and had fostered a wide range of children and teenagers. Most were working for independent fostering providers and our local authorities had great difficulty sourcing in-house foster placements. The placements provided to our young people were generally quite long term, with the purpose of preparing them for the transition to independent living. Most young people had been living in these placements for more than a year. Despite the fact that a small number of young people had recently moved on, most were still in regular contact with their foster carers.

5   Arrival, assessment and placement-making

This chapter begins to tell the stories of the young people. In doing so, it draws mainly upon our interviews with young people, foster carers and social workers. It situates what is known about the diverse backgrounds of unaccompanied young people and their reasons for leaving their countries of origin, drawing on the available literature, and it describes (so far as we could ascertain it) the arrival, referral and assessment experiences of our sample. The chapter explores issues associated with the assessment process and its outcomes, providing a focus on placement-making and placement pathways.

Coming to the UK

Only a small number of studies have explored the pre-flight experiences of unaccompanied asylum-seeking children and their reasons for leaving their countries of origin (see also Ayotte and Williamson, 2001; Thomas *et al*, 2004; Hopkins and Hill, 2008). Thomas and colleagues found that among the young people in their study the main reasons for flight included death or persecution of family members, persecution of the young person, forced recruitment, war, being trafficked, and education. In addition to the dangers experienced in their countries of origin, many young people also experience long, complex and hazardous journeys to the UK and are often vulnerable to exploitation and abuse at the hands of their agents (Russell, 1999; Ayotte, 2000; Candappa and Egharevba, 2000; Chase *et al*, 2008).

While there is limited research exploring reasons for flight, it has also been noted that research with refugees, including unaccompanied minors, often begins their stories from the point of departure and very little indeed is known about the ordinary lives of young people during the time before they became asylum seekers (Kohli, 2007; Sirriyeh, 2010b). As Kohli suggests:

By only beginning a story from the point of departure, the chance to see unaccompanied minors as 'ordinary people driven by ordinary desires, such as wanting to live in peace in a democracy that allows free speech' (Robinson and Segrott, 2002) has not yet been grasped by researchers. (Kohli, 2006a)

There are a small number of accounts of ordinary (and generally happy) pre-migration lives given by earlier generations of young refugees (Minority Rights Group International, 1998; Harris and Openheimer, 2001). While more of these accounts would be helpful to gain a holistic view of young people's lives, in reviewing these accounts it is also important to consider the construction of memory and narrative and the context in which these stories are told. How might the re-telling of these stories have been influenced by the process of exile from countries of origin and families? How might they also have been influenced by different life-course journeys as well as migration journeys? Narratives are selective and fragmentary and so are the memories from which the narratives are derived. They are formed and reformed in the context of more recent events, in the context in which they are being told, and in ways that fit with the plot of the wider narrative (Davidson, 2008). Meanwhile, Summerfield (1998) writes of forced exile as leading to rupture and the loss of 'narrative thread'. Bearing in mind their young age, their experiences of protracted conflict or of multiple moves prior to arrival in the UK, "ordinary" life may have been a more complex condition for some young people, while "rupture" or movement may not be a single event (Van Hear, 1998). Heterogeneity exists among all refugee populations and there is likely to be variation in pre-migration experiences and lives. As Kunz (1981) states:

It is reasonable to assume that within any refugee wave, individuals who constitute it are not equal in their social relationships; some feel more marginal than others toward the society which they leave behind.

Young refugees are often described as coming predominantly from middle-class or affluent backgrounds, although with a caution against generalisation (Rutter and Jones, 1998; Robinson and Segrott, 2002; Kohli, 2007). They are also often described as having had experiences of stable and secure family backgrounds and good parenting prior to their migration, usually in contrast to other looked after young people that social workers encounter (Williamson *et al*, 1998).

It is important to remember that despite the often traumatic circumstances surrounding the flight from their homeland the majority of these children are likely to have come from otherwise secure, stable family backgrounds. (Department of Health, 1995)

This is likely to be the case for many of the young people in our study. However, there were also some suggestions that a few young people had suffered earlier losses or more difficult relationships with birth families and that there was greater complexity in family relationships and histories (see also Sirriyeh, 2010b; Wade *et al*, 2005).[21] Kidane (2001) recommends that practitioners gather information about the family histories of unaccompanied minors, although this can be a difficult task to accomplish, given the difficulties often found by practitioners when talking with young people about their past (Wade *et al*, 2005).

Hopkins and Hill (2008) state that most of the young people in their study appeared to have played a "passive role" in the decision to migrate. Many young people described this decision as being made by relatives, family friends or neighbours and the vast majority spoke of being accompanied by an agent during their migration journey. Robinson and Segrott (2002) suggest that family and friends in the UK may also shape migration journeys by acting as a primary reason for choosing the UK (if it is indeed chosen) and by passing on information about the UK to potential asylum seekers in their country of origin.

In her study with adults and young people seeking asylum, Crawley (2010) found that migration routes and final destinations had often been decided by agents who facilitated these migration journeys. Gilbert and Koser (2006) have also argued that people seeking asylum

---

21 These issues are discussed further in Chapter 10.

generally know little about the UK and its welfare system and therefore surmise that asylum seekers rarely travel to the UK with the specific aim of benefiting from the welfare state (see also Crawley, 2010). While it seems that people seeking asylum are not generally drawn to the UK because of the welfare state, some young people in our study had perceived that there were likely to be good education and employment opportunities here and some appeared to bear the weight of family expectations that there would eventually be a return on this educational investment (see Kohli, 2007). There are often multiple reasons for migration which co-exist and the "genuineness" of asylum claims are not necessarily bound up with a lack of knowledge, agency or strategic thinking.

There were differing views among social workers over the degree to which young people were aware of their migration destination and what conditions would be like on arrival.

> *They're obviously sold the idea of coming to the UK before they leave . . . I mean it varies . . . not all young people will admit to it but one or two will say, yes, we've discussed it . . . They then get to the "Jungle" or wherever they're going to stop off before they hit the Channel or the Tunnel and they get more briefing. You've got to say you're 14 . . .' (Social worker, Area 1)*

> *I don't think they choose a destination . . . or the agents . . . Quite often they have a number of agents. It's not just one agent who delivers them . . . and, depending on who you meet and where you are and what happens at the time, you end up on a lorry . . . and that takes you wherever you end up. (Social worker, Area 2)*

People seeking asylum may be identified at ports of entry to the UK or "in country", where agents deliver them to a location somewhere within the UK. Most young people had apparently arrived overland by lorry.

> *From France I came. I went into a lorry in the wheels. From there I arrived in [place name] . . . The police found me there and they took me to the Home Office. (Abraham)*

This may be connected to the countries of origin of young people seeking asylum at this time, the routes available, and the young people's sex. The largest country of origin represented in the current study was Afghanistan and most young people in our study were male, reflecting the gender balance in the wider population of unaccompanied minors. One social worker said that a number of young people from Afghanistan spoke of arriving via Greece. One young Afghan person had told his foster carer about his journey and had shown her on the map where he travelled through Turkey. Some young people from Eritrea had spent periods of time in Sudan and Libya on route to Europe. Journeys therefore tended to be individualised and fragmented; some transits were rapid and others lengthy, requiring short or long stays in different countries.

Referral

Under the Children Act 1989, local authority children's services departments are responsible for providing support for unaccompanied children. Responsibility for an unaccompanied minor lies with the local authority in which they first present themselves. The Home Office provides a funding grant to local authorities to help with the cost of care, but is not directly responsible for providing this care. In many areas (all of those in the current study) unaccompanied minors come under the responsibility of a specialist children's asylum service. Three of the areas in the current study had duty social workers or social work teams within this service who received referrals. Referrals may arise directly at ports of entry or "in country", from agencies or individuals with whom young people have contact, or by young people requesting help themselves.

Around three-quarters of young people (74%) in the survey sample were thought by their current foster carers to have been referred to the local authority immediately on arriving in the UK.[22] Most of the young

---

22 For 16% of young people, the current carer did not know the story of their initial referral. Some others were confused and only related the young person's referral to them or their particular fostering agency.

people we interviewed confirmed this. Some were met by immigration officers. A number of others described being found by police after they had arrived, usually by lorry. They were initially taken to police stations before being referred from there to children's services. Others were directed to the police or United Kingdom Border Agency (UKBA) information centres by people they had encountered. Mahmud said he arrived with other Afghan boys. He described how he got off a lorry and found a man who helped him. It is unclear who this man was.

> This man he said to me, 'I [will] show you the Home Office or I'll tell the police, this guy is coming today new, to a different country'... He and me together go to, I don't know, wherever. I don't know. But just he said that. This boy told to police, 'Excuse me, this boy is coming today new from Afghanistan'. (Mahmud)

Two young people, not immediately referred, had found their way to their local authority's children's services department through a relative or a stranger they had met some time after their arrival: 'The young lady was left at the police station by a lady no one can contact.' Others had been taken initially to their local Home Office centre and were referred on from there. Two other young people had had their ages disputed by the Home Office and were only accepted finally by the local authority for a longer-term placement once this had been settled.

> The child initially lived in a bed and breakfast as the Home Office wanted an age assessment. He was deemed to be a minor and placed in foster care a few weeks after arriving. (Survey)

Finally, four young people had lived in intermediate settings before being referred to the current local authority. These cases included a young male who had lived with an older brother and a girl (perhaps trafficked for exploitation) who had lived with a family who exploited and abused her.

> She came with a Congolese family who did not treat her well.

She suffered domestic and sexual abuse. The police and social services intervened and she was eventually taken into care. (Female, aged 14 at arrival) (Survey)

He was seen by (children's) services at the airport and then went to live with his older brother for six months who was not able to look after him. He eventually moved to a foster placement. (Male, aged 11 at arrival) (Survey)

Two other young males had also eventually run out of places to stay. One had been abandoned when he arrived in the UK and had moved from house to house for a year until a woman he stayed with advised him to contact the Home Office.

I'm destitute for a while 'cos I didn't have nowhere to stay at all 'cos I got abandoned, so. Then, like, I've been . . . here since I was 14 but I was, like, on the road till I was about 15 years, then . . . someone advised me to go to the Home Office, the Home Office contacted [Area 4]. (Ayotunde)

The other had arrived in the UK with a man he said was his uncle. He lived with him in a hotel until he was also abandoned sometime later.

Although most of our young people were considered by their foster carers to have been referred to the local authority immediately on arriving in the UK, some social workers harboured suspicions that young people may not always reveal time spent in the UK before referral or where they have first spent time in other European countries, such as France or Italy. Young people may be wary of sharing such information. The Dublin II Regulation means there is a risk of removal to the first country in the European Union where the young person claimed asylum (Dorling, 2009). Asylum applicants are fingerprinted and checked against a European-wide database that informs the UKBA whether they have previously made a claim for asylum in another member state (Refugee Council, 2006). As one social worker commented: 'They try to keep quiet . . . Initially, they are afraid of disclosing this information because it has an impact on their status in the UK.' Social workers described how they determined whether a young person had just arrived in the UK or had been here for some time longer.

You can usually tell those that have been here longer. I mean some have just arrived because you can tell when you take them out to the car park they've got no idea where the cars are coming from . . . Others, you know, they recognise everywhere and could probably give me the route back to be honest. (Social worker, Area 3)

Some young people will turn up washed and clean and then they'll tell you they just got off a lorry, they've been in a lorry for 40 hours . . . Then other people will genuinely look like they've had a rough journey to get here. (Social worker, Area 2)

However, irrespective of these doubts, as children in need these young people were entitled to an assessment of their need for services.

Assessment

Local authority children's services departments hold responsibility for the welfare and resettlement of unaccompanied asylum-seeking young people as children in need under the Children Act 1989. Once an unaccompanied asylum-seeking young person is assessed as being "in need" they are entitled to the same level and range of services as citizen young people. To be eligible to receive these services, however, an unaccompanied young person has to meet three essential criteria during assessment: first, as a child (i.e., under 18 years of age); second, as a separated child (lacking the presence of parents or customary caregivers); and, third, as an asylum seeker. Once these criteria are met successfully, local authorities have clearly defined responsibilities and are able to claim payment for accommodation and support services through the Special Grant from the Home Office (Wade *et al*, 2005; Brownlees and Finch, 2010).

Assessment of age

Age determination has therefore assumed an important place in assessment. It has implications both for determining eligibility for support from children's services and for young people's subsequent placement pathways. Approaches to assessment have been marked by variation, with some focusing more strongly on eligibility and others, generally found within specialist children's asylum teams, focusing more on the needs of young people as lone children (Mitchell, 2007). It was evident in this study that there were variations in the extent to which there was a focus on age and its positioning compared to other aspects of assessment.

How old they are is the biggest concern because that then determines what's available to those young people in terms of our responsibility. To be blatantly obvious, depending on how old they are that would dictate our level of responsibility, so that's what we're interested in getting to the bottom of. (Social worker, Area 2)

Sometimes there's an issue about age, although we try not to do "over the counter" age assessments, if at all possible. Very occasionally we'll get into a situation where we do refuse to take somebody on the basis that there's overwhelming evidence that they are an adult, but unless that's the case then we would normally accept responsibility for them. And the immediate situation is to make an assessment of how they are [with respect to] immediate health needs and . . . where we would want to place them. (Team manager, Area 1)

Where a young person claims to be a minor, but is considered by the UK Border Agency to be older than 18, they are treated as an adult until they provide evidence that proves otherwise. Age assessments are generally undertaken by social workers (Home Office, 2000). Assessments are linked to identifying not only need, but also eligibility for services, and the relationship between these factors and order of prioritisation was sometimes a difficult issue to address. Some of the young people we interviewed had undergone age assessments.

Social workers described a context in which they, but also young people, were attuned to the issue of age. Some (though not all) felt that young people were generally aware that they needed to appear younger in order to assist their claim for leave to remain and to obtain services. Some young people also acknowledged this need for fear of the consequences if they were categorised as being older.

> Because the service they get, not only the service they get [but] a major part of their future depends on their age. (Social worker, Area 1)

> I think this is an illusion that young people latch on to [the idea] that we've got to say we're 14 because we're children and therefore they will accept us. (Social worker, Area 1)

> When I was coming before to England, I was afraid if you say your exact age, which my age was 15 and a half, then the social say you're 18, they're likely to send you back. So I said a bit younger, which what I said 13. So then I went to doctor and doctor said I'm 15 as well, which was my real age . . . Basically from my saying at the time I was 13, but they said, you're 15. So that's how it was. (Omid)

Young people were provided with accommodation while their age was assessed. If they were thought to be over 16 years old, they could be placed in short-term residential units or supported hostel accommodation for a few days or weeks while these assessments took place and other placements were located. Although some young people were accommodated in these units, social workers and young people in two local authorities indicated that bed and breakfast or hotel placements were also sometimes used during assessment. Young people who were thought to be under the age of 16 were generally placed in foster care.

The conduct of age assessments is known to be challenging and there has been considerable debate about the adequacy and accuracy of existing procedures, perhaps especially those relying on physiological assessment (Levenson and Sharma, 1999; Crawley, 2007).

There is no prescribed way in which local authorities are obliged to carry out age assessments. Local authority approaches have tended to evolve through practice development, the development of practice guidelines and emerging case law (Walker, 2011). The Merton judgment in 2003 was influential and commented favourably on age assessment practice guidelines developed jointly by the London boroughs of Hillingdon and Croydon.[23] In consequence, all local authority age assessments are required to be "Merton compliant" and to follow subsequent legal judgments (Crawley, 2007).

Young people's ages are normally assessed by social workers and are based on the young person's appearance, behaviour and interaction, documentary evidence, social history, family composition, health, level of independence and developmental considerations (Crawley, 2007). In line with current practice guidelines, social workers in Area 2 described how age assessments were undertaken by two qualified social workers, experienced in the conduct of age assessments. They outlined the process and some of the challenges involved in conducting assessments, in particular the pressure to make an informed assessment in a short timescale.

We follow the guidelines. We look at their physical appearance, their demeanour, how they conduct themselves in the interview. We look at their history, education, family background, religion and any documentation they might present to us.

I guess it's just that it's not an exact science, is it? . . . I think that the more you do work in this area and the more you . . . get accustomed to what, generally, people are like from specific countries and build up your experience and information. Working with interpreters can be difficult [because] they're not always translating everything that's being said [or] maybe they're interpreting it in their way . . . And, you know, it's questioning that . . . The other thing [is] just the timescale . . . they want them to be produced in, but then they want them to be

---

23 *B v The London Borough of Merton [2003] EWHC 1689 (Admin)* (14 July 2003)

good documents and detail why you have made that decision and the analysis on that.

Difficulties in conducting age assessments were noted by all social work teams, including the challenges of considering different life histories and experiences, cultural understandings of age and age-related behaviour, the impact of traumatic events, difficult journeys and the approximate nature of the assessment. Re-assessments could occur later on during the young person's time in the UK. An important issue here was change over time, the arrhythmic growth of the young person and, therefore, the need to take into account moving pictures rather than relying solely on an initial static image. One social worker said, 'There is a spurt when they come into foster care; they bloom.' It was noted that, in addition to the physical impact of difficult experiences on young people's appearance, some young people had to "act up" during their journey as a survival tactic. An example was given of a young boy who seemed mature among his peers, but it became evident he was much younger when placed in a family context and was able to draw on this support to "act his age". The examples given point to the importance of viewing age assessments as a process rather than a single event (Stanley, 2001) and of taking a holistic approach to reviewing markers of age. However, it also highlights the inexact and approximate nature of the science of age determination.

Young people's responses to the outcomes of age assessments varied. Some young people chose to appeal decisions while others were more accepting of them. Age assessment not only impacted on whether the young person was treated as a minor and the form of placement they received, but could also affect their emotional well-being and entitlement to other services. A social worker commented on the stress and ill-health experienced by some young people appealing decisions. Meanwhile, when we interviewed Rahim, he was preparing to move on from his foster placement for independent living. However, he was still insistent that he was only 15 years old, two years younger than his assessed age of 17. He felt very anxious about moving on and doubted his ability to manage the level of responsibility that would be needed. He had unsuccessfully appealed the decision to move him into shared housing.

Assessment of need

The Children Act 1989 places a duty on local authorities to assess and meet the needs of children assessed as being "in need". Where an unaccompanied asylum-seeking young person lacks the presence of a parent or other customary caregiver, they are by definition "in need". As such, government guidance suggests that they should be accommodated under Section 20 of the Act pending completion of initial and core assessments in line with the *Framework for the Assessment of Children in Need and their Families*, within which unaccompanied minors are mentioned as a group requiring special care and attention (Department of Health, 2000; Department of Health, 2003).

A range of additional guidance has also been developed to assist local authorities when considering care arrangements for these young people. Official guidance was first issued in 1995 (Department of Health, 1995) and an updated guide, endorsed by government, was published in 2001 (Kidane, 2001a). Guidelines to support good practice have also been issued by the Separated Children in Europe Programme (2004), the United Nations High Commissioner for Refugees (1994) and the Council of the European Union (2003). Training resources for foster carers and social workers have also been made available (Kidane and Amarena, 2004, 2005). Taken as a whole, this body of guidance emphasises the importance of speedy but well-informed responses to children's immediate placement needs, backed up by careful core assessments undertaken over time, of listening to children's views about placement, of taking account of their past experiences and of their cultural, linguistic and religious needs. It also emphasises the need for careful assessment and the value of ongoing monitoring and support to provide continuity for children and young people, to respond to changing needs and to minimise the need for further movement.

A number of studies in the early 2000s exploring service provision and placement pathways for unaccompanied minors, however, have

69

highlighted the variability between local authorities in the quality of needs assessments that were undertaken (Stanley, 2001; The Children's Legal centre, 2003). It was found that many young people aged 16 and 17 did not receive full needs assessments (Wade *et al*, 2005), or these were not adequately implemented to meet their needs (Kidane, 2001a; Stanley, 2001; Dennis, 2002). Age was found to be a determining factor in assessment and in the level of support then provided (Stanley, 2001). As we saw in Chapter 3, however, developments in government guidance and case law have subsequently brought about a significant change in the legal care pathways of unaccompanied young people, with the vast majority now looked after (under s20) rather than supported in the community (s17).[24] Most research has focused on the age dimension of assessment and much less attention has been given to conduct of the wider needs assessment process (see Wade *et al*, 2005).

The Munro Review on child protection has recommended de-limiting the timescales for assessment and combining initial and core assessments into a single process (Munro, 2011). Movement towards merging these stages was evident among some teams in our study.

[We] will complete an initial assessment, which will . . . become a core assessment, basically. So we've sort of combined the two because, in terms of timescales, because of actions that need to be taken, a majority of the time we would complete a core assessment. (Team manager, Area 1)

Initial meetings with young people were generally undertaken by duty social workers based at UKBA or children's services offices. The confusion, suspicion and anxiety felt by young people at this stage was frequently evident (Kohli and Mather, 2003; Chase, 2010).

They have no understanding or knowledge about social workers. They don't know what social workers can provide or how social

---

24 In particular, we refer to guidance on the accommodation of lone children (Department of Health, 2003) and to the findings of the Hillingdon judicial review in 2003.

workers can help them, and they see everybody as an authority that is there to impose power on them. Also they are very emotional, they experience trauma and it is quite difficult for them to present themselves fully and openly, and we have to be careful not to go into too many details about their social backgrounds . . . So we have to take it step by step to gather this important information. (Social worker, Area 3)

The initial meeting tended to focus on stabilisation and immediate welfare needs. Practitioners sought to establish levels of vulnerability, identifying and attending to health needs, providing food and locating an initial placement for the young person (Wade *et al*, 2005). Recognising the anxiety and emotional distress young people may be feeling, this was also a time in which social workers attempted to calm fears and reassure young people. One social worker said: 'I mean a lot of them are very distressed when they come here and it's about making them feel secure.' Another described how she tried to make sure that young people were initially given a comfortable and welcoming environment in the offices to rest while a placement was being found. She avoided delving into immigration questions at this point in order to help reinforce the distinction between social workers and immigration officers.

The initial meeting was also an opportunity for social workers to clarify their role. Young people encounter a range of organisations after arrival in the UK and may be uncertain about their objectives. Social workers commented on the large number of appointments young people needed to attend in their first few weeks in the UK, including immigration screening and interviews, solicitors, education workers, registering with doctors, dentists and so on. Therefore, young people were coming into contact with a large number of professionals and being asked for information from all these sources (Kohli, 2006a). Sabir had found his assessment to be a tiring and confusing, although ultimately reassuring, experience:

They were asking too many questions. I didn't know what they were saying. Many questions for a long time there. I said, 'Who

71

are they?' I don't know why they needed that. But after that, I know they were helping me, yeah. (Sabir)

Social workers described how they explained their role to young people and differentiated themselves from immigration officers by briefly explaining to young people the different roles of the police, Home Office and social workers (Kidane, 2001a).

I tell them my job is to look after children and make sure that children are safe. That's it. (Social worker, Area 3)

We talk about taking on the parenting role. We're not going to look after you ourselves but our job is to make sure you're looked after, because your mum and dad aren't able to look after you here and we need to do what a good mother and father would do. That's our role. (Social worker, Area 3)

Social workers faced limitations in the degree of information they could gather to inform assessment and placement-making for young people. Young people are usually the sole source of information about their family and social histories, about themselves and their needs (Kohli, 2006b). Unaccompanied minors are by definition separated from family members and other social networks that might be able to provide further details. Like many asylum seekers, unaccompanied minors may also not have documents that could shed further light on their history and needs, including proof of age (Mitchell, 2003). In addition, they may be feeling emotional or wary of disclosing information and placing their trust in social workers, especially at this early stage when they are still finding their bearings and establishing who different professionals are. Indeed, this silence may continue further on into the relationship as young people make use of silence as 'functional distrust' (Kohli, 2006a) or as a means of maintaining agency and protecting their privacy (Chase, 2010).Young people and social workers communicated through interpreters at this point and although this helped alleviate some of the language barriers, there were still a few reports of communication difficulties where interpreters did not transmit exact translations.

Placement-making

There were clear time constraints faced in gathering information to guide placement-making. In most cases, placements are needed on the day of referral and, in these circumstances, choices are heavily constrained (see Wade, 2009). The level of information gathered at an initial meeting could simply depend on the time of day that a young person arrived.

> *If, for example, a client has gone to a screening unit at 12 o'clock, by 4.30–5 o'clock that person could be in a foster placement. That isn't time to get a lot of information.* (Social worker, Area 4)

> *It depends upon what time the referral will come into our building. For example, if the referrals come early morning then our team sometimes have time to assess their basic needs . . . to ask some information from the young person which can help us to find the appropriate foster placement or hostel.* (Social worker, Area 3)

Of course, as we shall see further in later chapters, working within these constraints also meant that the information passed to foster carers ahead of placement could be severely limited, affecting the degree to which carers felt prepared and ready to accept a young person into their home.

Local authorities also tend to receive conflicting messages from central government on the provision of care to unaccompanied minors. While being advised to offer greater support to 16/17-year-olds by looking after them under Section 20, there is still a lower level of grant available to look after these young people compared to those under the age of 16 (Watters, 2008). Therefore, resources for funding foster care for the older age groups are restricted.

As we saw in Chapter 3, while there has been a significant change in the legal pathways of unaccompanied young people, age still tends to determine whether young people move into foster care (under 16), a residential placement (approaching 16) or to supported or independent accommodation (16 or over). Having said this, room is made at the margins for young people who appear to have particular vulnerabilities (see also Brownlees and Finch, 2010). Practitioners were often tuned into the circumstances in which they might be able to advocate for placements, such as foster or residential care, that offered higher levels of support to young people. This was usually reserved for young people who were thought to be victims of trafficking, who had particular health concerns or who otherwise were thought to be particularly vulnerable.

> *Typically with young women if, for example, there's evidence of them having been abused on route . . . that would be one example, or just generally, for either sex, whether there's . . . a level of stress and distress that they're indicating.* (Team manager, Area 3)

The limited information available to social workers from initial assessments could make it difficult to assess self-care skills and support needs.

> *Because they're new arrivals, we don't have that much inform-ation about them. Obviously they're telling us their basic story about where they've come from and how they've travelled here. But we don't know the individual incidence of their coping skills.* (Team manager, Area 4)

Referring to cases of young people who had been placed initially in a residential unit, one social work team noted some of the rapid developmental changes that took place in young people and the differences identified in their needs and coping capacity compared with what had been seen during their assessment on arrival. This finding points to the potential benefits that can accrue in initial supportive placements of this kind and to the value of sustained assessment over a period of time.

Resources and "matching"

The children's asylum teams used commissioning and resources teams to procure foster placements for young people. Two local authorities had policies whereby they first tried to locate foster carers through the internal fostering team before contacting independent fostering providers (IFPs). However, due to the general shortage of foster carers, the majority of young people were placed with foster carers from IFPs (83% overall). Team managers reported that not only were these placements more expensive for the local authority but there was considerable variation in the quality of care provided.

Finding foster carers with the requisite skills and experience to care for refugee children was a particular challenge, especially in areas with small minority ethnic populations, and despite the efforts that have been made in many areas to recruit from refugee and minority ethnic communities (Williamson *et al*, 1998; Wilson *et al*, 2004; Wade, 2009).

> *It seems to be harder to get suitable foster carers, so we're . . . getting not only foster carers referred who've never taken an unaccompanied young person, but they've never fostered at all, which is quite difficult . . . So it's usually only foster carers taking their first placement.* (Team manager, Area 3)

Lack of time created limitations in locating and selecting placements. There was a broad consensus among social workers that, in these circumstances, the potential for matching, especially for an "ideal" or holistic match, was very often not possible. This reflects wider research findings on limitations in placement choice, especially when foster placements have to be made on an emergency basis, with choice of placement only being available in around 30 per cent of cases (Sinclair, 2005; Schofield and Beek, 2006).

> *We don't have much of a choice. So we take on what we have and, let's say, 50 per cent of the time it works well and young people stay there for quite some time. Now, not having the time to match is a result of two things. First of all, it is the time factor,*

so young people have arrived at, say, 5 o'clock . . . and you only have a limited number of carers . . . The choices are just not there. So there is a time factor, plus the availability factor. (Team manager, Area 1)

Schofield and Beek (2006) suggest that the matching process draws on often unspoken assumptions or beliefs about the most important aspects of children's needs and about the most important elements in family characteristics and quality of care-giving. When the question of matching was raised in our focus groups with social workers, discussion was centred on notions of "ethnic" or "cultural" matching. One issue to consider here is what is encompassed by the concept of a "cultural match".

A range of criteria was referred to, including religion, ethnicity, nationality and language. However, some social workers also displayed an awareness of the risks involved in making broad generalisations about the meaning of a "cultural" match.

There shouldn't be the assumption that Afghan children will be settled with a Pakistani family and it will work wonderfully because they're all from this Asian area . . . Some people still have this viewpoint. (Social worker, Area 2)

It has been suggested that matching purely by ethnicity is inevitably crude (Wilson *et al*, 2004). In the fields of identity and ethnicity studies, critiques of essentialist and fixed categories of "race" and "ethnicity" have developed and studies have been critical of a tendency in social work to view ethnicity in this way during placement-making (Tizard and Phoenix, 1993; Gilroy, 1993a; Macey, 1995; Selwyn *et al*, 2010). Anthias (2006) suggests that the notion of identity as a stable marker of sameness or difference assumes that it is a fixed and possessive property of individuals rather than a process. Social constructionist approaches to identity formation have viewed it as a 'narrative of the self' and an ongoing process of construction or 'becoming' (Hall, 1996; Ghorashi, 2007). Jenkins (2008) suggests that, as interactional episodes, processes of identification are temporary checkpoints rather than concrete walls. Therefore, it is perhaps helpful to consider taking "routes" rather than solely a "roots" approach (Gilroy, 1993b) to explore young people's identity in order to understand it as a process and to explore their own self-definitions of identity (Biehal *et al*, 1995).

Essentialist approaches to matching may therefore not be helpful. Accounts given by social workers, young people and foster carers in the current study illustrated that there were often also successful outcomes in placements that were not matched on these terms (see also Chase *et al*, 2008). Social workers noted that there was variation in the extent to which individual young people sought these cultural 'matches' and identified the importance of working on a case-by-case basis on the issue of matching rather than taking a blanket approach (Hek, 2007; Wade, 2009). This was usually discussed in comparison to young people's prioritisation of other factors in the placement rather than as a critique of "cultural" matching *per se*. Other aspects of matching that were mentioned by social workers, foster carers and young people as affecting placement choice and progress included, for example, the extent to which they thought they would speak and therefore learn English in the placement, "family fit" (Sinclair *et al*, 2005), the location of placements, and lifestyle and house rules. These issues are discussed further in Chapters 6 and 7.

Most young people were in cross-cultural placements (placed with foster carers of a different ethnicity or religion to that of the young person), although in one local authority a high proportion of young people were placed with minority ethnic carers. The ethnicity of foster carers was unsurprisingly strongly linked to the different demographics in local populations.

I'd say the majority of our carers are from ethnic minorities. They're varied . . . [We have] a lot of Asian and Black carers. So I think the majority are from other ethnic groups. [Team manager, Area 4]

We don't have a wealth of carers that want to look after unaccompanied minors or who have a similar background, because the ethnic population [in our area] is quite limited. It's a fairly white European area, and we're trying to focus on the recruitment side so we've got more suitable carers. But we have very few ethnically matched carers for young people coming through. (Social worker, Area 3)

However, it was recognised that a "cultural" match could be viewed in a broader sense that took into account foster carers' wider experiences of working with unaccompanied minors and their willingness to support young people in maintaining and developing aspects of their identity. Some examples of these practices are explored further in later chapters.

Past placements

Most young people in our survey sample had been living in the UK for some time when our survey of foster carers was conducted (see Table 5.1). Duration of stay ranged from 5–84 months, with a median length of stay of 22 months, although only seven young people had been resident for five years or more.

Table 5.1
Length of time in the UK (n = 133)*

Time in months	Per cent (n)
Less than 12 months	20 (26)
13–24 months	41 (54)
25–36 months	18 (24)
More than 36 months	17 (22)
Missing	5 (7)

* Percentage column rounded

It was not surprising to find that there was an association between age and length of time in the UK, with older young people having been here longer.[25] In similar vein, where there was some dispute about the young person's age (official or otherwise), these young people tended to have arrived more recently.[26] Females tended to have been living in the UK for a longer period, probably reflecting the high proportion of young males that have arrived from Afghanistan in recent years and the fact that nine (out of the ten) females had arrived from African countries.[27] Five of these females had been in the UK for three or more years.

For well over two-fifths of young people (46%) their current placement was their first, but for just over half (52%) it was not.[28] Where foster carers knew the child's history, they reported that their young people had experienced one (n = 52), two (n = 11) or, more exceptionally, three (n = 3) prior placements.

Table 5.2 provides a breakdown of primary reasons for previous placements having ended. These have been divided into broadly positive or negative reasons.[29] Around one-fifth of the sample had moved from temporary foster or residential placements to a longer-term foster placement or to a placement with a cultural match that was considered more appropriate (19%). In addition, two young people had requested a move to be closer to their friends or relatives and one had made a brief attempt at independent living before returning to their foster placement.

Around one-fifth of the sample (19%) had moved for broadly negative reasons. The categories reflected comments made by young people's current foster carers, although it may be that each of these could be interpreted as forms of placement breakdown. Carers made reference to conflicts or tensions in the relationships between young

---

25 Kendall's tau-b test (p<0.001, t 0.381, n = 121)

26 Mann Whitney U exact test (p = 0.006, n = 117)

27 Mann Whitney U exact test (p = 0.02, n = 126)

28 Three foster carers reported that they did not know their child's placement history.

29 For the small number of young people with two or three previous moves, an overall primary reason was ascribed (mostly negative). Only two of this group had made two brief temporary moves before entering a long-term foster place-ment. Most had experienced past breakdowns or unsatisfactory placements.

people and their foster carers, to poor quality of care or unsatisfactory living conditions or to difficulties in their relationships with foster carers' birth children. In other scenarios, the young person was simply described as having been unhappy. As we will see in Chapter 10, past placement movement was one of the factors associated with young people not doing so well in their current placements and in other domains of their lives.

Summary

This chapter has explored the limited research available on the pre-migration and flight experiences of unaccompanied minors and has considered aspects of the referral, assessment and placement-making process for young people in our study.

From the accounts available it is apparent that such young people come from diverse socio-economic backgrounds. Although the "ordinary" lives of many may (often) have been lived in relative affluence and within settled and relatively secure family relationships, some others have occupied more marginal positions within families and wider society prior to leaving their country of origin. Forced exile can result in breaks with, and loss of, these narrative threads. Reasons for flight are mainly connected to death or persecution, dislocation through poverty or civic breakdown, personal fear of safety, and/or to a desire to improve life through education.

Most of the young people in the current study had been referred to children's services on arrival in the UK. Considerable attention has been given to the issue of age assessment as one criteria determining eligibility for services and subsequent care pathways. Social workers and young people were attuned to the importance of age. Older young people may face pressure to appear younger. Appearing to be under 16 was a key determinant of placement pathways – whether or not young people would access foster or residential care or move to independent living with less support. Age assessments were challenging to conduct, they tended to take account of a wide range of developmental factors, and most practitioners appeared to be mindful of the developing guidance in this area. Timescales were often short and

Table 5.2
Reasons for previous placement moves (n = 133)*

Reasons for placements ending	Per cent (n)
Broadly positive reasons	
Planned move from short-term placement	14 (19)
Move for cultural/religious reasons (improved match)	5 (6)
Move to independent living (returned later to foster care)	1 (1)
Wanting to move to a different area (that is, close to friends or relatives)	2 (2)
Broadly negative reasons	
Young person unhappy in placement	6 (8)
Placement breakdown	8 (11)
Unsatisfactory placement	2 (3)
Young person absconded	1 (1)
Poor relationships with other children in placement	2 (2)
Missing information	
Not sure	8 (11)
Not applicable (no placement moves)	46 (61)
Missing	6 (8)

* Percentage column rounded

developmental changes became apparent once young people had settled into placements. Holistic approaches for assessing age, moving beyond appearance and demeanour, and assessments conducted over a period of time can help to reduce inaccuracies.

Initial meetings between social workers and young people focused on stabilisation and immediate welfare needs, establishing levels of vulnerability, identifying health needs, and locating an initial placement. These meetings provided opportunities for social workers to clarify their role and distance themselves from other authorities (police and immigration). Social workers faced limitations in the degree of information-gathering they could conduct to inform assessment and placement-making for young people. Young people are usually the sole source of information about their family and social histories, about themselves and their needs. Independent sources of information are rare. Young people may also be confused, emotional or wary of disclosing information and placing trust in social workers.

Opportunities for matching young people to foster placements were limited due to short timescales and the limited availability of placements. Most young people were placed in trans-cultural foster placements. Matching is a complex process and there is heterogeneity among young people who may be categorised under the same ethnic or religious identity. It is likely to be helpful if identity is not treated as a fixed category, but rather as a fluid and constructed process.

6 Transitions into foster care

Asylum-seeking young people, like all looked after young people entering foster care, face changes, adjustments and new experiences as they settle into a new household and family. However, in contrast to the experiences of most young people entering foster care in the UK, asylum-seeking young people's experiences of transition into foster families are also intertwined with a wider process of arrival and settlement in a new country. Many of the young people in this study had entered their first foster placement within days or, in many cases, within hours of their arrival in the UK. Therefore, their experiences of transition into foster care need to be considered within this wider experience of transition, which encapsulated, but also extended beyond, the domains of household and family.

This chapter first explores how young people were prepared for entering foster care and how their foster carers were prepared to receive them into their homes. We then move on to examine early experiences in placements, including foster carers' and young people's expectations and feelings at this point and some of the key adjustments and challenges which they encountered.

Preparing young people for foster placements

First placements

In order to gain an insight into young people's experiences and feelings on arrival into placements it is necessary to consider what understanding and expectations they had of foster care and how they were prepared for entering these placements. Fostering may be an unfamiliar and confusing concept to many unaccompanied asylum-seeking young people who have often not encountered it before and may not know what to expect (Hek, 2007). In different countries, notions of what fostering means can vary and there may be different traditions and experiences of fostering (Steinbock, 1996; Tolfree, 2004). Referring to case studies in Tanzania, Democratic

Republic of Congo, Rwanda and El Salvador, Mann and Tolfree (2003) found some children feared discrimination, being treated less favourably than the foster carer's children, not being allowed to attend school, and being made to work (see also Dona, 2001; Abdullai *et al*, 2002).

We asked young people about the extent to which they had understood the concept of foster care prior to their arrival at their first foster care placement. None had heard of foster care before arriving in the UK. Some thought it might be like a hostel. Aarif's foster carer described how he had initially thought her house was part of the Home Office and that she worked for the Home Office.

One social worker commented that unaccompanied young people 'don't even know what a social worker is, so they have no perception whatsoever what a foster placement is'. This is an issue that differs in comparison with the experiences of other adolescents entering foster care in the UK. Most adolescent entrants come into care because of a breakdown in relationships with families, abuse, neglect, the young person's behaviour, or a combination of these factors (Biehal, 2009). In many cases, even when admitted for the first time, young people have been known to social care services for a number of years and so have some experience of the process involved and the roles of different professionals (Farmer *et al*, 2004; Biehal, 2009).

Although some young people had lived with extended family after losing or becoming separated from their parents in their countries of origin, none had been cared for by non-relatives. One social worker said that some young people ask why they are moving in with someone they don't even know. Comparing the experiences of unaccompanied minors with those of other looked after young people, another social worker said:

It's really difficult because British children would understand the fostering system, whereas in other countries you'd be looked after by somebody who's your auntie or uncle but not necessarily a relative. (Social worker, Area 2)

Therefore, a key task for social workers at this time is to explain the concept of foster care and what can be expected from this form of placement. Explanations generally focused on two main themes. The first centred on the reasons why young people were being placed in foster care. Young people were told that because they were minors, children's social care services had to ensure they were looked after in a supported setting and, since they were under 16, this would be in foster care.

> *We first explain to them that when they're in this country if you're under 18 that you need a guardian and we act as a guardian, and that because they're under 16 they obviously need somebody to look after them and look after their needs.* (Social worker, Area 2)

> *When I came to the UK she [social worker] said that when the young people come to the UK, they [foster carers] have to, like, be caring for them, 'cos it's not enough age to do what I want to.* (Ermir)

The second centred on a description of what happens in foster care. Foster care was usually described as living with, and being cared for, by a family.

> *They understand when you tell them you will be with the family and they are going to look after you like their son or daughter, because they don't have these kind of things [foster care] back home. But explaining about the family and you will be part of the family, like their son, and so they will have an idea.* (Social worker, Area 2)

> *They just said you will live here with them and they will take care of you. They are like your family from today.* (Young women's focus group)

Some young people were also given a description of some of the kinds of tasks that foster carers would undertake during the placement.

The social worker said . . . [your] foster carer will help you with shopping, school, food, teaching you to study, homework. (Young men's focus group)

They explained to me it's like mums. They wash your clothes. They cook your food. They take you out. They give you money so you keep your studies. (Young women's focus group)

Peers were also a source of information. A young Afghan said that while he was waiting to find out where he would be going, a group of Afghan boys who had already been in the UK for a while talked to him and gave him information about what was likely to happen, based on their own experiences.

The children say to me, like, they ask for my age and I say 'I'm 13 or 14.' He said that 'When you are under 16 the council, Home Office, give to you family and the family will look after you.' (Rashid)

While most of the young people remembered being given a broad explanation of the concept of foster care, none recalled being told about the characteristics of their particular foster family. Therefore, they had little idea of what to expect on their arrival at the placement. This included factors such as the personalities of foster carers and the composition of the foster family. However, a specific consideration for this group of young people was often the limited prior knowledge young people had about the ethnic diversity of the UK population.

They do have this idea that England's going to be white British and we suddenly move people into very multi-cultural areas . . . and it's quite a shock at the beginning to some. (Social worker, Area 3)

They were from Jamaica! I was very excited. They are black people . . . I thought it might be a white family. They treat me like family. (Young men's focus group)

Some young people were surprised when they arrived at the placement and found out more about their foster family. Rashid, from Afghanistan, described how he saw another Afghan foster child in the window of the house when he arrived. He had, therefore, assumed he would be living with an Afghan family.

> When I saw him I thought, it's an Afghan family. When I saw uncle [Ghanaian foster carer], I thought, no, maybe it's a hotel... He's white, he's black, how can you say to me, it's family and I live here, or something, 'cos I didn't understand his family. (Rashid)

Although Rashid was very happy in his placement, this had initially confused him. In contrast, prior to moving into his second placement, Ban-hwa had been provided with information about his new foster carer's ethnicity.

> I asked him [Ban-hwa] if he knew I was black, and he said, 'yes', because I know a lot of children don't want to go to black carers and he was coming from a black carer to a black carer... So I said, 'Did you know that I was black?'... He says that when he came he liked that the house was clean and he liked me, you know, and I felt the same with him. (Jasmine, Ban-hwa's foster carer)

Young people are always likely to feel a degree of anxiety about a move to a new placement, but if they have little information about the people who live there this uncertainty will be heightened (Farmer *et al*, 2004). In research on transitions into foster care, Mitchell and colleagues (2010) found that children want to be informed not only about the meaning of foster care, but also about the foster carers and what the foster home would be like. While some young people in our study were excited at the prospect of meeting their foster family, feelings of anxiety arising from lack of knowledge were not uncommon.

I have no idea what it would be like. So I was thinking and plus a bit nervous that, ah, there was a foster family and what they would be like because they are not like . . . so they are like special parents. So they are not like real parents and mother and father. (Young men's focus group)

I think they have a lot of anxieties about who will be looking after them and will they understand them and what kind of food they'll be eating. (Social worker, Area 2)

I stayed in a hotel for three days. The owner says they will transfer me to a family who will look after me 'til I get old. I thought this is wonderful. I was really happy. I was excited, happy like I would have my own family. I was so happy. (Young men's focus group)

I was talking to myself, oh, it's going to be hard. I imagine I was going to be sharing with other people – bathroom, kitchen and toilet and I don't even know people. (Ban-hwa)

Moving between foster placements

Good preparation was therefore important for young people moving into their first foster placement, but it was also significant for ensuring smooth transitions between foster placements. As described in Chapter 4, 52 per cent of young people in the survey sample had lived in a previous placement. Six young people we interviewed and some participants in the young people's focus groups had lived in more than one foster placement. Key issues arising from their accounts of place-ment change centred on the degree of choice they had when plans were being made and the extent to which these were planned or emergency moves. This influenced the degree to which young people felt prepared for the transition and how comfortable they felt about the prospect of moving.

The degree to which young people were consulted about placement changes varied. Although all the social work teams moved young people out of placements that were not considered satisfactory, there was variation in the speed at which such moves took place, the factors which prompted moves, and the extent to which young people were consulted. This is likely to reflect a range of issues, including individual judgement and practice, team policies and, not least, the availability of local foster placements. Sabir had asked to move to another area in the local authority where he had more social connections. He was told initially that he could not leave his foster placement, but was later moved at very short notice to another placement about which he had little information.

In contrast, when Majeed asked to live closer to his cousin, who was also in the UK, a planned transition was arranged to his current foster carers who lived nearby. Arian was also eventually moved to an alternative placement that took account of concerns he had raised with his social worker. Arian and his foster sibling, who was also Albanian, requested a move to a white British family because they thought they would have more opportunity to practise their English, after being placed initially with a foster family who did not speak English in the home. The boys were Muslim and they had been originally matched with a Muslim foster family who had a different ethnic origin. They had found that, although they were all Muslim, their religious and cultural identities and lifestyles were not compatible. The boys felt isolated, as they did not share a first language with their carers, and, lacking sufficient opportunity to learn and practise English, they struggled to communicate.

Two interviewees and one focus group participant had the opportunity to visit their current foster placement prior to moving in.

She [social worker] said: 'Would you like to visit them?' I visited and she was very good and the same day I visited her and I felt comfortable and she said: 'Would you like to live with me?' and I said, 'yes', and after one week I moved in. (Young men's focus group)

We showed him round; we explained how we operate as a family and this is what we expect, and we asked him if he had any questions. And I think he told his social worker he was happy to come here. (Isobel, Majeed's foster carer)

Meanwhile, another young person was taken to visit a placement which he was able to refuse because it was too far from social connections he had made in his first placement.

In contrast, where placement moves are made in emergency circumstances, there is likely to be less opportunity to visit first (Farmer *et al*, 2004). Sabir's move from his second to his third (and current) foster placement had come about more suddenly. It was a disturbing experience for him as he did not appear to have had the opportunity to explore his options, to consider the consequences, and to prepare for the transition (Kidane, 2001).

> *He actually got moved very suddenly then. He didn't even know he was moving. They just told him and said that they'd packed all his stuff and they were moving him on, and so with that, he got a bit frightened, I think, and ran away.* (Elizabeth, Sabir's foster carer)

Preparing foster carers for placements

So far we have explored young people's experiences at the point of entry into foster care. Chapter 13 examines in greater detail the preparation, training and support of foster carers who care for asylum-seeking young people. However, in this section we outline briefly some of the key concerns foster carers raised about their own experiences of preparation for receiving these young people into their homes.

There is a predominance of "crisis" admissions to the care system for teenagers. Approximately 60 per cent of admissions are unplanned and take place shortly after referral (Farmer *et al*, 2004; Biehal, 2009). This means there is rarely time to consider a choice of placements, for young people to meet their foster carers in advance, or for social workers to share detailed information with foster carers. Although entering care for different reasons, this pattern was not dissimilar for asylum-seeking teenage entrants into care. Most foster carers in the current study were given a few hours' notice of the young person's arrival and only basic information about the young person.

The wider literature on foster care has highlighted foster carers' concerns about the limited information they receive about some young people coming into their care (Farmer *et al*, 2004). However, many of these citizen young people, even if new to foster care, will have been known to children's services for some time and so information about them may have been gathered during this period. In contrast, social workers of unaccompanied minors may have very little information to pass on to foster carers because the young person has recently arrived in the UK, is the sole source of her/his story and, for various reasons, may be inhibited about revealing much about themselves at this stage (Kohli, 2006?which one?; Chase, 2010). Most foster carers in our study had been informed of the young person's nationality, sex, age (sometimes approximate), religion, health conditions (although not in all cases) and asylum status. Beyond these basic details, however, information was limited.

> *They told me he was a unaccompanied minor and he was a Muslim.* (Grace, Ayotunde's foster carer)

> *I didn't know anything yet, 'cos normally they [fostering agency] don't even know themselves yet.* (Jasmine, Ban-hwa's foster carer)

> *The Home Office, they give [information] to the agency, and they haven't got too much information from people who have come from the war. They know their age, their name, that's it. They come from the war. Not much information . . . some children [they know] their medical problems, they will let you know.* (Sarah, Nabil's foster carer)

Often young people in our study had arrived at their placement late at night after undergoing initial assessments and waiting while a placement was found. Social workers usually visited the young person and foster carer within the next few days with an interpreter to hold a planning meeting. Practical information was exchanged at that point and expectations about the foster placement were discussed. However, it was apparent that much of the detailed information-gathering took place over a period of time once the young person had settled into the foster placement and as the young people and foster carers got to know one another (see also Wade *et al*, 2005). Foster carers played a key role working with young people to compile information and knowledge about their needs and experiences and they were often the main person in whom young people confided.

Given this limited notice period, when asked about how they prepared to receive the young person, most foster carers described generic practical preparations they made for any foster child who was to be placed with them; making sure their room was ready and preparing food for when they arrived. Foster carers who had previous experience of fostering unaccompanied minors incorporated additional elements into their "checklist" based on their knowledge of previous young people who had arrived and who were sometimes from the same countries.

We had two Afghan boys before we had Rafi, so we knew a little bit of the culture . . . what they liked and didn't like and what they could and couldn't have . . . So we had a little idea. (Katherine, foster carer)

When I'd done it for a few years, [I had] a checklist for when they arrived. Find them a school, find them a mosque, get them a school uniform, clothe them. 'Cos they only came in what they stood up in. So, you know, I had a checklist which applied to all the young people. (Laura, Samir's foster carer)

I asked him . . . what he doesn't eat . . . I know that anyway because they . . . he's from Nigeria as well and I am from Nigeria and you know a little bit of the culture of the other side. I am a Christian and like the Muslims, we know they don't eat pork and they pray five times a day and also little things like that. (Grace, Ayotunde's foster carer)

In these ways, in the absence of more detailed information about the young people, foster carers developed their own guidance and routines to prepare as best they could. This amalgamated their general fostering knowledge and checklists based on more specific knowledge about asylum-seeking young people that they had built up over time from personal experience. Team managers and social workers recognised the need for foster carers at this point to utilise generic foster care knowledge and approaches in combination with an understanding of the particular issues relevant to asylum-seeking young people.

> *I think warmth, welcoming . . . all of those things that you would have for any foster child coming into care, but also having an understanding of what the young person has potentially been through; [that] . . . this young person . . . has lost orientation . . . they may have come to a new place . . . understanding the stresses and the pressures . . . on this young person and [understanding that] it isn't that they're now saved, which other foster carers have once said, and that their future's fine now that they're in the UK. So maybe a little bit of understanding of the asylum process.* (Senior social worker, Area 2)

Settling into the foster placement

Mitchell and colleagues (2010) note that there is little research on young people's perspectives on transitions into foster care. Here we examine how young people in the current study experienced their arrival into foster care, the adjustments and challenges that arose over the first few weeks and how they were supported during this transition.

Arrival

Most looked after young people find the transition into foster care stressful due to the separation from their families, the effects of the difficult circumstances and events leading up to placement, and their feelings of uncertainty about what lies ahead (Sinclair, 2005; Wilson *et al*, 2005). Although the causes and contexts may be different, asylum-seeking young people have also experienced considerable adversity and hold feelings of loss. Many young people also felt a degree of uncertainty as they faced the prospect of living in new families, starting new schools and generally settling into life in a new country (see also Kohli and Connolly, 2009). All this took place within the context of the uncertainty and precariousness of their immigration status. Some foster carers expressed awareness of the feelings their foster children might experience at this point and empathised with them.

You don't know what to expect. You don't know whether the Home Office will accept you ... Going to school, what type of school? What year group? Everybody would feel that way. Where are you going? Who are you going to meet? (Daniel, Rashid's foster carer)

What the houses are going to look like? What these people are going to look like? Shall I trust these people? Are they good? (Eva, foster carer)

Many citizen young people express relief on entering care, even though most would prefer to have remained with their families, and appreciate the feelings of safety, care and affection provided by foster carers (Sinclair, 2005; Selwyn *et al*, 2010; Wade *et al*, 2011). These views were evident in this study. Young people recalled feeling relieved that they had finally arrived at a destination after long and arduous journeys from their countries of origin. Some were excited about the prospect of being looked after in a family. However, many were also disorientated and anxious. Most had been given some information about the nature of foster care and why they were being placed there. However, as mentioned earlier, they usually did not have more detailed information about the characteristics of their foster carers and were unsure what to expect (Farmer *et al*, 2004).

This anxiety and disorientation was also exacerbated by logistical aspects of their arrival. First, by the time young people arrived in the foster care placement it was often late at night and they were exhausted from travelling and from administrative processes they had encountered on referral to the Home Office and children's services. They were often also very hungry. Haaroon's foster carer recalled how he had arrived at her house at midnight, having entered the UK and been referred to children's services earlier that morning.

There was this boy, his face covered in mud, his shoes, every-thing, with this plastic bag with all his dirty things, belongings and whatever and he said, 'Hello' [laughs] and he was so tired. (Eva, Haaroon's foster carer)

Second, almost all of the young people in this study spoke very little, or no, English. Abbas described his experience of arriving at his foster carer's house saying, 'I can't understand anything and then I come here, and some lady brings me and it was night, two o'clock.'

While some young people were described as presenting cheerful demeanours on arrival, others were quiet or appeared visibly anxious and in "survival mode" after they had developed defences and mechanisms for coping with events leading to migration and during their journeys to the UK (Kohli and Mather, 2003). They needed to (re)acclimatise into a more "ordinary" rhythm of life.

They're in survival mode . . . because they've had to live like this for so long . . . and been through so much when they come here, they're in a real state . . . They've got to almost be debriefed. (Ann, foster carer)

Ann gave an example in her description of her foster child's reaction to her attempts to estimate his size so she could provide him with a change of clothes when he arrived. Unable to understand English and communicate with her, when she approached to measure him he had raised his arms as if her intention was to search him.

So far, we have outlined some of the experiences and contexts in which young people arrive into foster placements. The following sections begin to explore some of the main activities which took place during this early stage of the foster placement, looking at the key functions of the foster care task. Tasks broadly fell into two themes: first, establishing an initial core base of familiarity and refuge and, second, supporting young people with transitions to more unfamiliar and new experiences.

It's that balance, isn't it, of getting what they're used to and what they're familiar with and actually then branching out to the things that they're less familiar with. (Social worker, Area 3)

Refuge and familiarity

A key function of everyday practical tasks carried out by foster carers at this stage was to contain, reassure and welcome these young people. They also helped to establish a break from previous precarious ways of living that enabled the young person to begin to settle and resume a more ordinary rhythm of life (Kohli and Mather, 2003).

Rest and refuge

Foster carers and young people spoke positively of some of the immediate practical responses made by foster carers in their attempts to make young people feel physically comfortable and recover from their journey, such as making them food, showing them around the house and how to use the appliances, and allowing them to rest.

She asked if I was hungry, like, how I am, and then after, straight after, I had a shower . . . then after, she showed me the bedroom and everything. (Omid)

She said to me, 'Do you want any food?' I said, 'Yeah.' I was starving. And then, she said to me, 'Do you want to go to sleep?' I said, 'Yeah, I want to go to sleep,' because I was really tired. And then I went to sleep and it was like a dream, like, I was feeling so nice. (Abbas)

Young people advised that it was better for foster carers to avoid asking too many questions at this stage, as they found these easier to answer when they got to know their foster carers and felt more comfortable.

When you're used to a foster carer or someone that you know, you're better then, anyone's coming to ask you a question that is alright, 'cos you're comfortable. First place, you're not comfortable. (Aarif)

Unaccompanied young people in foster care, while frequently the sole keeper of their stories, can feel that being asked lots of questions by foster carers is an intrusive and unsettling experience (Wade *et al*, 2005; Chase *et al*, 2008). Over time, however, as trusting relationships are built, many young people become willing to share information and confide in foster carers who are able to listen to them and bear witness to their experiences (Kohli and Mather, 2003).

Communication and welcome

In the face of a number of new and often challenging experiences, many young people felt comforted by familiar points of reference that offered spaces of refuge within wider experiences of displacement. An immediate concern for many young people was the challenge of communicating in another language. Osman's foster carer described how he spoke no English on his arrival from Eritrea and yearned for contact with someone who could speak his language:

> *He was trying to see if he could get someone to relate to and he asked if he could get the interpreter's number and they said: 'No, you don't do that.'* (Marion, Osman's foster carer)

While most young people were in cross-cultural placements, some were able to find points of familiarity in the languages spoken in the home. This helped them settle as well as providing foster carers with a means of communicating and welcoming them. Many of the young people from Afghanistan told us how foster carers who spoke Farsi or Urdu were able to communicate to some extent with them because some Afghans understood a little of these languages. As mentioned earlier, young people were sometimes surprised by the multicultural nature of UK society. A focus group participant described his experience of living with a British Pakistani family.

> *I think maybe [in] England people [are] different. When I go there they [are] Pakistani people. I know a little Urdu and they speak to me, but at that time I can't speak English properly. So they ask me: 'Do you know Urdu?' I said: 'A little bit.' They were very good people. They treat me like a son.* (Young men's focus group)

Although most foster carers did not speak the same or related languages, some young people were placed in households which already had other foster children from their country of origin. Where this was the case, these children were able to provide further explanations of what foster care was like and new arrivals could communicate and be understood.

It's maybe two, three days. After this, you know one Afghan guy, he's living here. It's my language. He's told me about everything. And after that, I'm okay. I'm not scared after that. (Mahmud)

The other young person; that one was speaking a little bit of English. So they were speaking their own language, but if I want something I have to ask the other one, he was a little bit understanding. (Sarah, Nabil's foster carer)

Young people felt reassured when they encountered young people who spoke their language and could offer them explanations and guidance about their environment. Some social workers tried to look for placements where this support was available. Reflecting on his own experience of being supported, and also supporting others, one young person suggested that a buddy scheme could be helpful for new arrivals for the mutual peer support it could provide.

Even when foster carers did not speak a shared language, some were aware of the symbolic significance of familiar language as a means of welcome and found ways to make use of this. The young daughter of Arian's white British foster carer had drawn a "welcome" sign in Albanian in preparation for his arrival. Arian used this example to contrast this foster family with his experience in a previous foster placement where he had not felt welcome or included in family life. Nabil also singled out the use of language as a means through which his foster carer had welcomed him. When asked how his foster carer had helped him at the beginning of the placement, Nabil recalled how his foster carer had said, "good morning" to him in Arabic on his first day, which is similar to the phrase in Pashto, his first language. Although unable to communicate in a shared language, this effort to speak a few familiar words had a symbolic importance and communicated the foster carer's desire to welcome Nabil into her home. Some fostering agencies also provided resources to support foster carers welcoming new arrivals. One young person remembered that his foster carer's agency had provided him with a welcome pack on his arrival, which he still kept.

> *Still I have it ... welcome boxes ... bag, wallet, camera, a pencil, you know ... Books to read. Was good ... I was happy, you know. (Samuel)*

Finally, foster carers also displayed creative and thoughtful approaches in working around communication difficulties to find points of commonality, looking more broadly at communication beyond language to find familiar points of reference and welcome. Nadir and his foster carer, Steve, discovered they shared a common interest and used this as a basis for beginning to develop their relationship.

> *We have got a lot of things in common. If I'm working in the back garden he knows exactly what I'm doing ... when he came here, the first week I was building a shed at the back, when he didn't know a word in English. But every tool I wanted, he knew what I wanted and would pass it to me. Which, if it was my son I would have to say: 'Can you pass me the saw? Can you pass me the hammer?' He knew exactly what I wanted and he'd pick it up and would join in and cut a bit of wood for me and things like that ... I think he enjoyed that. I think that's really where the bond started. (Steve, Nadir's foster carer)*

These practical skills, although familiar and reassuring to Nadir, were also a form of cultural capital that migrated across borders with him (Bourdieu, 1984).[30] The skills, knowledge and interests were recognised and valued in his new environment and were drawn on to enable him to take an active role in the household in the early days of his placement.

---

30 "Cultural capital" refers to educational, social or intellectual knowledge used as a resource in the production of social positions in society. Bourdieu argued that cultural capital helped to reproduce social class distinctions and privileges.

Culture and religion

Some young people had been placed with foster carers of the same ethnic, religious or national origin. In our interviews, some Afghans and Iranians were placed with Pakistani or Iranian foster carers[31] or with Muslims from other ethnic origins. Some Eritrean, Ghanaian and Nigerian young people were placed with foster carers from the same countries of origin. While some young people reported tensions in these placements, many settled well into relationships with foster carers of the same nationality or faith, and often mentioned cultural factors that facilitated this, citing the benefits of shared language, food tastes or values. Ayotunde said: 'I think it was all right because she [my foster carer], she's Nigerian and I'm Nigerian as well . . . we kind of have the same values and norms so.'[32]

Where foster carers and young people did not share the same nationality, ethnic origin or religion, foster carers often made an effort to develop their knowledge of the young person's country of origin and religion and tried to provide familiar points of reference by accessing information and pictures on the internet or in library books, often as part of a shared activity with young people. Social workers generally informed foster carers about young people's religious needs so they could provide basic considerations such as food that met dietary requirements, prayer mats and religious books and could show young people where places of worship were located. Some foster carers who had begun placements more recently had been given booklets about the young person's country of origin. Others said they were given these a year or so into the placement, by which time they had already built up this knowledge themselves. Foster carers began with this initial guidance and their own research on countries of origin. Religious and cultural identities are not homogenous or

---

31 Although from predominantly Muslim countries, some Shia young people may have been placed with Sunni foster carers and vice versa; there may well also have been different degrees of commitment to religious identifications and practices. These contexts were not explored in detail in this study. Christian young people placed with Christian foster carers were often also from different traditions within this faith.

32 These issues will be picked up again in Chapter 8.

interpreted and practised in uniform ways by young people (Hall, 1996; Anthias, 2006). Some foster carers went beyond a "cultural checklist" and began a complex and interactive process of refinement with young people during the placement where, through trial, error and negotiation, they were able to create an experience that was more familiar in the context of that young person's particular social history and took account of their expressed needs and wishes.

Food

Research in social anthropology has for a long time recognised the social role of food beyond its nutritional, physical value. This knowledge has more recently been incorporated into research on the topics of migration and settlement, families and foster care (Hage, 1997; Mankekar, 2005; Kohli *et al*, 2010; Rees *et al*, 2010). Kohli and colleagues (2010) explore the social role of food in work with refugee and asylum-seeking young people in foster care, which lies at the intersections of these research fields. In addition to being necessary for basic survival, comfort and well-being, food and food practices hold wider symbolic significance and can be tools and measurements of settlement, of inclusion and feelings of belonging and home.

Food featured in a number of ways throughout accounts of foster care placements and these are explored further in Chapter 8. However, with respect to the early stages of the placement, it was evident that food could act as a "first refuge" for unaccompanied minors where 'in such contexts of uncertainty and flux' it provided 'a practical and psychological fix that allowed them to find their bearings' (Kohli *et al*, 2010). Providing young people with a familiar environment enabled them to feel safe and secure and created a stable base from which to deal with transitions into aspects of life in the UK which may be less familiar.

First to make them feel safe and secure . . . get as much as they can about what reminds them of home . . . I like carers that really take an awful lot of effort to cook exactly what the young person likes, and to go all round the place trying to get the tastes that they like. (Social worker, Area 3)

Food generated lively discussion amongst young people in focus groups and interviews. Many of the Afghan young people who lived with Pakistani or Iranian foster carers mentioned the pleasure of having familiar food. An Eritrean young person described the food and Eritrean coffee his Eritrean foster carer prepared for him and spoke about the first meal he had on his arrival at the house. Two other foster carers had lived in the Middle East for a number of years and had some understanding of regional food tastes. However, there were also many successful food experiences in other foster placements where foster carers who were less familiar with young people's cuisine demonstrated early on that they were prepared to provide food the young people liked and encouraged them to become involved in food choices and preparation. Arian's foster carer described how this was also a useful tool through which she could display her commitment and care to Arian (Finch, 2007) and build a relationship of trust.

So you want a tangible, early win ... So things like, you know, we would try and find out what kind of food that they liked and make it. (Eleanor, Arian's foster carer)

Samir's foster carer enjoyed cooking and he and his partner described how they enjoyed trying out new food and had developed their eating to accommodate new flavours. Some foster carers found Afghan recipe books and began to experiment. A number of foster carers commented on their enjoyment of the new experiences they had through fostering young people from a different cultural background to their own (Brown *et al*, 2010). Eva encouraged her foster children to suggest ingredients she might incorporate, which they suggested based on ingredients they remembered their families using. While familiarity was important to many young people, choice and control was also significant, whether in choosing food from countries of origin or other new kinds of "comfort" food. A person's choice and control over their environment, decisions and lifestyle have also been identified as key criteria for establishing feelings of "home" (Watson and Austerberry, 1986; Van Horst, 2004; Sirriyeh, 2010a).

Communication difficulties early on in the placement sometimes created challenges in negotiating food arrangements. Abraham and his foster carer described how a process of trial and error established which food Abraham enjoyed. His foster carer said: 'Sometimes you'd put food in front of him and he wouldn't touch it . . . It made you feel really bad and you'd open the cupboards and the fridge and that and he'd pick out what he liked.' Abraham said: 'Some day if I didn't like it I'd just go (makes vomiting noise) in the toilet.' Young people were often included in family food shopping trips and were asked to choose things they might like to eat. This also helped to clarify anxieties and answer questions. For example, some young people were cautious about eating food early on in the placement because they were unsure of their foster carer's knowledge of halal food, but were unable to discuss this with them. One focus group participant described how he only ate bread when he first arrived and his foster carer was concerned. The young person explained to his social worker through an interpreter that he did not eat because he did not know if the food was halal. Subsequently, the foster carer took him shopping to show she bought meat from a halal butcher.

Another obstacle in providing familiar food occurred when young people had not learned how to cook in their countries of origin and were unable to explain what meals they were used to eating or how to prepare them. Rafi, who arrived in the UK when he was ten years old, said: 'They have tried, but I couldn't really remember what I had in Afghanistan . . . They have tried to cook rice or something but I wouldn't know.' An Eritrean focus group participant chose to move out of her foster placement after two weeks in order to live in a shared flat with another Eritrean young person in an area with a larger Eritrean population where she would have closer cultural links and support. Speaking about her experience in foster care she said:

> She [foster carer] was telling me to cook your country food and sometimes I don't know how to cook very well so, yeah, I was confused. And I don't see another from my country people and there is no neighbour . . . so no one show me how to cook.
> (Young women's focus group)

Finally, the Muslim holy month of Ramadan was raised as a point of adjustment for foster carers attempting to provide support for young people while they were fasting. While some Muslim young people chose not to fast, the majority appeared to do so. Social workers and foster carers raised this issue as an area that sometimes caused tensions. During Ramadan young people needed to eat later in the evening and very early in the morning, which had an impact on family food routines and food preparation.

> *The foster parent is not going to wake up at four o'clock in the morning . . . Food then becomes an issue. Who's going to pre-pare the food? Are you going to disturb the rest of the household? So that's a huge conflict area.* (Social worker, Area 1)

However, although foster carers in our study mentioned that accom-modating young people's food needs during Ramadan could be challenging, most were flexible in their approach. Foster carers usually prepared food in advance for young people so that it was available when they needed to eat, but did not disrupt the food routines of other members of the family, and their foster children seemed happy with this. Some young people also visited friends for meals on some evenings during Ramadan – often friends who lived in independent accommodation and knew how to cook. In one case, several Afghan young people lived in one foster placement and chose to prepare food and break their fast together during this month. Finally, two foster carers chose to change their routines and woke up with the young people to support them during this period.

As we have seen, some foster carers had pre-existing resources within their individual backgrounds and prior experience that they were able to utilise in providing a "first refuge" for young people based around familiarity and security. However, other foster carers demonstrated that, while helpful, these resources were not a necessity and there were examples of how foster carers' creativity enabled them to construct alternative ways of helping young people to feel welcomed and secure.

Supporting transitions to unfamiliar territory

In addition to providing a "first refuge" based around familiarity and security, a key role for foster carers was to support young people through new experiences and transitions into less familiar territory. In Chapters 9 to 11 we explore how foster carers supported young people's attempts to establish themselves in domains outside the foster home. However, in this chapter we begin by exploring how unfamiliar territory was also encountered within the foster care home itself.

A key task for foster carers was to support young people's efforts to learn English in order to integrate into the household as well as the outside world. In their study on transitions into foster care among the wider population of looked after children, Mitchell and colleagues (2010) found that young people's experiences of anxiety and discomfort were minimised when they were able to tell their foster carers about their likes and dislikes. They suggest that this may help the bonding process during these early stages as foster carers and young people become more familiar about each others' interests and objects of significance. As mentioned earlier, a key challenge was the difficulty of communication. In situations where no one in the house spoke the young person's language, verbal communication was a struggle that could leave young people feeling isolated: 'At that time I don't know much English so I don't understand her. Every day I was sad because I don't understand English.'

Social work teams provided interpreters for meetings soon after placing a young person. However, for day-to-day interactions young people and foster carers had to find ways to communicate without this service. Two foster carers used a telephone interpreting service in the early days of placement, although there were mixed views on its helpfulness, given that the quality of interpreting was variable.

Some foster carers and young people waited several days for the initial meeting with a social worker and interpreter to transmit information between foster carer and young person and to make plans. One foster carer described how they waited three days for this first planning meeting (others had waited up to ten days). In the meantime, as she lived in an area with an Afghan population, she took the young person to a local Afghan shop where the staff could pass on basic information.

Where foster carers and young people did not have a shared language, some carers made use of dictionaries, phrase books and sign language to communicate and begin teaching young people English. Some were given a phrase book by their local authority. However, most foster carers used resources on the internet or in their local library. Aarif's foster carer made her own flashcards to help newly-arrived foster children to communicate with her. It was notable that in this process of communication foster carers sometimes met young people part way in the early days, as they also encountered new experiences, made adaptations and learned some basic words and phrases in other languages. Mark and Susan fostered an Eritrean young person. They had used a Tigrinya phrase book that Mark ordered from the local library and described how these early attempts to communicate with their foster child were incorporated into their daily activities:

We took snippets out of the Tigrinya phrase book, pinned up on the fridge. That's how we communicated to start with, which was extremely hard work. (Mark, Abraham's foster carer)

A few of the Afghan young people came from nomadic backgrounds or had lived in very rural areas. Therefore, as well as the difficulties of adjusting to the challenges of a new language, being away from their families and dealing with the immigration system, even some "everyday" and taken-for-granted features of life in the UK represented new experiences. Nadir said he used to live in a tent in Afghanistan, was not used to being in a house with electricity and central heating and had to learn how these worked. Leena, Mahmud's foster carer, said: 'I can imagine it was like being dropped on another planet, you know. He didn't know absolutely anything at all about how anything worked, and they kept flicking the lights on and off.'

However, not all young people face such adjustments. As mentioned in Chapter 5, even young people from the same countries of origin have heterogeneous backgrounds. For example, young people from Afghanistan came from different regions in the country and different ethnic groups and socio-economic classes. However, even for young people from more affluent backgrounds or urban areas, who did not find this lifestyle such a big change from their previous experience, simply being in a new house and unfamiliar surroundings could be a daunting experience (Sinclair, 2005; Mitchell *et al*, 2010). Aarif's foster carer remembered how Aarif had appeared anxious and uncertain at this time. She highlighted the importance of being aware of this and described the prompts and encouragement she provided to him at this stage to help him settle into the house.

> *It's the expressions on his face, just a look of shock and bewilderment. Frightened to move, having to say, like: 'If you want a drink, help yourself, just ask me'... And getting up in the morning, they wouldn't move 'til I knocked on the door.*
> (Lisa, Aarif's foster carer)

As for many other young people entering foster care, a key area of adjustment for young people in our study was around lifestyles, family culture, practices and "rules" in the foster care household (Sinclair *et al*, 2005). Allocation of space in the home and attitudes to shared space were discussed both in relation to adjustments necessary between individuals with differing lifestyles but also to ways in which culturally informed attitudes may be incorporated into fostering regulations and practice. While guided primarily by safeguarding concerns, approaches to sleeping arrangements perhaps also reflect particular cultural understandings of space, the individual, and communal living. Stephanie described how her Afghan foster children chose to share a room, although two bedrooms were available, because in Afghanistan they had both been used to sharing rooms with other members of their family. Following their social worker's insistence that they should not share as they were not siblings, the boys were made to have separate rooms, which they were unhappy with. In contrast Aarif, who was fostered in another area in the study, said he had been able to share his room with another Afghan boy in his placement. One social worker described how these adjustments could cause some confusion for young people, social workers and foster carers.

He said the worst part was having to sleep in a bedroom by himself. He'd never have done that, he'd always slept with his family. He said that was really frightening and, you know, we actually think, oh, it's important for them to have their own room. (Social worker, Area 3)

The issue of "house rules" and boundaries were frequently raised. Social workers and foster carers spoke of the difficulties some young people had in adapting to a more controlled environment if they had been used to greater levels of independence at a young age. While some young people felt relief and security at the prospect of settling in an environment where they were contained and looked after in this way, others struggled to return or adjust to this experience of dependence and regulation (Yaya, 1998; Luster *et al*, 2009).

Some social workers said they usually asked foster carers about their house rules at initial placement meetings. It was suggested that as young people were not familiar with the household, being given an outline of the rules upfront could clarify things for them and help them to settle. This practice was evident amongst some young people and foster carers. A young woman from a focus group said: 'She told me her rules. What she likes and what she don't like; the house; bathroom; everything.' While some foster carers said that they did have an explicit discussion about "rules" with young people early in the placement, others expressed discomfort at the terminology of "rules" and the notions of discipline and rigidity that they felt these implied. While not dismissing a concept of boundaries and structure, they described a process whereby the order and practices of the household were arrived at gradually through a pathway of negotiation and flexibility which took account of, and was moulded to, the needs and characteristics of that particular young person. Mahmud's foster carer described how setting too many rules and restrictions on young people was not appropriate due to their emotional well-being at this stage, while Samuel's foster carer described the gradual and negotiated process through which boundaries became established in their household:

> *They suggest that I put down rules, which I do . . . nothing strong, nothing petty, you know, I mean, they're free. I mean, they've had enough trauma without me adding to it, you know, I'm really laid back. And I give them respect and I get loads of respect back.* (Leena, Mahmood's foster carer)

> *We just let them come in. We just accept them, talk to them, get to know how they got here, and things like that. Let the boundaries come gradually, obviously.* (Michael, Samuel's foster carer)

Summary

Most unaccompanied asylum-seeking young people entering their first foster placement have only limited (if any) knowledge of the concept of foster care. Therefore, it is helpful for social workers to explain the meaning of foster care in simple terms at this point. Greater information about the nature of the specific placement and foster carers may also help to prepare them. Foster carers often receive only limited information about the young people. However, the time limitations in preparing emergency placements, the fact that young people are often only recently arrived in the country, and the challenges of gathering information at this stage mean that social workers face significant difficulties in providing information to fostering agencies and foster carers at this point.

Transitioning into foster care is often an anxious time for young people. They may feel a great deal of uncertainty as they face the prospect of living in a new family, starting a new school and generally settling into life in a new country. All of this takes place within the context of an uncertain and precarious immigration status. Communication is often a key issue at this point. Young people may find it helpful to live with foster carers or foster siblings from their countries of origin who speak the same or related languages. However, there were many examples of cross-cultural placements which were success-ful because foster carers actively sought out resources to assist them with communication, took on creative approaches and invested significant amounts of time. Provision of phrase books and country information by children's services and fostering agencies can be useful for foster carers when young people first arrive and own-language introductions to foster care for young people may be equally helpful.

In the early stages of placement, two key tasks of foster care were, first, to provide stable, secure, familiar and welcoming surroundings and, second, to support young people with their transitions to new and unfamiliar territory. Foster carers and young people spoke positively of some of the immediate practical responses foster carers can provide to make young people feel physically comfortable and recover from their journey, such as making them food, displaying a calm, relaxed and non-intrusive manner, introducing them to the household, and allowing them to rest. Providing familiar food can help to create a more "homelike" environment, and provide security and comfort on arrival. It is also a way through which foster carers can display to young people that they are welcome and included in the home and family. Adjustments and negotiations around house rules were also a common theme discussed in relation to transitions. To avoid misunderstandings as young people and foster carers adjust to their new circumstances, it appears to be helpful if the order, boundaries and practices of the household are arrived at gradually through a pathway of negotiation and flexibility which takes account of, and is moulded to, the needs and characteristics of that particular young person.

7 Placement relationships: how young people were getting on

Our last chapter explored young people's initial transitions into foster care. The current chapter moves on to explore some of the expectations and hopes young people held for successful foster care relationships. An overview is then provided of progress in placements after the initial settlement period and we explore the quality of relationships between foster children, foster carers and other children in the household.

The young people in this study were in relatively long-term foster placements. Only 37 per cent of the survey sample had been in their current placement for one year or less and for nearly half of them (46%) their current placement was their first placement. Often these had begun as emergency placements that were made when the young person first arrived in the country and then developed into longer-term placements. The primary aim of this form of foster care was to provide a secure base, to nurture and support young people in the resettlement process, and to prepare them for independent living (Beek and Schofield, 2004).[33]

What do young people want from foster care?

In order to understand young people's perspectives on how successful placements had been, we asked them about their criteria for measuring a "good" placement. Although unaccompanied young people have needs and experiences that are particular and unique, they also have much in common with those of other looked after children. Referring to this wider population, Sinclair (2005) suggests that young people have five main requirements from foster care. Broadly they want

---

33 This may only have been a temporary period of resettlement for many young people who faced the prospect of being returned to their country of origin when they reach the age of 18.

"normality", "family care", "respect for their origins", "control" and "opportunity". The unaccompanied young people in our study voiced similar needs that fell broadly within these categories, but also included some additional features and perspectives.

Like other looked after young people, our young people expressed a desire for a "normal" life (Hek, 2007). So far as was possible in a care setting, young people wanted an environment where they had the opportunity to recover and rebuild their lives following challenging migration experiences. They sought opportunities for the 'return of the rhythm of ordinary life after having lived through extraordinary events' (Kohli and Connolly, 2009, p88). Rashid said: 'I leave my family, everything to save my life. When I came here I feel safe, no fighting and no killing.' A central aspect of having a "normal" life was feeling safe. One social worker described how a young person he worked with felt safe and protected living with his foster carer:

He runs home or cycles home as quick as he can now to see the foster father, 'cos as long as he knows he's there he knows he's safe. (Social worker, Area 1)

When asked about the advantages of being in foster care, young people often described how it enabled them to be looked after and sheltered from some of the more adult responsibilities they would otherwise have to face or may have faced in the past. In foster care they could focus on education, and many of them were able to develop active social lives. Foster carers could also operate as guides and advisers through pathways in a new country (Luster *et al*, 2010). Obstacles to achieving a sense of normality were seen by young people as being imposed by some of the practice regulations in foster care and social work. However, challenges also arose from these young people's social and legal position as refugee and asylum-seeking young people. This included anxiety about potentially negative outcomes to their asylum claims, barriers to planning for the future, feelings of sadness about past events and missing families and countries of origin (Chase *et al*, 2008).

Where young people are able to develop a sense of belonging

within the family, this is likely to help them establish a "psychosocial secure base" in foster care (Schofield and Beek, 2005). Young people in our study generally wanted to feel this sense of belonging in the foster home, to feel cared for and to be treated the same as the other young people living in the home (Selwyn *et al*, 2010). They wanted to know that their foster carers were not just doing it for the money:

If you have foster children you should give them all the freedom, all the access in your house. You are allowed to go to the main place to sit in, so that is what you are going into foster care for, to be treated as their own. (Young women's focus group)

I think the placements that go really, really well are where young people are made to feel part of the family, they're, you know, really taken on board in what the family routine is. (Team manager, Area 4)

Looked after children hold differing views over the ways in which they want to belong to a foster family and some may feel a conflict of loyalty between foster and birth families (Sinclair, 2005). The context is somewhat different for unaccompanied minors as their birth families are not in the UK, although a few young people had established contact with some members of their extended family or with family friends. Young people sought different degrees of attachment and belonging in their foster families. Many young people chose to refer to foster carers using family-like titles, such as "mum" and "dad" or "auntie" and "uncle". Auntie and uncle were often terms of respect they had used for adult friends of family in their countries of origin. These young people were often keen to be included in family activities and to cultivate "family-like" relationships.

Others did not seek this level of intimacy and simply wanted caring, respectful relationships.

They should just care about you and we care about them . . . 'cos you're not, you know, their child anyway, but at least [they should] show you just some respect. (Young men's focus group)

Most young people were keen to clarify that their foster families were not their real family, although two young people appeared to have more complex and ambivalent feelings towards their birth family. Some young people had contact with their birth family through the telephone and internet. Sometimes foster carers were included in this contact, as the young people sought to connect these two different families into their family network. Abbas sent a photograph of himself with his foster carer to his mother to keep her informed and included in his current life in the UK. 'Respect for their origins' was important to these young people, as it also is for other looked after children (Sinclair, 2005). However, this included not only family origins, but also countries of origin. Most young people wanted to develop contacts, networks and activities in the UK that would enable them to maintain links to their countries of origin and to their cultural or faith heritage. They often wanted to be able to include and tell their foster family about this heritage. Other young people were less interested in developing these contacts, sometimes due to fear of information filtering back to their country of origin (Sirriyeh, 2008), because they had ambivalent feelings about their origins or because they did not want to feel different from their foster family.

In comparison to other looked after children, unaccompanied minors are frequently reported as tending to have high educational aspirations and good attendance and to enjoy and work hard in school (Hek, 2005; Wade *et al*, 2005; Kohli, 2007; Sinclair *et al*, 2007). This was also reflected in comments from social workers, team managers and foster carers.

Young people in our study often emphasised support with education as a key benefit of being in foster care and one of the reasons why they wanted to live there.[34] They spoke of foster carers and foster siblings supporting their access to and progress in school and encouraging them to do well (Wade *et al*, 2005).

I find this client group quite compliant . . . They're quite motiva-
ted to try and do well for themselves . . . There might be

---

34 The theme of education forms the substance of Chapter 9.

a . . . small handful, that . . . lose their way. But, on the whole, this client group tend to be very focused . . . wanting to remain in the UK and . . . do quite well . . . On the whole, they would be OK . . . in foster placements because of their attitude and focus to do better for themselves. (Team manager, Area 4)

Some young people were concerned about potential limitations on their autonomy and control as looked after children, but also as asylum seekers where access to services and their ability to plan for the future was strongly tied to decisions made by those dealing with their asylum claims. They thought it was important for social workers to elicit their views about how they were faring in their placement and to take these views into account in pathway planning (Farmer *et al*, 2004; Sinclair, 2005).

How well were the placements going?

Our survey of foster carers provided information, from their perspective, on how the placement was working out. As Table 7.1 shows, most rated overall progress positively. Most foster carers felt that the placement had gone 'very well' for them and for the young person in their care. In most other cases, placements were judged by carers to have gone 'as well as could be expected'.

Table 7.1
How well has the placement gone for the foster carer and young person?

	How well for foster carer – % (n = 132)	*How well for young person – % (n = 124)*
Very well	79.5 (105)	77 (95)
As well as could be expected	19 (25)	20 (25)
Not very well	1.5 (2)	3 (4)

While most young people were therefore thought to have settled very well, where foster carers reported that things might have gone better for young people (n = 29) the comments provided by them reflect a range of concerns. In some instances, carers worried about the traumatic effects of young people's past experiences and how these may be affecting them in the present (Kohli and Mather, 2003). Comments pointed to the potential effects of loss and separation and the difficult transitions needed to settle in a new country, often in a context where the young people lacked language skills and their futures were generally uncertain. Some may therefore have been rather better placed than others to meet these challenges and not all were thought to have been supported adequately.

> *He has very little English and understands some things by default. I have only just learned of his immigration issues and realise he must be under great stress. He has no friends and any mentoring is done by English speakers. I feel more work needs to be done to support him.*[35]

> *The young person in our care is a very pleasant character and he is embraced by the other members in the household. With regard to the young person, it must have been traumatic to be taken away from your birth family and sent to a different country where cultures and lifestyles are radically different.*

In relation to some young people, carers reported feelings of transience or dissatisfaction. Although the placements were often going quite well, some carers were aware that young people wanted to move away, either now or in the near future. This could have implications for the quality of care that could be provided.

> *It is very difficult to care for a child who does not want to stay.*

---

35 Written comments provided by foster carers on questionnaires are not attributed.

He appears settled in the home, but he has mentioned that he would like to be with a Muslim family. He has stated that he wants to leave when he is finished at school at 16 years of age.

Finally, some carers expressed concern about the extent to which some young people had become integrated into the family. Some young people were described as being withdrawn, as being unable or unwilling to interact with family members or as being secretive about themselves, their families and their personal histories (see also Kohli, 2006a; Chase, 2010). Sometimes cultural differences also created tensions and constrained the quality of relationships in the home, at least until time allowed for the development of more shared understandings of these differences.

The child has made complaints in the past and continually seems unhappy. He is doing well academically but has made no attempts to integrate into the family or the English-speaking community.

Unaccompanied minors have so many secrets, it's hard to get to know them properly and this can reflect on the relationship.

[Tensions have existed] ... due to differences in culture, language and the child's attitude, especially a lack of respect for females, although this is settling down.

Quality of the carer and young person relationship

The survey asked foster carers to provide answers to a series of questions about their relationships with the young people they were looking after. Overall, these provided proxy measures of the extent to which young people were perceived to be easy to care for, to have integrated into the foster family and to have a sense of belonging and attachment to their carers. Table 7.2 provides a breakdown of their responses.

By all accounts young people were thought to have settled into their placements quite well. Most foster carers reported that they

Table 7.2
Foster carer assessment of relationship with young person – per cent[36]

	Not at all	To some degree	Very much so
Is easy to care for (n = 131	4	31	65
* Feels part of family (n = 131)	5	33	62
* Trusts you (n = 131)	2	24	73
Feels the odd one out (n = 117)	67	24	9
* Feels you care for her/him (n = 131)	2	18	80

found the young people relatively easy to care for and that the emotional bonds between them were reasonably strong. Few carers reported strongly negative experiences in relation to the young people, although over one-third of the young people were reported to have some desire to leave (now or in the future) and a similar proportion to feel like the odd one out in the family, at least to some degree. In general, the central column points to some ambivalence about the extent to which young people were perceived to be completely comfortable within the family setting and, perhaps in particular, about the degree to which young people were thought able to communicate about personal aspects of their lives.

Young people's prior experiences of placement movement or breakdown had no significant effect on the quality of relationships in the current placement. However, it was not surprising to find that those who had been living in these placements for a longer period of

---

36 Items marked with an asterisk were subsequently combined into a Family Integration Measure (Cronbach's alpha 0.788). This measure has been used in previous York studies on foster care (see Sinclair et al, 2005; Biehal et al, 2010). Multivariate analysis using this measure suggested that, as discussed below, length of time in placement and the absence of emotional or behavioural difficulties were the two most important predictors of family integration, accounting in combination for 22% of the variation in this measure (Adjusted r^2 = 0.226 for linear regression with Family Integration as the dependent variable).

time were rated more highly in relation to many of these domains. Although they were no more likely than others to be reported as easy to care for, to feel part of the family or to feel encouraged, those who had been in placement longer were significantly more likely to have trust in their carer, to feel well cared for and to talk to their carers about things that were personal to them.[37] They were also rather less likely to feel like the odd one out or to feel picked on.[38] Finally, it was also marginally more likely that foster carers would consider that these young people had gradually integrated into the family better over time when compared to those who had more recently arrived.[39] As the qualitative material has suggested, the passage of time therefore helped to create the conditions in which confidence, trust and communication could grow, provided relationships were not unduly affected by other doubts and challenges.

The quality of these family relationships was also not greatly affected by young people's personal characteristics. There were no differences according to gender or the young person's age. However, in Chapter 3 we saw that for around one-fifth of young people (21%) there was uncertainty about their official age. Where this uncertainty existed, it appeared to have some knock-on effect for placement relationships. In these circumstances, carers' perceptions of their relationships with young people were significantly more negative.[40] It may therefore be likely that, for some foster carers at least, where these doubts about age remain, they can have a negative effect on the quality of relationships within the placement.

---

37 Kendall's tau b tests for placement duration and "trusts you" ($p<0.001$, t 0.273, n =115); "feels you care" ($p = 0.003$, t 0.234, n = 115); "talks to you about personal things" ($p = 0.001$, t 0.260, n = 115)

38 Kendall's tau b test for placement duration and "feels the odd one out" ($p = 0.015$, t 0.195, n = 103); "feels picked on" ($p = 0.06$, t 0.150, n = 108)

39 Kendall's tau b test for placement duration and "fits in better" now ($p = 0.06$, t 0.149, n = 115)

40 Mann Whitney U exact tests for age uncertainty and "easy to care for" ($p<0.001$, n = 122); "feels part of family" ($p = 0.038$, n = 122); "trusts you" ($p = 0.005$, n = 122), "feels cared for" ($p = 0.006$, n = 122); "talks to you" ($p = 0.002$); n = 122); "feels the odd one out" ($p = 0.033$, n = 109). Although the other three variables were not significantly associated, they were all in the expected direction.

Where young people were reported by foster carers to display emotional or behavioural difficulties, this was also associated with young people being less integrated into the foster family in some important respects. They were considered less easy to care for, presumably due to the behaviour management issues they raised. However, they were also reported by carers as being less likely to feel part of the family, to feel less cared for and less trustful, and more likely to feel like the odd one out and to want to leave.[41] Where no emotional or behavioural problems were reported by carers, over four-fifths of young people (85%) were considered to be highly integrated into the family. Where these difficulties were reported as being moderate to severe, two-thirds (65%) were rated as being quite poorly integrated. Coping with children's challenging behaviour is one of the factors that foster carers find particularly difficult, that may create carer strain and reduce their responsiveness to children. Negative spirals of this kind have also been linked to a heightened risk of placement breakdown and instability (Quinton *et al*, 1998; Farmer *et al*, 2004; Sinclair *et al*, 2004, 2005b.)

Relationships with other children living in the placement

In Chapter 3 we saw that young people needed to establish relationships with a range of other children, including other fostered, adopted or non-related children living in the foster home. In the survey, foster carers were asked to indicate how well they were getting on together. Table 7.3 shows that foster carers felt that these relationships, in most instances, were generally positive.

---

41 Emotional or behavioural difficulties were measured using a four-point scale (from no problems to serious problems). Kendall's tau b tests for these difficulties and "easy to care for" (p = 0.007, t 0.226, n = 124); "part of family" (p = 0.016, t .202, n = 124); "trusts you" (p = 0.013, 0.252, , n = 124), "feels cared for" (p = 0.011, t 0.216, n = 124); "odd one out" (p = 0.009, t 0.231, n = 111); "wants to leave" (p = 0.008, t 0.229, n = 114)

Table 7.3
Relationship with other children in the foster placement

	With foster carer's own birth children (n = 110)	*With other children in the household (n = 99)*
Very well	69 (76)	70 (69)
As well as could be expected	26 (28)	26 (26)
Not very well	6 (6)	4 (4)

The brief comments of foster carers in response to these questions reveal the complex nature of family relationships and the adjustments that are required to make them work. Young people were frequently portrayed as friendly, outgoing, respectful and polite (Kohli, 2007). In these circumstances they were able to reach out and cement relationships with other children and adults.

He is an easygoing young person who is able to mix with a wide range of people.

The child is very friendly and quite outgoing, which makes her fit in very well with other kids.

In our interviews, most young people and foster carers spoke of very positive relationships between unaccompanied young people and the foster carer's birth children, grandchildren and other foster children in the household. Extended family and foster carers' birth children played an important role in welcoming young people into the household (Triseliotis *et al*, 2000; Sinclair *et al*, 2004, 2005b). Ayotunde's foster carer described how her son and grandson had similar interests to Ayotunde and how they had befriended him and included him in their activities. Rafi's foster carers also described the close bonds that had developed between him and her older birth children.

He's very good with him . . . they exercise together, like running around, because my son's an exercise fanatic and it's the same too with Ayotunde. (Grace, Ayotunde's foster carer)

All our own children love him to bits and will take him off and do things with them all the time. (Andrew, Rafi's foster carer)

In a number of cases, young people were included in visits to foster carers' grown-up birth children and extended family and had developed good relationships with them. Eleanor described a scenario that symbolised to her the foster children's place within her family. Soon after her Albanian foster children arrived in the placement, Eleanor took them to her relative's birthday dinner:

We were taking some photos and we said, 'Oh yeah, let's get the family', and they [foster children] stood away and everyone else went, 'Oh no, no, no, in, in!' It was just one of those moments where you think, OK, yeah, that's it, you are. (Eleanor, Arian's foster carer)

Where young people had been successfully integrated into family life, the nature of the relationships that were formed with children and foster carers were family-like, with strong expressions of care and affection expressed in otherwise simple comments. As mentioned earlier, creative kinship was often in evidence where kin terms, such as "brother", "auntie", "like a mum", had been used by young people, carers and their families to symbolise closeness and construct a form of kinship status (Mason and Tipper, 2008):

He gets on well with the whole family: our grandchildren, with our other foster child living here, with our foster children who have left and come to visit and, when we go out, he likes it if we refer to him as our grandson. (Survey)

We were like sister and brother. (Samuel, young person interviewee)

Oh it's just like my big brother now. We go out a lot, he takes me to the cinema and stuff, and we go around and he's really cool. (Ayotunde)

She called me son and I called her mum. (Young men's focus group)

That family also have two sons that are younger than what I am. We live like brothers doing things between us all. (Young men's focus group)

While young people's adjustment to the everyday life of new families was not always easy, some comments suggested that a close cultural or ethnic match with foster carers or other fostered children could help young people to settle in and feel more at home.

Our other foster child is also Vietnamese. They both enjoy the ease of communication and socialise together and with us whenever possible. Our own children no longer live with us but have regular contact and mix in well with our foster children. (Survey)

He's like my brother ... most of the time we speak Pashto. (Rashid)

We have no birth children living with us. However, he gets on very well with another Afghan boy. He was placed at the same time, as they were already friends. Our other boy is from a different culture, being Kurdish, and they are not so close but get on OK. (Survey)

Where young people have formed prior relationships with other unaccompanied young people soon after arriving in the UK, finding ways of enabling them to keep together, as this last example showed, may be very important in providing them with companionship and solidarity on the journey towards resettlement. However, this example simultaneously points to circumstances where cultural differences between young people may lead to placement tensions. There were also one or two examples of tensions between Hazara and Pashtun young people from Afghanistan who were placed together but appeared unable to develop positive relationships. However, this was certainly not always the case and some cross-cultural (or cross-faith) relationships seemed to flourish.

The two boys I foster do lots of things together and never fall out. They are true friends, despite one being Hazara and the other Christian. (Survey)

Meanwhile, shared nationality and ethnicity did not guarantee an absence of tension, which sometimes arose simply from having a group of young people of a close age living in a shared space. Ann was fostering three Afghan boys:

They're very volatile. We've had a few little ups and downs, because with them it's all about status and who's the top man . . . They're not brothers, they're not related. They've all got different personalities and they can't 100 per cent always get on. (Ann, Abbas' foster carer)

Nevertheless, these boys also chose to prepare food and eat together during Ramadan and these relationships enabled them to perform communal and social aspects of their religious practices.

The discourse of asylum seekers as threatening "others" has often been embedded in the image of the racialised and sexualised young male body (Hubbard, 2005; Judge, 2010). In one placement, there was evidence of tensions among young people around perceptions of gender roles, age and culture. Here, a foster carer who had fostered Afghan boys had fitted alarms on the doors of her teenage daughters' bedrooms. She spoke of a sense of discomfort when the girls were around the boys. In another case, the birth and foster children had eventually developed close and positive relationships, but the foster carer's daughters had initially been anxious and expressed doubts, having been aware of negative portrayals of Afghans:

When we knew that they were both on their way over, both my daughters were a little bit concerned, which I suppose is under-standable when, you know, the situation, like, in Afghanistan. My daughter, my oldest one, was like, 'Oh my God, what if they try and bomb the house, or they do this or they do that? I want a lock on my door,' and stuff like that. But once they came and we got to know them, you know, everyone was fine. (Stephanie, foster carer)

Tensions in relationships also appeared to arise from differences in age, from limitations of language that inhibited communication and, in some instances, from cultural perceptions of gender roles.

He is slightly uncomfortable in the presence of our other foster child, who is a 15-year-old female, who is also very independent. It was expressed to us as being about a different understanding of female upbringing. There was never any tension between them, just an acceptance of both parties sharing the home. (Survey)

He didn't get on with my daughter because back home in their country women don't speak or say anything out of turn to the men. (Survey)

In similar vein to the last comment, some foster carers appeared more accusatory, suggesting that young people in their care made little effort to cross cultural borders and form relationships, preferring to remain withdrawn and sullen.

The other child living with us is also from Afghanistan, but not related. He says he doesn't like him. He doesn't make any effort to interact with my birth children. (Survey)

With our children and our other foster children, he would never relate. He would always fight and argue. He would only speak with our other Afghan foster child. (Survey)

In a softer tone, some foster carers described the emotional distance maintained by some young people as stemming from reticence, shyness or simply from a lack of shared interests.

He has very different interests to my own children and he spends a lot of time with his own friends. He is very easy to get on with. (Survey)

He is a friendly young person, but cautious with young people or adults he doesn't know. (Survey)

Ermir also maintained his distance from another unaccompanied young person who had recently arrived in the foster placement. Although not in conflict, they had not sought to develop a relationship with each other. Ermir said: 'I only once spoke to him and never do things [with him]. I don't know him, like, how he is or stuff.'

One of the young people we interviewed had moved into his current placement because he had found it difficult living with a foster child in a previous placement. However, in the interviews and focus groups there were no other reports of placement breakdowns due to difficult relationships with foster siblings. Some young people stayed in touch with foster siblings whom they had shared placements with and they kept in touch through social networking websites and visits. Other young people had reasonable relationships while they were sharing placements, but did not stay in touch after placements ended.

Finally, in evaluating their relationships with other young people in the household, it was important for foster children to feel that they were being treated equally with other young people in the household (Abdullai *et al*, 2002; Sinclair *et al*, 2005a). Although there were some exceptions, most of the young people we spoke to felt that they had been treated equally to other young people and this was another way in which care and inclusion had been displayed.

They treat me same, the way they treat her. If they buy her [foster sibling] something, as well, they buy me something. I'm not left out. (Samuel)

He is quite shy, so it is very difficult to get too close to him, but yeah, I mean, you know, he's part of our family now. We treat him like we do our daughters. (Elizabeth, Sabir's foster carer)

Social workers discussed the equal treatment of foster children and birth children and highlighted the importance of this in displaying care to young people. They identified a range of experiences they had encountered, with foster children being treated differently in some homes, but more equally in others.

> *If it's a good placement, they normally always say, 'I'm just treated like a member of the family, I'm just the same as their children', and they're always pleased about that. And if it's a bad placement, we always hear them say, you know, 'I'm not allowed to do that, their children do that. I actually do all the jobs, their children don't have to do any.'* (Social worker focus group)

Summary

The young people in this study were in relatively long-term foster placements. The primary aim of this form of foster care is to provide a secure base to nurture and support young people in the resettlement process and prepare them for independent living.

Like other looked after young people, the young people in our study expressed a desire for a "normal" life. Young people wanted an environment where they had the opportunity to recover and rebuild their lives following challenging pre-migration experiences and journeys to the UK. They wanted to feel a sense of belonging in the foster home, to feel cared for and to be treated equally in comparison to the other young people living in the home. Respect for their origins was also important, including not only family origins, but also their countries of origin.

Most foster carers felt that the placement had gone very well for them and for the young person in their care. In some instances, carers worried about the traumatic effects of young people's past experiences and how these may be affecting them in the present. In relation to some young people, carers also reported young people's feelings of transience or dissatisfaction. Although the placements were often going quite well, some carers were aware that these young people wanted to move away, either now or in the near future.

Most young people were thought to have settled well into their placements. Their foster carers generally found these young people relatively easy to care for and that the emotional bonds between them were reasonably strong. This was particularly so for those who had been living in these placements for a longer period of time, where there were not continuing doubts about the age of young people that could erode relationships and where they did not exhibit moderate to severe emotional or behavioural difficulties. Where these factors did exist, however, young people were perceived to be less integrated into the life of the family.

While young people's adjustment to the everyday rhythms of new families was not always easy, there was some evidence that a close cultural or ethnic match with foster carers or other fostered children could help young people to settle in and feel more at home. However, shared nationality and ethnicity did not guarantee an absence of tension and some cross-cultural (or cross-religious) relationships also seemed to flourish.

Finally, young people needed to establish relationships with a range of other children, including other fostered, adopted or non-related children living in the foster home. Foster carers felt that these relationships in most cases had been generally positive, and extended family and foster carers' birth children played an important role in welcoming young people into the household and increasing their identification with the family network.

8   Placement relationships: making them work

Chapter 7 provided an overview of the progress and quality of relationships within foster care households. This chapter explores how these relationships were built and negotiated by foster carers and young people. It considers the extent to which young people and foster carers were able to develop close attachments and how these were achieved. Consideration is also given to the tensions and dilemmas that arose in these relationships, and the ways in which relationships were cemented through participation in shared activities of one kind or another.

Doing and displaying family in foster care

Rees and Pithouse (2008) describe foster care as 'the coming together of strangers' where 'the key participants in fostering have to co-construct and learn new understandings about intimacy within a relatively short and limited span of time'. In exploring how relationships developed between young people and their foster carers, we will examine how family practices were "made" and "displayed" to establish "family-like" attachments, or more ambivalent and distant relationships (Morgan, 1996; Finch, 2007; Mason and Tipper, 2008). It has been argued that contemporary families are defined more by "doing" family than "being" family (Morgan, 1996). Research on family and kinship now increasingly explores family practices and intimacy and how people are related and located in social networks and networks of intimacy through creative identity work (Carsten, 2000; Lawler, 2008; Kramer, 2011). There has been a shift from a primary focus on biological connectedness to examining the social construction of families and the way people "do" family in the regular routines and interactions that become embedded into daily life. Recently, Jones and Hackett (2011) have applied this approach to explore relationships in adoption, although foster care is still yet to be examined within this literature.

In addition to taking account of how people "do" family, the ways in which family is "displayed" must also be considered (Finch, 2007). The concept of "display" examines how family practices are created and established. Sometimes acts need to be displayed so they can be conveyed to and understood by others in order to become established and embedded as a family activity. This is also the case in foster care, where new members of the family learn about and become included in existing family practices, but also co-create new practices.

Relationships in foster placements in the current study had changed and developed over time (Linowitz and Boothby, 1988). While particular experiences varied from placement to placement, it was common for a period of adjustment and shifts in relationships to occur both in the early and end stages of placements, with a more stable (although sometimes still fluctuating) period in the middle. There was usually a gradual development in relationships, but changes also occurred at "fateful moments" (Giddens, 1991) or turning points when certain events and responses produced crossroads at which point young people and foster carers made key choices about routes to take in the relationship. Often there was some combination of the two. There were broadly three forms of relationships in the foster placements described to us. These included:

"Family-like" relationships – here young people and foster carers established new "family-like" connections, bonds and status (Mason and Tipper, 2008). There was usually an expectation that this bond would endure beyond the end of placement.

Temporary home bases – here good relationships existed between foster carers and young people, but without a tight bond. The relationship was seen as time limited until the end of the placement.

Lodgings – here the foster carer delivered the service they thought they were contracted to do. The young person did not feel at home, but instead more of a lodger in someone else's house.

The largest proportion of our interviewees spoke of "family-like" relationships, only two might be classed as "lodgings", and a very small number were "temporary home bases". In the focus groups with young care leavers, there was more of an even split across the categories.

Work on attachment and resilience has highlighted the necessity of establishing a secure base in which young people can develop their self-esteem, resilience and secure patterns of attachment (Rutter, 1999; Gilligan, 2001; Schofield and Beek, 2006). Resilience refers to a set of qualities that enable a person to cope with negative effects of risk and adversity and make positive adaptations (Gilligan, 2001; Masten and Powell, 2003). It can be built through retaining and developing positive factors in young people's lives in an attempt to counterbalance more negative factors (Gilligan, 2001). For unaccompanied minors this may mean making the most of their current environment and the resources available to them by developing their social relationships, achieving their potential in education and developing a strong base for transitions into adulthood. This may take place in the context of more negative factors such as immigration uncertainty and the impact of experiences of trauma and other challenges to their emotional well-being.

Building a safe and secure home base through foster care can help to create a basis from which resilience can be retained and developed to enable young people to make positive adjustments to life both within and beyond the foster home.

Young people emphasised the importance of the foster carer's display of love and care and their availability. Aarif said: 'If you give [young people] love, then they're going to notice. If they're in a bad way, then they're going to come in a good way.'

Foster carers also commented on the significance of their caring and nurturing roles, providing young people with a loving and secure base.

It wasn't easy for him at first, but he quickly adapted to it because we offered him a loving home. He was safe to be with us you know. We give him the best. [A] loving home. (Daniel, Rashid's foster carer)

The most important thing is that I've offered him somewhere safe, secure and homely to live in. (Stephanie, Omid's foster carer)

He can see that people do care, and I think that goes a long way. I think if you see that you're not just an item, you're somebody, I think people should grasp it and Samuel's grasping it. (Michael, Samuel's foster carer)

Some foster carers referred to unaccompanied young people within comments about the needs of young people in general. Others pointed to specific care, nurturing and support that unaccompanied minors needed in the context of their past experiences and challenges of resettlement in the UK.

Developing trust

Being available and helping young people to trust is an important aspect of a secure base (Schofield and Beek, 2006). Both foster carers and young people acknowledged the importance of developing trust in order to build successful relationships in placements. There were two main interconnected themes in this. First, foster carers and young people discussed the degree to which foster carers trusted the young people and the ways in which this was displayed to them. Second, they discussed the degree to which young people trusted foster carers and how this was also displayed. These relationships were built in the aftermath of experiences of conflict and forced migration where young people may have been subject to "cultures of mistrust" in countries of origin (Fink, 2001) and may have had to be cautious themselves about whom to trust in order to ensure their survival and safety (Robinson and Segrott, 2002; Hynes, 2003).

Young people and foster carers often illustrated the levels of trust foster carers had in young people by describing the levels of responsibility they were given, the extent to which they were entrusted with valuables, and their access to space in the home. Nabil's foster carer said:

I respect him. I trust him, with all my heart I trust him. I leave the house for him because . . . the house you find is left the same when you come back. (Sarah)

Nabil recognised this action as a display of trust (Finch, 2007) and said that he chose to reciprocate by not bringing friends to the house when his foster carer was out as a mark of respect for her. Another common measure of trust was having a key to the house and young people often compared their foster carers favourably to others they had heard of through friends. One participant in a young men's focus group said: 'Some of the family don't trust so they don't give [them] a key.' Finally, some young people were given money by their foster carers to buy clothes and were asked to return with change and the receipts, which they also understood as a sign of trust. A participant in a young men's focus group said: 'They did trust me to take money to buy clothes, take money and come back.'

In return, young people usually displayed trust in foster carers by confiding in them. Young people frequently described their foster carer as their primary confidante and spoke to them about a wide range of issues. Mahmud said: 'She is like my mum. I tell Leena many things.' Many young people in family-like relationships had spoken to their foster carers about their lives in their countries of origin and about their journeys to the UK. It was important for foster carers to be able listen and bear witness to young people's memories and reflections on experiences (Kohli and Mather, 2003). Often these stories emerged gradually through conversations over time as foster carers and young people came to know one another and relationships gradually developed. However, there were also key turning points in developing relationships of trust. Some foster carers were actively involved in supporting young people in their immigration cases and many had worked with the young person to tell and record their story for their immigration case.[42] This activity required a high level of trust

---

42 See Chapter 12 for further discussion of foster carers' role in the immigration process.

and openness from the young person and trust, empathy and understanding from the foster carer. Often this contributed to, and also resulted from, building a close bond. Turning-point moments were also noted in other situations when foster carers proved to the young person that they were on their side and would support them. This included, for example, advocating for them in securing access to services, helping them to make and resolve complaints, and helping them to arrange or maintain contact with relatives and friends.

> *I think where the turning point was in January where we supported him with his cousin, and then after that then he's sort of trusted us.* (Isobel, Majeed's foster carer)

Foster carers regarded advocating for young people as a central aspect of their role as foster carers.

> *You just do what you do, and you try and fight for them . . . and advocate.* (Ann, foster carer)

> *If you're doing fostering properly, every child should matter a hundred per cent and you go the extra mile for every child.* (Andrew, foster carer)

Young people spoke very positively about foster carers who were seen to go beyond a narrow or limited definition of their role. One example was the extensive work and emotional support given to them by foster carers in relation to their immigration cases. Another key area of advocacy was around access to education. Here, some foster carers had not simply found a school that was "good enough", but instead looked for the "best" school and made a concerted effort to get young people into that school, as they might do for their birth children.

> *My foster parents didn't want me to go to the school here because it wasn't really a good school. I applied in a couple of other schools, which they didn't accept me, then I got into [name of current school], so, yeah, I went there.* (Haaroon)

I said: 'I am a foster carer, I can choose any school I like for these young people. They are the highest priority . . . So if you think I'd choose this school think again, I wouldn't dream of it.' I wouldn't send my own children there, why would I send my foster children there? (Eleanor, Arian's foster carer)

She [foster carer] really pushed hard and . . . that's not just at school, that's on a lot of things, with social workers and . . . there's been a problem, or anything, she's been helping me. (Arian)

Young people's trust in the availability of emotional and practical support from their foster carer can reduce anxiety (Schofield and Beek, 2006). Some young people were also reassured and pleased when their foster carer displayed some understanding of their experiences and an openness and genuine interest in finding out more about them. Omid had spoken to his foster carer about his journey to the UK. This experience had helped his foster carer to engage her next Afghan foster child, who was less forthcoming:

We got him a big map and said there's a . . . certain stretch of water on a Turkish border, and it's really, really rough . . . When I said this to the new little lad I've got, he was really pleased that I had a bit of understanding of his journey. (Stephanie, Omid's foster carer)

Haaroon's foster carer, Eva, went to the library with her foster children to search for books about Afghanistan and they used the internet to find out information together. She encouraged young people to talk about their backgrounds by making conversations reciprocal and exchanging stories from her own childhood in another country.

While some young people named foster carers as key confidantes and described very open channels of communication with them, other young people were more guarded, at least initially.

He isn't very forthcoming. I mean he has said some things, but it was like pulling teeth to get that information. (Rachel, Nadir's foster carer)

Attachment issues can arise when a young person wants a closer or less close relationship than the carer wants to provide (Sinclair *et al*, 2005b) or when young people and foster carers have divergent perceptions and expectations of foster care relationships (Linowitz and Boothby, 1988). Some young people who were more guarded did not necessarily regard the foster carer–young person relationship as the context in which such personal feelings and confidences would be expressed. A participant in the young women's focus group said, '[The foster carer] said I am very quiet and I have something inside. But why am I going to tell her? She [is] not the same as my age. She is old. I am not going to talk to her like a friend.' Meanwhile, Ermir had chosen not to confide in anyone, including his foster carer, because he was reluctant to place trust in people he did not know. He said: 'When I don't know people, really, how am I going to trust them?'

These comments were made in the context of more strained relationships with foster carers. However, this cautious approach was not always an indication of difficult relationships. Some young people were simply more selective about the topics they spoke about and, although they were silent or gave limited information on their pre-migration lives and journeys to the UK, they could be open about their daily experiences and personal life in the UK. Some confided in foster carers about school and relationships and asked for advice on these issues. Nadir did not tell his foster carers much about his pre-migration experiences (see above), but confided in them about more day-to-day issues such as school and personal relationships:

> We'll talk about his day and like he'll tell us about girls, you know, 'Oh I've seen a nice girl, oh she's beautiful. You know, we'll say, 'Ooh that's good. But, you know, young ladies are very tricky, so you have to be careful what you say and what you do'. So we've had all those conversations. (Rachel, Nadir's foster carer)

Age, asylum and mistrust

Most foster carers and young people we spoke to had developed trust in each other to some degree. However, there were also some examples of scepticism, degrees of mistrust or, more commonly, acknowledgement of doubts or questions foster carers had about aspects of young people's accounts. On this topic, foster carers often referred to previous placements, but some also spoke about their current situation. Foster carers' explanations usually centred on issues connected to age disputes and immigration. Some expressed doubts as to whether young people were the age they claimed. It was thought that some young people claimed to be younger than they were because of their (often understandable) expectations that they would be treated more favourably in the asylum system.

Foster carers who expressed these concerns mentioned a) the lack of documented evidence of their age, b) older physical appearances and c) behaviour they associated with older ages or early adulthood. In some instances, it was evident that carers were conducting their own unofficial age assessments during the placements and these carers sometimes expressed limited confidence in the accuracy of social work assessments.

> As a foster carer, I couldn't very well say he's a man because they [social workers] start: 'You can't judge people just because you think they're a man. I know when they're men and when they're young boys, and everybody else did. The dentist said his teeth were rotten at the back, his wisdom teeth. (Lisa, foster carer)

In these unofficial age assessments, foster carers reflected on the young people's appearance and behaviour. Some sought advice or back-up from other professionals. Four foster carers had inappropriately spoken to their foster children's dentists to ask their opinions on the young person's age, even though, as one foster carer pointed out, this is a contested form of age assessment and has been widely discredited as being inaccurate. As we saw in Chapter 7, once the young people's official age had been settled, a continuing process of surveillance and assessment tended to have negative implications for relationships of trust and for young people's integration into the family structure. Age assessments should be conducted over time, taking account of physical and behavioural observations (Stanley, 2001; Crawley, 2007). However, once settled, continuing suspicions appear to have negative effects on building relationships.

Comments on previous placements also indicated that where foster carers had been preoccupied with age, placements had often been strained. Links between age and behaviour were noted by foster carers and non-compliant behaviour became linked to their suspicion that the young person was older than their claimed age. One foster carer said: 'That explains the reason why he's demanding.' Social workers also cited this as a potential area of conflict.

If you're saying you're 13 and you're possibly 15 or 16, then there's obviously going to be conflict around setting in place boundaries. (Team manager, Area 4)

If you've got a 14-year-old . . . you set boundaries in foster care that they should be in at a certain time. If you're 16 that is different . . . They will not in the long run function very well pretending they're someone who they're not. (Social worker, Area 1)

In contrast, other foster carers were sceptical about the ages young people claimed to be, but acknowledged the difficulties in conducting accurate age assessments. While aware of the complexity of this issue, their approach in this context was to work with the young person's official age and make a decision not to become involved in the process of age assessment. These carers had often built good relationships with the young people. Abbas' foster carer did not see age assessment as part of her role. She said: 'I don't get involved in the age assessment. It's nothing to do with me. Social services do that.' Housyar's foster carer decided not to become involved in this process in case it jeopardised Housyar's immigration case. She said:

I am on his side whatever happens . . . I told him that . . . because [the local authority] did ask me whether I think he's . . . For all I know he could be older . . . but then I didn't want to drop him in it because he's gone through all that. (Amina, Housyar's foster carer)

Some foster carers were aware of age disputes from social workers or schools, but chose to remain neutral on this topic. These foster carers focused on advocating for the young person and only spoke about age in terms of their concerns about the impact age assessments had on their foster children's well-being or access to education and other services.

In addition to concerns over age assessment, some foster carers were sceptical about whether young people had genuine grounds for claiming asylum. Social workers described how this could potentially place strain on relationships between young people and foster carers.

I've experienced foster carers who have a real air of suspicion about the young people they care for. They don't believe their stories, they almost minimise their whole experience . . . I don't see how a placement can really succeed when there's this air of that . . . How can they feel safe and wanted and thrive when they're always being suspected and doubted? (Social worker, Area 1)

However, while a few foster carers we interviewed expressed some scepticism about young people's asylum claims, this was generally without the mistrust and anxieties attached to many foster carers' comments on age. Reflections on asylum claims were often made by foster carers who had close relationships with young people. Foster carers and social workers who expressed this uncertainty thought that young people's motivations may not fit within the criteria of grounds for asylum or that they were not giving a full account of their reasons for migrating to the UK. In these circumstances, young people's accounts were sometimes inconsistent.

Young people are fleeing their countries, mostly not because of the political situation, but because of the economic situation. (Sanaz, Rahim's foster carer)

He went through interviews with Border Agency and also the solicitor and the same questions were put to him . . . Sometimes you can see there are discrepancies, so it makes you think. (Daniel, Rashid's foster carer)

Foster carers were often worried about young people's chances of receiving a positive decision on their asylum claim and how they would be able to support them through this process. Even when these foster carers were unsure about the legitimacy of young people's asylum claims, they had empathy for their needs and continued to support them and advocate on their behalf. They often chose not to focus on troubling specifics and found a point of empathy with the wider overall story. As with Kohli's "confederate" social workers (2006a), these foster carers accepted and worked with the complexity in young people's narratives, took the side of the young person and became trusted companions.

It's . . . trying to understand the loss. Whether the stories that they tell are true or not, you still have to appreciate the fact that they've made such a big journey by themselves, and they are still only young. (Stephanie, Omid's foster carer)

In contrast to foster carers' focus on asylum and age, young people often explained foster carers' mistrust as emanating from their status as looked after young people rather than as asylum-seeking young people. They felt that as looked after young people they had been regarded with mistrust as unknown strangers in the house.

While, as mentioned earlier, many young people were given keys to the house and invited to treat it as their own, some were denied a key or knew of friends who had been denied one. Speaking about his former foster placement, one focus group participant said: '[The foster carers'] rooms are locked and the only rooms that are open without no lock is ours.' Meanwhile, some young people also faced restrictions in access to space in the home because they were not trusted. Mahmud contrasted his own positive experience with that of a friend whose foster carers locked up the kitchen at night. Two focus group participants described how they had not been allowed to remain alone in the house. For one young person this meant leaving the house at 7am when his foster carer left for work and waiting in the streets until 9am when a community centre opened. Another young person was also made to leave their house when her foster carer went out:

> She said she would not keep me in her home because she don't know me. She just knew me through fostering so she will not leave me in her house. (Young women's focus group)

Young people discussed their difficulties in reporting these problems in contexts where they felt disempowered and voiceless in the networks of professionals they encountered, but also due to their marginal status as non-citizen or, in effect, "lesser youth" (Sinha and Uppal, 2009).

> When she knew my social worker was coming . . . she was going to the market and she was doing some shopping . . . The social worker think that she is good. (Young men's focus group)

> When my social worker comes she say: 'You know, you are lucky living with this family . . . This beautiful sitting room and nice people' . . . I say: 'Look, the family is very good . . . the problem I have is that this is not true for me. Everything is fake.' (Young men's focus group)

> Because [the foster carer] is British and they [are] going to listen to her. They don't know us. They [are] not going to listen to us. (Young women's focus group)

Several young people were anxious about what they perceived as collusion in professional relationships between foster carers and social workers. In these cases, they felt unable to confide in either their foster carers or social workers. A participant in a young men's focus group said: 'Foster carers should not be friends with key workers.' A young woman also described how her perception of the close relationship between her social worker and foster carer had inhibited her from revealing information about how she was being treated in her placement:

> *I didn't tell anyone. The social worker, you know what she did when there was a meeting? She said: 'Oh thank you'. Finish. [The foster carer] said she [will] cook rice for her and they sit down together. I am just so worried.* (Young women's focus group)

Aarif explained that the problem with such relationships between foster carers and social workers was that 'friends can't write a bad thing about other friends'. One foster carer, aware that concerns may exist about confidentiality and loyalty, was careful to maintain openness and trust with his foster child and also clarified to us his role with regard to the young person's confidentiality:

> *Some stuff he's asked us not to say to his social workers and we've respected that . . . Something that would endanger him or anything, we'd have talked to social workers. But certainly the stuff that he's told us in confidence . . . we've respected that.* (Mark, Abraham's foster carer)

However, information sharing is also important. Very little is known about young people at arrival and foster carers have a key role in gradually assembling this information. As one social worker noted:

> *We are giving them a limited amount of knowledge. It's very much a two-way process of that foster carer feeding back to us about how that young person is coming along and settling in.* (Social worker, Area 4)

This process of constructing a narrative of young people's histories, experiences and future needs can only be achieved by social workers and foster carers working together and sharing information. From the young person's perspective, however, there was sometimes mistrust or uncertainty about the purpose of these exchanges. How these interactions may be read and understood by young people, therefore, needs to be kept continuously in mind during placement visits and meetings. However, the importance of sharing information (within agreed limits) should also be made transparent to young people.

Inclusion and exclusion

In addition to trust, a key element in developing a secure base centred on inclusion in the foster care household. Foster care placements have been found to be less likely to be disrupted when foster carers take part in fun joint activities with their children (Sinclair, 2005). This means not only including foster children in existing family activities, but also being flexible and open about the nature of these activities. Schofield and Beek (2006) highlight the importance of the capacity of the foster family to absorb new members from backgrounds and experiences that may be very different to their own.

In the interviews and focus groups, many foster carers and social workers reflected on the importance of adopting some degree of flexibility in the organisation of household life and activities. They emphasised the particular need for this when working with unaccompanied minors who were adjusting to cultural and lifestyle differences in a new country, as well as a new household. Foster carers might also expect to accommodate some adjustments to their lifestyle to meet young people's needs and interests. Suggestions included incorporating young people's food practices within existing family food practices, celebrating events in young people's cultural traditions as well as those already celebrated by the foster family and finding out about the young person's hobbies or interests to organise some family social activities around these. There was criticism of foster carers who were regarded as too rigid and who expected young people to simply assimilate into their family's existing household and culture. This form of integration in the household involved both the young people and the foster carers taking action and making adaptations. This has parallels with the two-way integration model recommended by much of the research literature on immigration and settlement policy. In these integration models it is argued that adaptation is required by both new arrivals and host societies to facilitate integration (Castles *et al*, 2002).

In our survey, foster carers were asked to report on the amount of time they spent on a range of activities with the young person (see Table 8.1). The most common activities were connected to helping young people develop their language and communication skills, to emotional availability (listening to anxieties and memories of home) and to cementing relationships by (amongst other things) cooking and eating together. Other shared activities tended to be more occasional, as perhaps would be the case in many families. Specific shared cultural activities connected to the young person's religion or country of origin appeared to be rather less common, with 35–39 per cent of foster carers never attending these activities.

We were interested to see whether the range of shared activities enjoyed by young people and foster carers might vary according to the nature of their ethnic or religious match. This comparison is inevitably crude, being based only on our knowledge of the country of origin and religion of young people and carers.[43] Where placements did involve a match in this way, joint involvement in religious and cultural activities was higher than was the case for non-matched placements.[44] For example, well over four-fifths of matched carers (87%) reported

---

43 This produced a derived variable that included: a) a match by country of origin and/or religion (43); b) placement with a minority ethnic carer (not matched more closely – 50); c) placement with a white British carer (39). Obviously, we cannot say whether these placements were in any way the product of matching. They may simply have related to the availability of placements at the time required.

44 Kruskal Wallis test for "matched placement" and religious events (p<0.001, n=113); cultural activities (p<0.001, n = 120). Paired tests for "matched" and other minority ethnic carers (Mann Whitney U exact tests: religious events significant at p = <0.001, n = 79; cultural activities at p = 0.002, n = 84). For "matched" and white carers (religious events significant at p = 0.002, n = 71; cultural activities at p<0.001, n = 76). Differences between minority ethnic and white carers were not significant.

attending religious events with their young people sometimes or often compared to just over half of non-matched carers (white carers, 56%, and minority ethnic carers, 55%). Similar differences were evident in relation to participation in cultural activities.[45] It was in this cultural domain that our findings were most clear cut. Indeed, there were no other significant differences between matched and non-matched foster carers in the range of other shared activities undertaken with young people.

Despite these patterns of difference, however, there was no significant association between the match between carer and young person, and the extent to which young people felt integrated into the foster family.[46] They were as likely to feel a part of the family, to trust and confide in their carer, to share personal feelings or, conversely, to feel excluded irrespective of the type of placement they were living in. While a matched placement (at least in the terms that we were able to construct it) may therefore help young people to develop or reconstruct a sense of cultural connectedness, all placements appeared to have a similar potential to be inclusive and nurturing. This was suggested in comments by some social workers who pointed to the importance of looking at the wider outlook and attitudes in placements beyond cultural matching alone.

What we're looking for are people who've got the right outlook. So it's not necessarily a brilliant religious, cultural, ethnic match . . . it's the sort of people who will rise to the challenge and have an open, interested outlook on the circumstances that young people bring with them . . . Those are the carers who respond best . . . and young people are able to respond best to. They're not always the most sensitive or subtle of people but they rise to the occasion and that brings out the best in young people. (Team manager, Area 3)

---

45 87% of "matched" carers reported some or frequent participation compared to substantially fewer white (39%) and minority ethnic carers (61%).

46 See Table 7.2 for categories included in this analysis. Individually, none of the variables in that table were significantly associated with whether the placement was matched. Overall result, Kruskal Wallis exact test (p = 0.146).

Table 8.1
Time spent with young people on shared activities – per cent

	Often	*Sometimes*	*Never*
Having child's friends to visit (n = 118)	26	64	10
Cooking and eating together (n = 131)	70	29	1
Swimming/skating/other participant sports (n = 113)	28	58	14
Talking to child about their own family or homeland (n = 123)	63	30	7
Visits to cinema/theatre (n = 116)	25	57	18
Visits to park/going for picnics, etc (n = 114)	28	52	20
Going to football matches or other sporting events (n = 117)	18	42	40
Talking to child about their worries and fears (n = 129)	62	37	1
Helping child to develop her/his English skills (n = 129)	84	15	1
Taking child to special classes or clubs (n = 116)	38	43	19
Visits to church/mosque or to religious events (n = 114)	35	30	35
Attending cultural activities/events linked to child's country of origin (n = 121)	23	38	39

More generally, it was not surprising to find that where young people and foster carers spent time together in these ways it was more likely that young people would be considered to be closely integrated into the foster family on our Family Integration Measure (see Table 7.2). In this sense, time spent in shared activities both reflected and reinforced the quality of family relationships. Not all activities were significant.[47] However, the association was clearest where time was being spent on activities that might be expected to improve communication, create closeness and a sense of belonging. These included having friends to visit, preparing meals and eating together, talking to young people about their own families or homelands, and listening to their worries and fears. In addition, visits to the park for picnics and shared time at sporting events were also associated with greater family integration.[48]

In the interviews, many of the young people and foster carers described the activities they shared with one another and these were seen as a display of the affection and bonds that existed, creating closeness and a sense of belonging as suggested by the survey evidence. Types of activities varied according to the interests of the young person, their age and the length of time in the placement. For example, even where there were close bonds some older teenagers had less time or interest in taking part in activities with the foster carer outside the house (particularly those who had more established social networks). However, they described having done so in the past and both young people and foster carers spoke of sharing meals and regular conversations.

We were planning a big Christmas dinner together 'cos we used to look forward to that, but then he wanted to do his own thing with his girlfriend . . . But, I mean, if he comes in now and you weren't here and I said, 'Oh, I'm going to do this,' he would help, you know, he would chop up things if he's not busy going to meet her or other friends. I enjoy cooking with him. (Jasmine, Banhwa's foster carer)

---

47 There was no association between family integration and participant sports (p=0.15), helping with English language (p=0.153), going to classes or clubs (p=0.349), to mosque or church (p=0.139), to cultural events (p=0.096) and only a marginal link with visits to the cinema/theatre (p=0.054).

48 Kendall's tau b tests for our Family Integration Measure and friends to visit (p=0.004, t 0.232, n=118); eating together (p=0.037, t 0.162, n=131); talking about home (p<0.001, t 0.301, n=123); talking about worries (p=0.001, t 0.268, n=129); picnics (p=0.003, t 0.241, n=114); sporting events (p=0.025, t 0.177, n=117)

Many young people also spoke about their inclusion or exclusion from family holidays as a marker of their status as part of the family and an indication of the level of care shown to them by their foster carers.

We went two time[s] for holiday with my dad, my mum, we three boys we went on holiday for two weeks. And one time, we three boys and my mum went together. (Abbas)

Those who were not included noted their exclusion and felt sad because they regarded this as marking their status outside the family unit. A participant in one of the young men's focus groups had lived with his foster family for three years. Yet during this time he had not been invited on any family holidays. Instead, he was sent to stay with another foster family while his foster family were away. While the young person felt this as exclusion, young people are not able to travel abroad while they are waiting for a final decision on their asylum claim. Therefore, where foster families chose to holiday abroad this may have been an explanation as to why some young people were left behind. However, a number of the foster families in our study had also arranged to take some of their holidays within the UK specifically so that foster children could be included.

The survey findings demonstrated that higher levels of family integration were associated with shared activities. As mentioned in Chapter 6, food was often a way of establishing an "early win" and communicating care and affection across language divides, before levels of trust had been built up. Further on in the placement, it was also a way of finding out more about each other. Young people introduced their foster families to aspects of culture from their countries of origin, sometimes using food to talk to them about home.

The food, I think, was quite a good thing. And then he'd remember . . . he'd talk about the family, the people that looked after him through his journey and stuff. That was really interesting. (Stephanie, Omid's foster carer)

Sharing food preparation and meals together was also a means of checking in and updating each other on their day (Rees and Pithouse, 2008). Inclusion and exclusion at the dinner table was upheld as a strong symbol of inclusion and exclusion in the family. Young people were happy when they saw foster carers had made an extra effort to cook them separate food that they particularly liked and regarded this as a sign of care and commitment. However, they also spoke of forms of separation that were hurtful and marked their status as only "lodgers".

> She cooked separately for herself and her husband and we had separate food... She cooked once every month . . . and put them in the freezer... Ours was frozen and hers was cooked fresh. (Young men's focus group)

> We've had a lot of placements where it's been a fairly miserable experience . . . Essentially, you know, it's separate from the rest of the family, you know, those kind of things. And we've drawn those to a fairly rapid conclusion when it's become clear what's going on. (Team manager, Area 3)

Finally, access to food and the freedom to regulate their own consumption of food was also frequently used as an illustration of how "at home" young people felt and the degree to which the foster carer sought to help them feel at home. Some young people reported monitoring and limitations on access to food. A participant from one of the young men's focus group described food being locked away and said his foster carer had reproached him for inviting friends over and offering them a snack. Such examples of regulation and control were also given in relation to use of space in the household.

> The family gave us room especially for us there. I am allowed to live there but I am not allowed every day to come into the sitting room watching TV. I am not allowed. (Young person's focus group)

In contrast, Sanaz's foster children, as members of the household, had free movement and access to the resources in this space. Sanaz said: 'I provide everything for them, you know, everything is in the cupboard so they are free, they can take anything they want, you know, as a snack.'

Interpreting and responding to challenging behaviour

Despite some of the tensions we have described around feelings of mistrust and exclusion, most placements were viewed as going well and relationships between young people and their foster carers were positive. Although foster carers frequently noted fewer problems with difficult behaviour in comparison to other looked after young people (Farmer et al, 2004; Sinclair et al, 2007), some forms of challenging behaviour were identified. Three key areas of tension centred on setting boundaries, gender relations and the provision of financial allowances and material items. Divergent perspectives existed on the extent of these challenges, the causes and the interpretations that were made of behaviour in these contexts.

Setting boundaries

The first key area of conflict was in relation to house rules and boundaries, and also tensions between fulfilling social work regula-tions and facilitating "normal" life routines. Children in foster care can feel they are under greater regulation and scrutiny than their peers (Geenen and Powers, 2007). In some cases, this had been a source of tension throughout the placement and led to placement breakdown. As mentioned earlier, some foster carers and social workers also linked this to their suspicions that the young person was older than they claimed to be.

Sometimes there was a clash of expectations arising from young people's earlier life experiences of greater independence and the difficulties they had in adapting to the boundaries set in foster place-ments. Although unaccompanied minors are often described as being generally compliant and well behaved (Wade et al, 2005; Kohli, 2007), instances of conflict over what was seen as difficult teenage behaviour emerged in some placements. This kind of behaviour was not described as unique to unaccompanied minors or as culturally specific, but rather was in the realm of regular challenges carers might encounter with this age group. While teenagers may seek to test boundaries, young people in foster care tend to lack the security of doing so within the structure of solid and longstanding relationships with their carers (Sinclair *et al*, 2005b).

In most cases, tensions or conflict arose either at the start or towards the end of placements as young people were preparing to make transitions out of foster care. Bushra described how a previous foster child decided to leave the placement at the age of 16 because he would not abide by house rules, which he found restrictive. In some cases, this kind of conflict led to placement breakdowns or else was resolved when young people moved on to independent living. Some of these young people returned to visit foster carers and maintained contact with them.

In other cases, foster carers described how they tried to prevent tensions arising in the first place. They attempted to resolve difficulties by having open dialogue with young people in which each party could express their concerns and foster carers could explain fostering regulations and practices.

> *If I'd told him no for something, if he didn't get his own way, I knew if he felt down because of what I'd said, but then, we'd talk about it. I'd leave him for a little while . . . and I think a lot of the time, because if you said, 'No', he thought he was in trouble, but once he understood that no, you say no for a reason, he was easy to care for.* (Stephanie, Omid's foster carer)

> *He said to me he's still a bit scared that people might turn against him, and I said to him, 'I know that if you have a bad day . . . the next day you'll be okay, and you'll be nice, and everything will be okay. So if something happens it's not forever, you know, we can change.'* (Amina, Housyar's foster carer)

Gender relations

The issue of gender relations was often linked to the negotiation of boundaries and behaviour. Gender roles and relations were often mentioned by foster carers and social workers (although not young people) when discussing adjustments and tensions faced at the start of placements. Most unaccompanied minors were male, while most of the primary foster carers were female. Social workers described how tensions occurred in some placements when there were differences between young people's and foster carers' perceptions of appropriate gender roles.

They can be very disrespectful to some female foster carers and order them around and expect them to do all the work, running for them, clearing up after them . . . The foster carers object and then we have to renegotiate. (Social worker, Area 1)

I think that some young boys have had a lot of freedom in their country because of the difficulties in their country and also the male-dominated viewpoint . . . So then it's very difficult when you've got a foster carer, say a female, laying down the law, really, of that house and the rules and I know that a lot of older boys find that difficult. (Senior social worker, Area 2)

When asked about challenges they faced at the start of placements, several female foster carers commented on the need to respond to some young people's gendered expectations. Many foster carers responded by having open discussions about gender roles and finding out from young people why they held certain views. Young people told them about the gender roles they were used to, referring to women in their countries of origin and to the particular experiences of their mothers and other female relatives.

Foster carers were clear and firm in setting out the kinds of behaviour they found acceptable in their house, but in successful cases often used approaches that included and did not ostracise the young person. Mahmud's foster carer suggested how conflict could be minimised:

It's got to be your attitude towards them. I mean, if you're barking orders all the time, that's not good, you know. Communicating with rapport, you know, and humour, we laugh a lot. (Leena, Mahmud's foster carer)

Sometimes, foster children followed the example of other young people in the house and at times other foster children living in the house would intervene when they were upset by a young person's behaviour towards their foster carer. Osman's foster carer explained how Osman had responded to another foster child's behaviour:

I heard him saying to him, 'She's like mum.' That lad said, 'You don't listen to women, we boys stick together.' And Osman said, 'You are living in her house, she's like a mother.' (Marion, Osman's foster carer)

Meanwhile, it is important to note that although gender relations were a source of tension in some placements, this was by no means the case in all households and the accounts of other foster carers reflected quite different experiences.

Majeed is very considerate in that if I was walking down the road with some bags, he'd run up to me and take them off me and things like that ... He's very respectful. (Isobel, Majeed's foster carer)

They respect me like they would respect their mother, absolutely. (Leena, Mahmud's foster carer)

It was evident that some very close attachments had developed between many young people and female foster carers, who were very often referred to with care, respect and affection using the family-like terms of "mum" or "auntie".

Finance allowances and material possessions
Finally, a recurrent theme in discussions about challenging behaviour centred on tensions and conflict around the allocation and provision

of financial and material resources. A number of foster carers and social workers spoke of the difficulty foster carers had in managing requests for money or material items which exceeded the allowances provided to them by fostering agencies.

They are obsessed with money, about how much they are entitled to, what the foster carer should be buying for them, and it does cause massive tensions in the foster placement. (Senior social worker, Area 2)

[If] they [would] tell some of the kids that money doesn't drop off trees . . . At one point I gave him some money to buy something and he didn't bring anything back . . . and he's still complaining. So they got someone to sit with him and tell him it doesn't work like that. (Marion, foster carer)

However, these concerns had not been experienced by all foster carers. Approximately half of the foster carers we interviewed did not mention this issue as a concern, or specifically commented that the young people they were fostering were not demanding and were easy to care for in this respect. Abraham's foster carer said: 'He's not in your face continuously. Occasionally he'll say he needs a new pair of football boots or whatever he needs at the time and we sort that out.'

Explanations for these tensions appear to be complex and multifaceted. Although divergent interpretations and explanations were expressed by foster carers, young people and social workers, four broad cross-case themes were identified. These included: young people's perceptions of wealth in the UK; young people's burden of debt; pursuit of equality with peers; and, finally, symbolic proof of care and affection.

First, some foster carers and social workers felt that some young people viewed the UK as a wealthy country where, as Marion describes (above), money is easily available. Although this may be the case in comparison to some countries of origin, it was thought that there was a lack of understanding among some young people about fostering allowances and limitations on finances.

We are very clear about finances, about set amounts of pocket money and what will be bought out of that pocket money, you know, a bus ticket will be bought and clothing . . . The young person has this expectation that Britain is a very wealthy country and, yes, it is in some ways, but a foster carer cannot go out every weekend and buy brand new clothing for the young person. It's not realistic, nor should it be. (Senior social worker, Area 2)

Second, most social workers and some foster carers expressed an awareness that an interest in financial resources may not be simply about current consumption and consumer desires. They spoke about the burden of debt that young people's families had acquired to pay for young people's journeys to the UK. In these cases, it was thought that some birth families held expectations that young people would be able to earn money to help pay this back.

There's also the burden a lot of them carry that it may have cost £10,000 or so to get them here and that's a debt on the family, and I think there's an expectation . . . Well, I'm expected to earn some money to pay this back. (Social worker, Area 1)

Bushra's foster child, Navid, had expressed anxieties about the burden of debt on his mother. He had told Bushra he wanted to be able to work so that he could send money back to his mother. Abbas also referred to this in his plan for his future in the UK:

They need the money . . . so I try to do – find a job now, to do work and send the money to my mum. (Abbas)

Sometimes this desire to earn money was seen as outside the boundaries of "childlike" behaviour (see Aitkin, 2001). Bushra sought to reassure her foster child and encouraged him to enjoy the lifestyle she associated with childhood by focusing on his education, which she valued highly. Others viewed this interest in money in association with suspicions that young people were older than they claimed to be.

> *Children, when there is somebody that cares for them and they're in a safe environment, they are prepared to, you know, to fit in, they just want to fit in and be a child again, you know, but you won't get that from adults. And I believe that he has a family he is supporting 'cos of the demand for money.* (Adele, foster carer)

While the first two explanations centre on the financial value of resources, other explanations revolved around the symbolic value of these resources and their allocation. The third form of explanation centred on young people's apparent pursuit of equality with their citizen peers.

> *They will be, like, 'Well, you didn't have that in your country, so why do you want it in this country?' But why shouldn't they have it in this country? You know, you just treat everyone equal.* (Stephanie, Omid's foster carer)

> *Some foster carers will say . . . all they're interested in is money and what they can get and all this sort of stuff. And you think yeah, but if you've had absolutely nothing at all and you think I might only be here for two years, wouldn't you think . . . let's see what I can [get]. I don't think that's a totally unreasonable position . . .* (Eleanor, Arian's foster carer)

> *Even that [comparison] comes down to material things as well, which is always the bane of most social workers' lives, that he's got this and why, why haven't I got that?* (Social worker, Area 3)

This explanation has also arisen in research on foster care provision for the wider looked after population. Sinclair and colleagues (Sinclair *et al*, 2005a) have suggested that acquisition of material things could signify to the child that they were no longer different from other children and that they could take part in the good things of the consumer society. One foster carer in our study described how her foster child had gained confidence from having nice clothes and looking well presented, while another noted her foster children's desire to have the same technology that other young people accessed. It is possible that unaccompanied minors, in common with other looked after children, may feel the need to accumulate possessions quickly in order to catch up and achieve parity with their peers.

As the comments made by the social worker (above) illustrate, foster carers and social workers experienced challenges in attempting to respond to young people's requests for financial equality with their peers. These were difficult in a context where different fostering agencies had different financial allowances for foster children and when young people did not understand why young people in independent accommodation had a higher allowance than those in foster care.

The contractual process for delivery of foster care and its allowances may also be in tension with attempts to provide family care, which tends to evolve as a more individual, organic process. Arian's foster carer suggested that financial allowances should be managed and distributed in a more natural way so as to facilitate and support more family-like relationships, which in turn might be less likely to develop into business-like forms of negotiation and conflict:

Neither of them [foster children] have been like that at all, partly because we haven't been doling things out . . . and to be fair if that's how you deal with people then they're going to respond, aren't they? (Eleanor, Arian's foster carer)

Finally, young people offered an alternative perspective on the provision of material possessions that was closely linked to the building of relationships described earlier. While young people remarked on the physical and emotional pleasures of owning certain items, such as clothing and televisions, the symbolic value of these items was also important. Foster carers' generosity and small gifts were a means through which young people measured and confirmed the level of care and affection provided to them. One participant in a young men's focus group said: '[The foster carer] didn't cut my money, and when she went off for the holiday to Africa, she bring some present for me.' Samuel also described how his foster carer had brought small gifts back for him when she had been to visit family abroad. Extra small gifts that were not from the official financial allowance were appreciated. This demonstrated generosity on behalf of the foster carers, but also acted as proof to young people that foster carers were not 'just doing it for the money' (Sinclair *et al*, 2004). In contrast, a participant in a young men's focus group spoke of a foster carer's partner who had referred to fostering as "a business" following a disagreement about a clothes purchase. A participant in another focus group also remembered an incident that he held up as an example of the lack of care and kindness he had been shown in his placement:

> She [foster carer] used my money to get me a [birthday] card. When I was leaving she said, 'Minus that 'cos I used it to get you a card.' (Young men's focus group)

Summary

Relationships in foster placements changed and developed over time. While experiences varied between placements, it was common for a period of adjustment and shifts in relationships to occur, especially in the early and end stages of placements. There was usually a gradual progression in relationships over time, but changes also occurred at turning points when certain events and responses produced crossroads at which young people and foster carers made key choices about the route to take in their relationship.

Work on attachment and resilience has highlighted the necessity of establishing a secure base in which young people can develop their self-esteem, resilience and secure patterns of attachment, and fulfil their potential. Young people emphasised the importance of the availability of the foster carer and their display of love and care.

Being available and helping young people to trust is an important aspect of a secure base and both foster carers and young people acknowledged the importance of developing trust in order to build successful relationships.

Relationships were built through foster carers and young people displaying trust in each other and foster carers advocating for young people, demonstrating to them they were on their side and often showing care by going beyond a narrow and limited definition of their role. Relationships were more likely to be close when foster children took part in shared activities with foster carers and where they felt they were treated equally to other children in the household. Close bonds were more likely to develop where foster carers, as well as young people, made adjustments to their lifestyle and family practices were jointly developed. Meanwhile, tensions sometimes arose when foster carers became involved in age disputes, when they demonstrated a lack of trust in young people and when there was conflict over particular kinds of behaviour that were viewed as challenging, including boundaries, gendered assumptions and the provision of material possessions.

9 Education pathways

Alongside young people's need for a secure home base, access to education and a positive educational experience are crucial aspects of resettlement. Access to education provision is essential for English language acquisition and for academic progress. However, it offers not only an opportunity to build for the future, but is also a pivotal site through which young people can re-establish the rhythms of ordinary living and begin to develop friendships and social networks in the UK.

This chapter examines the educational experiences of young people in the sample, including their educational backgrounds, their academic and social experiences in education in the UK, and the support available from their foster carers, social workers and schools.

Educational backgrounds

Research with refugee and asylum-seeking young people has highlighted the diversity of their educational backgrounds and experiences (Candappa and Egharevba, 2000; Wade *et al*, 2005; Rutter, 2006). These experiences were reflected in our sample, which included young people who had no experience of education in their countries of origin but also young people who had been in school for several years, although this had often been disrupted by conflict and/or long migration journeys.

Educational systems and access to education may vary between countries of origin. However, differences aligned to socio-economic backgrounds were also apparent within countries. Among the Afghan young people (the largest nationality represented in the sample), some had never attended school in Afghanistan while others had been in school an average of 5–6 years. Nabil had not been to school in Afghanistan and remembered his entry to school in the UK as a very memorable occasion: 'Thirteenth of November I went to school for the first time. First day [was the] first time in my life.' In contrast, two focus group participants explained that they came from affluent families, were keen to challenge assumptions they thought existed connecting asylum seekers with poverty and pointed out that a significant sum of money is needed to travel to Europe (Van Hear, 2006): 'Before I came to [the UK] my dad was wealthy. I went to a private school. I had the best life.'

Young people also described differences between schools in their countries of origin and the UK. Although a few had studied English at school in their countries of origin, most had not. Young people highlighted key differences in approaches to teaching and in access to some technology, including computers and science labs, which some had not used before. Young people who had never attended school had to adjust not only to a new language, curriculum and educational approach, but also to the concept, routine and structure of school and to learning what it means to be a student. These young people were also unable to read and write in their first languages and so had to learn reading and writing skills for the first time.

Access to education

Around one-third (34%) of young people in the survey sample had experienced problems accessing education. Although refugee and asylum-seeking young people have a clear legal entitlement to places in mainstream education, there can be delays in accessing places and variations in the degree of co-operation between social care and education agencies in resolving these problems (Audit Commission, 2000; Candappa, 2000; Rutter, 2003b; Hek, 2005b).

Some of these patterns were confirmed by our interviews. Experiences of accessing education tended to vary according to the age of the young person at the time they arrived in the UK, the time of year they arrived, the degree to which local schools were oversubscribed and the degree to which foster carers and other professionals advocated for the young person to access a school place. Young people experienced waiting times ranging from a few weeks to six months before gaining admission to school or college, which caused frustration for some.

I keep asking my social worker... I know some boys, they live in a family, they went straightaway and I went after six, seven months and I said to my social worker: 'Why is that?' And they said: 'Because it's your age', or something like that... I want to learn English. I don't care if I can't read and write it, but I want to learn to talk, how to talk to people. (Abbas)

He went to school immediately... He came in December and he started school in January. (Bushra, Navid's foster carer)

Some young people had no access to education during this waiting period, while others attended short courses over the summer holidays or part-time language provision at voluntary sector organisations. Although young people mostly enjoyed and valued their time at these courses, they did not compare to full-time education.

I was learning in the refugee centre, just a bit in English, like two hours a day. That was nothing like a school. (Ermir)

Young people who arrived part way through Year 11 or were aged disputed, found it particularly difficult to get a school placement and often had a long waiting period before they could begin college (Wade *et al*, 2005). Those aged 16 or 17 were usually placed on English for Speakers of Other Languages (ESOL) courses at further education colleges rather than in school. Arian's foster carer said: '[The school] actually told me no school will give him a place in Year 11.' Young people who arrived in the final term of a school year also experienced difficulties attaining a place as the school year was winding down. Often these young people had a gap over the summer period while they waited for school to begin again in the autumn.

In addition to schools being oversubscribed, foster carers reported that some schools were reluctant to take on more refugee and asylum-seeking young people, either because they lacked the resources available to deal with language needs or because they already had a number of refugee and asylum-seeking young people enrolled in the school. Sabir's foster carer said: 'It took seven weeks to get him into school, because a lot of schools just didn't want to take any more asylum seekers, because they'd already taken a lot.'

Foster carers reported variations in the degree of co-operation and support between social work teams, foster carers and local authorities in facilitating young people's access to education (Candappa, 2000; The Children's Legal Centre, 2003; Wade *et al*, 2005). Abraham's foster carers described a relatively smooth transition into a placement at the local primary school, which was facilitated by joint action from the foster carers, social worker, the school and the local authority. Other foster carers mentioned assistance from particular practitioners. One foster carer was very satisfied with the support provided by the child's social worker. The social worker had ensured that the young person was able to access an appropriate school placement after an initial placement in a Pupil Referral Unit following rejections from mainstream schools. In contrast, other foster carers described situations where they were the sole advocates for young people and some found this experience challenging. In other cases, foster carers described how they "got on with it" because they regarded this as part of their role as foster carers. Others took this lead because it had to be done and no one else was doing it.

Attitudes towards education

There is evidence that education is a high priority for many refugee and asylum-seeking young people in the UK (Brownlees and Finch, 2010), who have been described by practitioners as often being highly motivated with regard to participation and progress in education (Wade *et al*, 2005; Kohli, 2007). This view was also prevalent among social workers in our study who described young people's high aspirations and commitment to 'making something of themselves' and having 'huge aspirations and dreams'. These were sometimes seen as being unrealistic in the context of limited previous education experience and English language skills and the potentially short period of time available in which to accomplish these tasks (Kohli, 2007; Watters, 2008). Social workers and foster carers admired young people's focus on education and the good progress they generally made. There were, however, also some echoes of the questions asked by practitioners in the study conducted by Wade and colleagues about the reasons behind this determination and the potentially complex and multiple reasons for young people's journeys (Wade *et al*, 2005).

The survey asked foster carers to report on whether young people were enjoying their studies, whether they attended regularly and whether the courses they were pursuing were appropriate for their academic abilities as foster carers understood them.

Table 9.1
Attendance, enjoyment and relevance of education – per cent

	Not at all true	To some extent true	To a large extent true	Number
S/he enjoys education now	2	33	65	129
S/he atttends regularly now	3	9	88	124
The courses s/he is doing are appropriate for his/her abilities	3	26	71	124

Table 9.1 shows that very few young people had attendance problems and that, from the perspective of foster carers, most were enjoying and receiving an appropriate education. However, in these latter respects, some ambivalence was reported for around one-quarter to one-third of young people.

There were no significant associations with whether or not young people were enjoying their studies. However, according to foster carers' reports, some groups of young people were rather more likely than others to be undertaking courses appropriate to their current abilities. This tended to be the case for older young people, for young people without moderate to severe emotional, social or behavioural difficulties, and for young people who had lived in the current place-ment for a longer period of time. Where young people had made more placement moves in the past, there was also some association with a poorer current attendance pattern and for current courses to be less appropriate for their abilities.[49] Some caution is needed here, since none of these associations is particularly strong. Overall, however, the findings are consistent with the fragmented evidence that currently exists on the motivation and commitment of unaccompanied young people to the pursuit of education as one crucial means of finding constructive resettlement pathways (Hek, 2005b; Rutter, 2006).

Young interviewees expressed their determination to succeed and spoke of their intention to stay out of trouble, work hard and focus on their education. Omid's foster carer said: 'The only way I can put it is he has an agenda . . . wants to learn and didn't want to get into trouble.' Some young people had high ambitions to become, for example, footballers, doctors, engineers or ambassadors. However, many also expressed interest in a wide range of other careers including construction, plumbing, mechanics, public services, football coaching, boxing, computer programming or business. Frequently, young people had made these choices in consultation with teachers, careers advisers at school and foster carers and these plans often came across as flexible, but considered, choices. Although often motivated and determined, young people were aware of the constraints they faced. While there was a need to be realistic in the face of a number of potential challenges, it was helpful when these were considered by practitioners without extinguishing the aspirations that motivated young people.

Although most young people were strongly motivated to succeed in their education, this was not without exception. There were some reports from foster carers of poor attendance, a reluctance to attend school or college and a lack of motivation in completing homework. One foster carer described his struggle to persuade a former Afghan foster child to attend school:

---

49 Kendall's tau-b tests for courses appropriate for current abilities and older age ($p = 0.04$, t 0.167, n = 119); emotional, social or behavioural difficulties ($p = 0.019$, t 0.201, n = 120); time in placement ($p = 0.024$, t 0.178, n = 111). Past placement moves and appropriateness of current course ($p = 0.046$, t -0.174, n = 118); attendance ($p = 0.035$, t -0.185, n = 118)

It was like trying to motivate . . . We did get him in to a school and we did get him to go most days. (Malik, foster carer)

Young people's aspirations to do well centred on a desire to make the most of their time in education and to achieve their potential. However, interests in educational progress were sometimes also tied to the recurring theme of future immigration pathways. Young people and foster carers held hope that educational progress might help young people with their asylum claim by demonstrating they were making a successful life in the UK. Banhwa's foster carer was concerned about the effect his poor attendance and performance at school was likely to have on his application to extend his leave to remain. She had told him: 'If you carry on like this, it's not going to be good when you go in front of the immigration judge'.

Education placement

At the time of data collection, the vast majority of young people in our survey sample were in mainstream schools (primary or secondary) or in further education (see Table 9.2). None had yet progressed to higher education, although some young people were preparing to do so. Only five young people were aged 18 at the point of data collection and all of these were completing courses in further education or at school. Two young people were reported by carers to have rejected

Table 9.2
Young people's education status (n = 130)

	Number	Per cent
Mainstream school	88	67.5
Special school	4	3
Further education	31	24
Higher education	0	0
English language provision (not school based)	4	3
Pupil referral unit	1	1

education. One young person had refused to consider college and was engaged in part-time employment. The other was reported to be receiving help through the Refugee Council.

All the young people we interviewed were in mainstream school or further education at the time of interview. Following an education assessment at school, three young people were placed a year below their age group, while another was able to repeat Year 10 after he struggled the first time around. All said they had found this experience helpful as it gave them an opportunity to settle. This was particularly helpful for those taking GCSEs, as they had time to develop English language skills and catch up with the curriculum. This meant they were able to gain the qualifications needed to progress to study for A Levels or BTEC courses.

Young people entered education through three main routes: entering straight into mainstream school placements; beginning in language units within or outside school before moving into mainstream classes; or enrolling directly on to courses at further education colleges. They were enrolled on a variety of courses, ranging from ESOL classes three days a week at college, ESOL in combination with vocational courses and GCSEs, BTECs, or A levels. Three young people were studying A levels at school and two others were studying for BTECs at college. Most of the other young people aged 16–18 were studying ESOL in college in combination with other vocational courses such as mechanics, bricklaying, IT or construction. They included young people who had not had previous experience of education in their country of origin, those who had arrived in the UK near the end of Year 11, those who had not attained the grades needed at GCSE to pursue studies in the Sixth Form at school, and those who expressed an interest in vocational courses. Of the younger age group (13–15-year-olds) who were still in school, two were in Year 9 and older ones were being entered for GCSE examinations or a mix of GCSE and BTEC examinations. Two young people, aged 16 and 15, were on ESOL-only programmes of study.

Language support

Many young people were in need of help to develop their English language skills. A large minority of young people in the survey who attended mainstream school (43%) were receiving additional classroom-based language support. A smaller proportion of school students also received language support outside school (21%). This provision was organised through schools or children's services and tended to comprise private home tuition or tuition organised in community education centres. In many cases, it provided a valuable supplement to help young people catch up and take better advantage of subject-based teaching in the classroom.

Young people and foster carers agreed that acquiring and developing English language skills was a crucial aspect of young people's resettlement needs (Candappa and Egharevba, 2000; Marriot, 2001; Stanley, 2001). First, it was important for future education progression. It enabled young people to participate and gain good qualifications, but also to move beyond ESOL courses to other academic and vocational subjects that would help them to pursue their chosen education and career paths.

Second, learning English was also very important for enabling social interactions in school and beyond (Wade *et al*, 2005). In addition to fears and anxieties about starting a new school in a new country, Omid spoke of the immediate practical barriers imposed by a lack of English language knowledge and the social isolation created by this: 'Even if you want to try and make a friend, you can't. When you don't know anything, how can you say something to them?'

Young people often had an intensive period of language learning after their initial arrival in the foster placement and in school. Foster carers spent time interacting with and supporting young people in developing English language skills in everyday routines in the home using, for example, dictionaries, flash cards and resources on the internet. Abraham's foster carers noticed that his language skills quickly developed once he started school. Although young people needed ongoing language support in school, most had been able eventually to move full time into the mainstream curriculum.

He's improved a lot now. Since two years now . . . he don't have no interpreter, he speaks by himself . . . He's shy a little bit for speaking. (Sarah)

However, as mentioned earlier, two young people were only studying ESOL. Wade and colleagues (2005) found that the part-time structure of many ESOL classes could be a source of frustration to young people who were wanting to progress at a faster pace.

The big ESOL trap can be quite demotivating for some young people who just get stuck on language courses. (Team manager, Area 3)

Educational progress

Many unaccompanied young people are reported to progress well in education both academically and socially (Wade *et al*, 2005; Kohli, 2007). It has been suggested that this level of engagement differs in comparison to many other looked after children who are frequently reported as performing poorly in education (Berridge, 2007; Kohli, 2007; Berridge and Saunders, 2009). However, as mentioned earlier, some unaccompanied young people may face significant challenges due to limited past educational experience or interruptions in their education. When young people arrive in the UK, it is important, when assessing their academic progress, to consider young people's starting points and education background (Ofsted, 2003).

Young people's central focus on education and drive to succeed appeared to place some under considerable pressure. The term "temporal panic" has been used to describe a reaction to time passing more rapidly than the person's ability to finish the present act requires (Lewis and Weigert, 1981). With insecure immigration status, the precariousness of plans for future residence in the UK, and interruptions in earlier education experience, the time in which young people can achieve and progress in education is often compressed both by their past experiences and future possibilities. There was a sense that many young people felt the pressure of the clock ticking away as they sought to achieve their education goals. Samuel, who was 17 years old, hoped to become a paramedic, but after finding out from his teacher about the qualifications he would need in order to do this, he was unsure if he could achieve this in time. He said: 'If it happened here when I was a kid, if I started here, so it could be alright, but now it's really, I think so, already my life's passed.' Where a young person's age is disputed there may also be implications for education trajectories and the creation of a compressed time period in which to achieve goals. Rashid was initially placed in Year 9 before being age assessed and moved to Year 11 after his school suggested he might be older than the age he claimed. Rashid's foster carer said: 'It affected him in terms of his education. Not enough time to prepare for his exams.'

Young people often worked very hard and showed a determination to not only catch up, but also to excel.

I don't want to get anything below a C. I want to pass everything I do and, yeah, I did pressurise myself a little bit, and especially Year 11 'cos it was putting more work on top of me. (Haaroon)

There was a feeling among many of the young people that there was little time to waste and that they needed to focus on their education. There was a sense this had to be achieved within a timeframe determined not only by young people's age and time left in school, but also by the time limits imposed by the asylum system. Young people spoke about the uncertainty they felt about their future education and employment prospects in the context of unresolved asylum claims and the pressure they felt to make the most of their time in education.

Table 9.3 shows the assessments made by foster carers of the educational progress being made by young people. Most young people were considered to be doing reasonably or very well and less than one-third of young people were performing at a level below which foster carers might have expected.

Most foster carers reported that young people's educational circumstances had improved since they had first come to live with them, 'to a large extent' (75%) or at least 'to some degree' (21%). There was an obvious association between young people being rated as doing

Table 9.3
Assessment of young people's educational progress

	Per cent (n = 126)
Very good (well above average for ability)	25
Quite good	46
Quite poor	22
Very poor (well below average for ability)	7

well educationally and them enjoying their studies, attending regularly and participating in courses that were appropriate for their skills and abilities. It was in relation to the relevance of the educational programme for the young people, however, that the association with good educational progress was strongest.[50] Where this programme was considered strongly relevant, four-fifths of young people (81%) were thought to be making good educational progress compared to one-half (50%) where it was considered less relevant.

A number of other child and social work factors were also associated with educational progress. Young people were more likely to be rated as making good progress where:

- they were not considered to have emotional or behavioural difficulties (p<0.001);
- they had a range of hobbies and interests (p = 0.015);
- they had made fewer past placement moves (p = 0.034);[51]
- there was some evidence of positive social work planning (p = 0.01);[52]

---

50 Kendall's tau-b tests for educational progress and enjoying education (p = 0.02, t 0.194, n = 123); attending regularly (p = 0.02, t 0.196, n = 120); appropriateness of courses for ability (p<0.001, t 0.352, n = 120)

51 We also checked to make sure that past placement moves was not simply an effect of length of time in the UK (p = 0.88) or of the young person's age (p = 0.16).

52 Our planning score provided a proxy measure of social work planning. It was based on responses to whether foster carers had received written copies of the child's care plan, personal education plan and health plan. These were combined to provide the 0–3 score. Possession of these provided an admittedly crude indication that social work planning was taking place.

- contact with the young person's social worker was considered to be helpful for the young person (p = 0.002) and for the foster carer (p = 0.03).

The first three points relate to the young person, taking account of aspects of their characteristics, care careers and current interests. The second set refers to the framework of social work support that surrounded the young person and foster carer. Proactive social work support and planning for the child, combined with foster carers themselves feeling reasonably well supported and confident, presumably helped to provide an environment in which young people could harness their own motivation to succeed. However, this was less likely to be the case where young people presented significant emotional and behavioural challenges or, to some extent, where they had been unsettled by past placement moves.

In order to identify which of these factors were most closely associated with young people making good educational progress, further multivariate analysis was undertaken. The above list of variables was included in a stepwise linear regression. We also included the foster carers' assessment of whether the education the young person was receiving now was appropriate for their current abilities. As we have seen, this was closely associated with educational progress (p<0.001) while, a priori, retaining some independence from it.[53]

This analysis produced a final model that identified two factors that contributed most to young people's educational progress. Good progress was more likely where:

- the young person was not considered to have emotional or behavioural difficulties (p = 0.001, Beta 0.305);
- the course s/he was doing was appropriate for his/her current abilities (p<0.001, Beta 0.388).[54]

---

53 Whether the young person enjoys education (p = 0.07) or attends regularly (p = 0.3) were excluded. The appropriateness of the course was much more strongly associated with educational progress (p<0.001) than either of these in multivariate analysis.

54 This model explained 29% of the variation in educational progress (R2 0.288).

The first reinforces what is known about risks of poor educational attainment for young people with emotional and behavioural difficulties in adolescence (Farmer *et al*, 2008). In relation to looked after young people generally, studies have revealed relatively high levels of mental health, emotional and behavioural problems amongst young people in the care system (McCann *et al*, 1996; Meltzer, 2003). If these cannot be ameliorated there is also evidence of their lasting effects for young people leaving care (Dixon *et al*, 2006). There is some evidence that unaccompanied young people may fare rather better than UK children while they are looked after and may be less likely to display challenging behaviours and emotional disturbance (Dixon *et al*, 2006; Sinclair *et al*, 2007). However, this study provides some evidence that where unaccompanied young people do display challenging behaviour they are more likely to struggle educationally. The second brings the question of assessment and matching to the fore, as discussed earlier. Once young people arrive in the UK, therefore, the diversity of their social and educational backgrounds signals the need for careful assessment of their educational backgrounds, capabilities, interests and aspirations as a prelude to identifying appropriate education and training opportunities.

Wade and colleagues' (2005) study, which analysed the social work case files of 212 unaccompanied young people, highlighted considerable variation in these assessments. Although some educational assessment was undertaken in the vast majority of cases (80%), the extent and range of information that was recorded was highly variable. Thorough assessment is important, not least because many education professionals feel they receive insufficient information about refugee children's education histories and needs when they are referred to schools (Ofsted, 2003; Remsbury, 2003).

Our current evidence suggests that the educational progress of young people may suffer where insufficient attention is paid to finding an appropriate match. It would not be surprising to find that young people would find less enjoyment and motivation in education where they had been routinely allocated to courses that were not consistent with their interests and aspirations. Abbas, for example, was having difficulty staying motivated at college. He said: 'They teach something like I done before. So it's a little bit boring for me because I've already done it.' The association between educational progress and social work support may therefore stem from the activities of social workers directed at helping young people to access and manage courses that are reasonably well matched to their abilities and interests and/or by facilitating foster carers to provide that day-to-day support. In these circumstances, the prospects for educational success appeared to be propitious.

Supporting education

Unaccompanied young people, who may be coping with a number of difficult situations outside school, can often benefit if there is provision of strong levels of support in school (Jones, 1998). Given their varied education histories and the context of the broader resettlement process, some initial period of adjustment is likely to take place and support may be particularly helpful at this time. Placing young people in well-supported educational placements as early as possible has been found to be important for young people's sense of well-being (Chase *et al*, 2008).

The interest and encouragement of adults who are important to the young person (including teachers, foster carers and social workers) play a key role in supporting their educational progress (Gilligan, 2007a). When asked about who helped them with their education the most, while young people in our study focused on particular teachers or foster carers, others described more of a 360-degree base of support. Samir, for example, said he was "surrounded" by support from his foster family, friends and college.

Schools can provide a safe and benevolent environment where students can have intensive contact with the teachers who have the potential to function as guides in a new society (Ruuk, 2002) . Most young people in the current study reported having positive relations with their teachers and felt encouraged and supported by them. Teachers were often described as kind, helpful and encouraging. Young people especially valued extra help they were given by language support staff, although occasionally there were more negative experiences. Nabil was happy with the teacher he had at the time of the fieldwork, who he described as helpful and kind. However, he had recently had a negative experience with another teacher at the college who had used racist language towards him and had not given permission for him to have a day's leave for Eid. His foster carer made a complaint on his behalf and he was moved to another class following a meeting at the college.

A few young people were receiving extra assistance from education professionals in addition to their teachers and language tutors. For example, Samuel had an education mentor who visited him twice at school and helped select his course options. Mahmud's education support worker had acquired a laptop for him to use for studying.

Young people reported that social workers supported them in accessing material resources such as laptops and Education Maintenance Allowances (no longer available as of February 2011), or gaining access to a school placement itself. One young person said that his social worker was helping him complete university course application forms. While a few young people spoke to the social worker about their progress at school, this day-to-day education support and nurturing outside school was generally provided by foster carers. One foster carer said: 'Well the social worker hasn't got time to do education with them, it's just social things; how things are improving and listen to their complaints.'

Unaccompanied minors in foster care and residential care have been found to be significantly more likely to be consistently engaged in education than those living in semi-independent or independent accommodation (Wade, 2009). Stanley (2001) found that young people living in semi-independent accommodation often had no one to show a day-to-day interest in their education progress. Gilligan (2007b) highlights the day-to-day mentoring role played by many foster carers and residential workers and explains how this can help to improve young people's educational performance (see also Jackson et al, 2005).

Foster carers in this study were generally providing this day-to-day support and showed considerable interest in young people's education. Most singled out educational progress as one of the main priorities they had for their foster children while they were in their care. They tried to encourage and motivate young people to fulfil their potential by making sure they attended school regularly, helping them with homework, giving them positive praise for their achievements, and supporting and raising their aspirations. The foster carers' birth children often also provided support (see Gilligan, 2007a). Most young people had felt encouraged by their foster families.

Education is very important to us to advise and help. Just helping his education and advising and counselling him to know what he wants to do in the future. (Daniel, Rashid's foster carer)

I've encouraged him to push himself, particularly intellectually, 'cos he's a bright boy . . . It's that thing that you do with your children, you try to raise their aspirations. You don't just sort of settle. (Eleanor, Arian's foster carer)

We did help in the early days. We helped him with his reading and words and what they mean and so forth . . . even now we still do that. (Rachel, Nadir's foster carer)

Foster carers also demonstrated their interest in young people's education by attending parents' evenings, maintaining regular contact with teachers and making sure they were up to date with how young people were progressing. Haaroon spoke to his foster carer every day about school during his first year in the UK:

I used to come home, especially at the beginning, she used to talk to me every day after school: 'What happened? You alright? How was your day'? And we used to talk. (Haaroon)

By maintaining regular communication with schools and young people, foster carers were able to advocate and provide support if problems occurred. Since, as we have seen, young people had just a relatively short space of time in which to achieve positive education outcomes, the role played by adults around them was imperative if young people were going to have the opportunity to realise their full potential.

Education and social relationships

School or college is a main site through which young people begin to construct their social networks in the UK (Candappa and Egharevba, 2000; Beirens *et al*, 2007; Kohli, 2007). Young people who were initially placed in language support units at school described the supportive environment this provided at that stage.

I could make some friends in that class as well because they all didn't know how to speak English so we had some funny conversations. It was all not even English but we had to talk to each other in English. It was really funny. (Ban-hwa)

[It was] a bit weird at the beginning like. I felt all right 'cos there was quite a lot of other people who, you know, didn't speak English. (Arian)

Other young people attended schools that already had students from their countries of origin and spoke of the social and language support provided by these young people.

When I was starting school there was two Afghan boys, they were speaking [the] same language . . . They would help me a lot and, you know, with meetings in the office or if I need to ask something. (Nabil)

Most young people had made friends at school or college. Rafi described the social aspect of school as 'Better than staying at home 'cos you get bored sometimes, and it's different at school 'cos you see your mates and play football.'

Although some young people had found it difficult starting at school when they were unable to communicate in English, most felt they had been welcomed by (at least some of) their peers. Studies have highlighted the importance of good welcome and induction procedures in schools and the development of a school ethos of inclusion and respect in order to enable refugee young people to settle in school (Richman, 1998; Rutter, 2003a; Ofsted, 2003; Hek, 2005b). A number of young people mentioned the value of peer mentors. When Samuel started school he was assigned a peer mentor who acted as a guide and introduced him to his friends, who invited him to play football at break time and after school. Samuel had moved on to college, but was still in regular contact with these school friends. Some Afghan young people had been paired with Afghan peer mentors who supported them with language and with developing a friendship group at school. Haaroon mentioned that being in the company of another Afghan young person who was popular in the school and doing well academically had encouraged and motivated him. Other young people had themselves taken an active role in welcoming other newcomers into their schools. At a parent's evening, Rashid's teacher had praised Rashid for approaching and supporting a new Afghan student at school who had been anxious and withdrawn.

The ethnicity and nationality of friends varied and, unsurprisingly, this was in part dependent on who young people came into contact with. Young people studying ESOL were mainly friends with refugee and migrant young people from their or other countries (Refugee Action, 2003). Young people who were in school were usually friends with young people from the ethnic backgrounds represented in their schools and neighbourhoods. Most Afghan young people living in areas where there was an Afghan population, or sharing a placement with another Afghan young person, had developed a group of Afghan friends. Beirens and colleagues (2007) found that young people in their study who attended after-school clubs for refugee young people often felt a sense of belonging and security there, particularly in cases where they were subjected to racism and prejudice in mainstream school. Some young people in our study chose to focus their friendships around young people of their nationality, perhaps because of the familiarity and security of shared language, cultural background and experiences, or because of experiences of racism and exclusion. However, in many cases these friendships were built alongside friendships with young people from other ethnic backgrounds.[55]

---

55 The social networks developed by young people form the principal focus of Chapter 11.

Most young people were reported to be well behaved in school, although there were some exceptions.

I got him put on report so that it controls his behaviour at school. He's done some bullying at school, but he's got hundreds of peer-group friends. (Mark, Abraham's foster carer)

From day one there were problems with him in school . . . He doesn't want to abide by the school rules. He doesn't want to wear the proper school uniform. He's using the phone in the middle of the class. (Adele, Ermir's foster carer)

Young people were often shocked by the bad behaviour of some students in the school.

They don't have respect for [the] teacher . . . In my country they have a different life, different kind of culture. (Abbas)

Mahmud, Aarif and their foster carers described a disruptive school environment where there was frequent disorder and fighting. At Mahmud's school, this was reported as taking place along ethnic divisions, although Mahmud and his foster carer said he had not experienced any bullying directly or been involved in the fighting. Both young people had struggled to concentrate and learn in this environment. The young people thought their further education colleges were better than their schools because students were more mature and tended to be well behaved. Aarif's foster carer commented that the college was more ethnically diverse, although Mahmud and his foster carer thought that the significant ethnic diversity in Mahmud's school was actually a key source of tension.

While education is often a primary location for social integration, there have also been reports of young people having to contend with bullying and racism in the school environment (Hek, 2005b; Kohli, 2007). Around one-third of young people in our survey (34%) were reported by their foster carers to have been the victims of bullying, at least occasionally. In contrast, fewer than one in ten (9%) were thought to have engaged in bullying.

It is not uncommon for asylum-seeking and refugee young people living in areas with a predominantly white population to experience racism at school (Brownlees and Finch, 2010) or in local neighbourhoods (Hemmerman *et al*, 2007; Spicer, 2008). In two schools, there had been hostile responses to the presence of a small number of Afghan boys who started at the school around the same time. Some young people had experienced verbal bullying and name calling at school. Navid was being verbally bullied by young people at his school because he could not speak English and was an asylum seeker. Rafi shortened his Afghan name in response to bullying at school.

Some of the Afghan boys had also experienced violent physical assaults. Abbas had been persuaded by a girl from school to meet her at a location where instead he found a group of boys waiting to attack him. In one school, following attacks on Afghan boys during and after school time, the school had arranged for Afghan pupils to leave early at the end of each day and a security guard was placed at the school gate as they were leaving. Majeed reported that he had been assaulted by a group of boys at a previous school he had attended, which had resulted in one of his teeth being knocked out. His foster carers said he had been the only Afghan boy at that school. They compared this with the school he was currently at where he had many friends from a range of ethnic backgrounds, and where there were other Afghan boys in the school. There were far fewer reports of racism in areas with multi-ethnic populations, although Navid (above) attended a school in a multi-ethnic neighbourhood and had experienced racist bullying there.

There was a mixed response from schools to racist behaviour and bullying. Some had strong anti-racism and anti-bullying policies and were swift to respond. Abraham's foster carers said: 'They have a zero tolerance of racism . . . The school phoned me up straight away and told me what had happened.' Sabir had also been able to talk to his teacher about bullying in the school and the police had responded to fighting between Afghan and white boys at the school. In contrast, Navid's school informed his foster carer that the bullying was not serious, but rather just children making fun of other children and therefore "normal" playground behaviour. Navid, however, was clearly distressed by the bullying and very unhappy with the school's response.

Some young people were keen to demonstrate that they could stand up to and deal with bullies on their own. Haaroon said: 'I was pretty self-confident and I had self-esteem and I was like, "You can't bully me, you know, I'm not that weak".' One foster carer also described this attitude among young people and thought that schools needed to be involved more pro-actively as some young people were reluctant to report incidents to teachers:

The school used to say, 'Well, any problems, come to me'. But I don't think they understand that the Afghan boys, they want to look after themselves, and even though they were really in trouble, they wouldn't ask for it. (Lisa, Aarif's foster carer)

Foster carers often advised young people to stay out of trouble, to walk away from the situation and to not retaliate. In addition to protecting young people from being harmed in violence and disorder, foster carers were also anxious about the effect any involvement could have on their status as asylum seekers and on the asylum process itself.

If trouble starts, you don't need it. Just get away as quick as possible . . . You know, because it's too dangerous for you to get mixed up in that with your asylum process going. (Leena, Mahmud's foster carer)

Summary

Unaccompanied minors come from diverse educational backgrounds, therefore education assessments play an important role in ensuring access to appropriate courses and support. Some young people had experienced delays in accessing school places. These were attributed to young people arriving in the UK either late in the school year or when they were approaching 16 years of age. When their age was subject to uncertainty and/or their appearance was older than their official age, they could also be caught in the gap between school and college.

Acquiring and developing English language skills were a crucial aspect of young people's resettlement needs. It was important for academic progression and also in enabling social interactions in school and beyond.

Education is a high priority for many young refugees in the UK and unaccompanied minors have been described as often being highly motivated with regard to participation and progress in education. Very few young people had attendance problems and most were enjoying and receiving an appropriate education. Most foster carers reported that young people's educational progress was on an upward curve. Good progress was less likely where young people had moderate to severe emotional, social or behavioural difficulties, where courses were considered inappropriate for their current needs and abilities, or where the packages of support provided by social workers and foster carers were weaker.

However, with insecure immigration status and interruptions in earlier education experience, the time in which young people can achieve and progress in education is often compressed by both their past experiences and future possibilities. Education was a key area in which foster carers provided support to young people. Foster carers' advocacy and support for young people in education were crucial during a period in which young people had a short timeframe in which to achieve positive education outcomes.

Education was also an important arena within which young people could strengthen their network of social relationships, although experiences of marginality, racism and bullying were not uncommon. The ways in which foster carers and schools managed these incidents affected young people's experiences of cross-cultural relationships.

10 Health and emotional well-being

This chapter explores the health and emotional well-being of the young people in our study. In doing so, it touches more broadly on young people's experiences of integration, settlement and feelings of belonging. Using the survey data, the first section examines overall progress and well-being, highlighting some factors associated with higher or lower levels of well-being. The second section then uses interview and focus-group data to explore more dynamically how young people's health and emotional well-being tended to vary over the course of placements and to consider the wide range of factors that tended to influence feelings of well-being.

The overall progress and well-being of young people

This section draws on information provided by foster carers in the survey to consider the progress and well-being of young people in some key developmental areas – health, education, emotional ties, friendships, skills, confidence and behaviour. Respondents were asked to rate their young person in relation to a number of well-being indicators according to how they had been getting on over the previous three months. These findings are presented in Table 10.1.

In overall terms, young people were perceived to be faring quite well at the point of data collection, especially in relation to their health, emotional well-being, friendships and ability to look after themselves in age-appropriate ways. However, variation was also evident in some areas. Over one-quarter of young people were rated as faring "quite" or "very" poorly in relation to their education, their development of skills and interests, their emotional ties with adults and, to a lesser extent, their connections with homeland cultures and communities.

Nine of these items were combined into an overall well-being score in order to see whether young people's progress and well-being were

Table 10.1
Child progress and well-being indicators – per cent (n = 126)

	Poor	Quite poor	Quite good	Good
Health (frequently ill and/or failing to thrive, normally well and thriving)	2	2	12	84
Educational progress (relative to age and ability)	7	22	46	25
Hobbies, skills and interests	10	18	48	25
Self-confidence	2	15	37	45
Emotional ties (to at least one adult)	9	18	33	41
Close friendships (none, several close friends)	4	8	29	59
Emotional and behavioural difficulties	5	9	32	55
Self-care skills (competent for age)	6	6	27	60
Emotional well-being (sad, unhappy; normally happy)	3	5	35	57
Links to home culture (or community of origin)	10	12	33	45

Not all rows total 100 per cent due to rounding.

linked to other aspects of their lives.[56] The overall progress of young people was not associated with their age or sex. However, there was an indication that young people experiencing mental health problems were faring less well.[57]

---

56 Links to "home" culture was dropped. Factor analysis suggested that it would not combine well with the other nine items. Reliability analysis also suggested that while these nine items made for a reliable measure (Cronbach's alpha 0.801), links to "home" culture was the only item that (if included) reduced this score. One outlier case was also removed. This created a scale from 9–36, with a higher score being positive.

57 Mann Whitney U exact test (p = 0.021, n = 125). Caution should be exercised with this finding, however, since only five young people were reported to have such problems.

There was also variation in overall progress according to young people's countries or regions of origin. Most young people in the survey sample had originated from Afghanistan (69%). The numbers from other countries were therefore relatively small. In consequence, the analyses we were able to undertake were inevitably quite crude. The sample was subdivided into three groups: Afghanistan (n = 91); Africa (n = 21) and "Other" areas (n = 20).[58] Young people from Afghanistan were tending to fare less well overall than either of the other two groups.[59] Amongst the list of indicators in Table 10.1, however, not all categories applied equally. Significant differences lay in relation to educational progress (p = 0.034), emotional and behavioural development (p = 0.043), and the development of emotional ties with adults (p = 0.007). In other words, relative to others, Afghan young people were more likely to have been perceived by foster carers as lacking attachment, as presenting behavioural challenges and as progressing less well in their studies.

It was not surprising to find that young people who were rated as "doing well" across these domains also scored highly on our Family Integration Measure.[60] There is likely to be a reciprocal relationship between these two measures. Where young people were considered by foster carers to be easy to care for, to feel part of the family, to be able to confide and communicate, and to have positive relationships with other children living in the household, it is also highly likely that they would be seen as doing well in their emotional, social and educational development.

Young people were also rated as doing well where:

- they had made fewer placement moves in the past (p = 0.019);

---

58 "Other" areas included: Asia other (Pakistan, Sri Lanka, Vietnam, Bangladesh); Europe (Albania, Kosovo); Middle East (Iran, Iraq).

59 Kruskal-Wallis test (p = 0.003, n = 125). Paired tests showed that this applied to both African (p = 0.042) and "Other" young people (p = 0.003).

60 Kendall's tau-b test (p<0.001, t 0.348, n = 123). The Family Integration Measure combined a number of factors designed to assess the extent to which the young people had become well embedded into the foster family. The measure was described in Chapter 6 (see Table 6.2 and its footnote).

- they had been resident in the UK for a longer period of time (p = 0.046);
- the placement was matched by religion and/or country of origin (p = 0.023);
- contact with the child's social worker was considered helpful for the young person (p = 0.014) and for the foster carer (p = 0.021);
- there was evidence of proactive social work planning (p = 0.015).[61]

Further analysis was undertaken in an effort to reduce this list of variables and identify those most closely associated with the overall progress of young people. This list, together with region of origin, was entered into a stepwise linear regression. The final model, presented in Table 10.2, highlights the influence of movement and the legacy of origins.

Table 10.2
Factors associated with the overall progress and well-being of young people (n = 110)

	B	S.E.	Beta	Sig.
Number of prior placements	−1.986	0.647	−0.295	0.003
Region of origin	2.101	0.650	0.310	0.002

Adjusted r^2 0.162

The model emphasises the importance of stability for young people's progress and development. To a much lesser extent, the findings also provide evidence about the value of an extended period of time in the UK to enable young people to adjust to life in this country, to learn English, to develop networks of support and to settle into a programme of learning. These positive benefits were considerably greater where

---

61 Our planning measure was based on whether the foster carer had written copies of the child's care, health and Personal Education Plans. Where this was so, this was taken as an admittedly crude proxy for planning.

young people had found a settled placement (and not moved around) and, to a lesser extent, where the support provided by their social workers had proved helpful to them and where they had a good connection (or match) with their foster carer.

The model also suggests that young people from Afghanistan may experience a more difficult period of adjustment to life in the UK than do some other groups of young people. This finding needs to be tested through further research. These difficulties may arise from past educational experiences that have a continuing legacy during the resettlement phase and/or to cultural or familial experiences that make the transition to foster care in the UK more troublesome for some of them or for their foster carers. These experiences may also include stereotypical or racist assumptions in the wider communities in which young people were living in the UK about Afghanistan and the young people who arrive here from that country during a time of war. At the very least, it warns us against the risk of treating unaccompanied young people as a homogeneous group. It makes us mindful of the diversity that exists within this population and of the need to develop a deeper understanding of differences in patterns of experience for young people from different national and ethnic backgrounds (see also Rutter, 2004; Wade et al, 2005).

While helpful, these findings explain just 16 per cent of the variance in the progress and well-being of young people and it may be that other factors (that we could not test) may be equally influential.[62] Previous chapters have highlighted some of the issues that contribute to young people's progress in foster care. The remainder of this chapter utilises data from interviews to explore the physical, mental and emotional health of our sample of young people living in foster care.

---

62 To give just one example, we were unable to test the effects of emotional and behavioural difficulties on progress, since this formed part of the composite progress measure. We know, however, that behaviour is strongly associated with the progress of looked after children (Sinclair et al, 2005; Biehal et al, 2010; Wade et al, 2011) and in this sample, for example, there was a strong correlation between behaviour difficulties, educational progress (p<0.001) and family integration (p = 0.009).

Health and emotional well-being

As the evidence from foster carers suggested above, very few of the young people were identified as having poor health. This was reconfirmed in the interviews, particularly in relation to physical health. However, while young people were described as being in overall good health, the interviews revealed some rather more nuanced accounts of emotional well-being.

Physical health

In line with the survey findings, most young people and foster carers reported that young people were in good physical health. Many were actively engaged in a range of sports and led healthy lifestyles. Foster carers' comments in relation to physical health most commonly made mention of the young people's lack of health and immunisation records. In addition to being without access to such documents following their migration, some young people may also have come from regions of conflict where access to healthcare may have been difficult (Kidane, 2001a; Wade *et al*, 2005). Therefore, one of the early tasks soon after arrival was to register the young person with a GP so that they could receive a health assessment and all the necessary immunisations.

Where young people were reported to have had physical health conditions, these had generally existed for a limited period of time in the initial stages of the placement, shortly after the young person's arrival in the UK. Two young people had sustained injuries during their journeys to the UK, although one of these, a problem with the toes, was reported to be a minor injury.

He'd had an accident or something in France. Someone had jumped on him in their boots, and he said . . . later on, when he could talk English . . . [that] he'd broken his foot. But we don't know whether he meant broke it or fractured it or what. (Susan, Abraham's foster carer)

He hurt his toe when he was on the lorry and he, you know, damaged his toe, but it seems to be getting better. The nail keeps coming off and growing again, but that's just a minor thing. (Leena, Mahmud's foster carer)

Two other young people had been admitted to hospital soon after they arrived, although we do not know the nature of their illness. One of these young people was living in foster care when she was admitted to hospital and had been pleased when her foster carers visited her regularly and offered her support during her stay. The other young person was in hospital prior to his referral to children's services, soon after he arrived in the UK.

Long and difficult journeys to the UK meant that a number of young people were hungry, tired and in a relatively weak physical state on arrival. The most common health complaints associated with the journey were skin infections, often scabies, which had developed as a result of harsh conditions young people had experienced.

A lot of them come with skin, scratching and itching . . . and they're really embarrassed about that. So we explain to them that's fine . . . You're bound to have done 'cos you've been on the journey. But we try to work out whether that's scabies or not, so, 'cos we have to alert the foster carers . . . So we try and sort that out. (Social worker, Area 3)

Foster carers who had looked after foster children with scabies reported that they had received advice from social workers on how to care for these young people. Apart from scabies, one young person had a skin condition which he had had since birth; another young person had recently developed alopecia; and some young people needed quite extensive dental treatment.

Emotional well-being and mental health
The emotional well-being and mental health of asylum-seeking and refugee children has received prominent attention in the international literature in this field. Studies have examined the effects of forced migration and resettlement and, within this, have explored levels of post-traumatic stress, anxiety and depression linked to pre-migration

and post-migration circumstances and have attempted to identify risks and protective factors for mental well-being (Bean *et al*, 2007a; Chase *et al*, 2008; Hodes *et al*, 2008; Bronstein and Montgomery, 2011).

Studies have found that self-reports of traumatic stress reactions and psychological distress are significantly higher among unaccompanied minors than among refugee young people living with their families and very much higher than is the case for normative populations of young people (Bean *et al*, 2007a; Hodes *et al*, 2008). However, risk levels may be broadly similar to those experienced by citizen young people in the looked after system (McMillen *et al*, 2005; Bean *et al*, 2007b).

Elevated levels of risk in the present are strongly associated with exposure to past trauma events and, while social demographic factors appear less influential, Bean and colleagues (2007b) found that older young people (who were likely to have experienced more cumulatively traumatic events and to have been less sheltered from war-related experiences in the past) had higher levels of distress than younger age groups. Placement in supported settings has also been shown to have some protective effects. When controlling for age, reports of psychological distress were lower for refugee young people living with family members and for unaccompanied young people living in foster care or small group homes compared to those living independently (Bean *et al*, 2007a; Hodes *et al*, 2008).

The impact of war on children and young people can vary, depending on their disposition and the circumstances that they have experienced (Boyden and de Berry, 2004). While some young people may need specialist therapeutic help, not all asylum-seeking young people are necessarily traumatised or require this form of support. Appropriate care and support can help young people to rebuild their lives and develop their resilience and capacity to cope with the uncertainties associated with forced migration (Richman, 1998; Kohli and Mather, 2003).

The journey . . . what's happened to them that's led them to . . . go down the asylum road . . . does have a major impact and will cause real continuing problems for them, but . . . we've got some people who from time to time . . . will struggle, but overall they're doing well . . . It's a question . . . of never completely ignoring that issue, but on the other hand not necessarily seeing it as . . . always going to have the impact that people think it might have . . . It's a huge strength of character . . . with a lot of young people, in terms of their ability to keep things together. (Team manager, Area 3)

While epidemiological and psychological studies have explored the prevalence of mental health conditions among refugee and asylum-seeking children and the characteristics associated with these, some qualitative studies have begun to explore young people's own accounts and perspectives on emotional well-being. These studies have tended to highlight young people's resilience in the context of forced migration (Rousseau *et al*, 1998; Goodman, 2004; Chase *et al*, 2008; Ni Raghallaigh and Gilligan, 2010; Groark *et al*, 2011). Ni Raghallaigh and Gilligan (2010) identify six coping strategies that may contribute to the development of resilience among unaccompanied minors. These include: maintaining continuity in a changed context; adjusting by learning and changing; adopting a positive outlook; suppressing emotions and seeking distraction; acting independently; and distrusting. Kohli (2006a) and Chase (2010) have written of silences and limited talking among unaccompanied young people, including the potential ways in which these may be used by young people to cope with their situation, and have highlighted the ways in which social workers understand and work with these silences over time.

Levels of emotional well-being

Government guidance on promoting the health and well-being of looked after children emphasises the importance of having the physical, emotional and mental health needs of young people assessed by appropriately trained professionals (National Institute for Health and Clinical Excellence, 2010). However, research has found that while unaccompanied young people's physical health needs are quite routinely assessed, assessment of emotional well-being may be more variable (Wade *et al*, 2005; Barrie and Mendes, 2011).

In overall statements about young people's progress, foster carers often described them as cheerful and pleasant young people who were easy to care for. Abraham's foster carer said: 'He's such a happy-go-lucky lad. He's very laid back.' Only one foster carer in the interview sample was currently looking after a young person diagnosed with a mental health condition:[63]

> *He does self-harming and all that sort of thing . . . In the first two weeks we had to go to hospital, stay there all night, because he was banging his head against the stairs, and he had a knife in his hand.* (Amina, Housyar's foster carer)

Young people were frequently described as resilient and were often admired for doing well in spite of the adversities they had faced. Samir's foster carer said: 'I think it's safe to say that he, he takes things in his stride,' while Omid's foster carer compared the resilience of unaccompanied young people with that of citizen young people:

> *They have a built-in resilience. They're completely different and I think they've probably been doing and seeing a whole lot more [and are more] hardened to loss than . . . you know, other kids in care. But that's not to say they haven't, obviously, got feelings and emotions and memories, and things trigger certain things off and you just have to be there really.* (Stephanie, Omid's foster carer)

Although there were few reports of severe mental health conditions, comments made by foster carers and young people indicated that the full picture was rather more complex and multifaceted. While not all asylum-seeing young people are necessarily traumatised or experience severe mental health conditions, other challenges to their emotional

---

63 Another foster carer reported that a previous placement had ended after they had struggled to cope with a young person who was self-harming.

well-being may be less immediately discernible or visible. One social worker cautioned against taking apparent resilience and well-being at face value:

> I think . . . understanding the system and understanding what the young person has been through . . . Because our young people seem very resilient, not to just take that resilience at face value . . . They may think, oh, everything's fine, but, obviously, there's that loss from their parents and, you know, I think sometimes that resilience is there because of the good attachment that they've had in their early lives, but, you know, they've lost family and they've left their homeland. (Senior social worker, Area 2)

Young people described a mixed picture in terms of their emotional well-being. When asked on a scale of 1 to 10 how good they felt about their life, some young people placed themselves reasonably high on the scale, but said they could be higher if they were not worried about their family or their asylum claims. Others described a happy day-to-day life in the UK, but then gave a low score on the scale due to the anxieties they had about their future. Where young people were able to focus on the present, as distinct from the worries of the past or future, their self-report well-being ratings tended to be higher.

> My family, I mean, basically just I don't know nothing, but I'm, like, a bit worried about my brothers as well, so that makes it, like, eight, nine, but otherwise it could be more than ten . . . [I'm] not worried about life, you know, like no worries, no problems here . . . I have friends so it's good. (Omid)

> I think after one year I made a family so I [am] very happy. (Rahim)

> Well he's OK, he's doing well, as far as I can see, but I mean I know distress inside him because I mean when he's got to do it, is he going to be here, if he goes to Nigeria that will be the end of his education. (Grace, Ayotunde's foster carer)

Samuel described two scales that existed side by side. One scale described his everyday life in the present in the UK. The other one extended ahead into the future and revolved around the outcome of his asylum claim.

> *The way they've treated me and the way I've been in this home, and the way I go with my friends, all that, that's wonderful, 10 out of 10. But I am a bit worried . . . When I'm 18, I don't know where I live.* (Samuel)

Emotional well-being was undermined by the impact of past traumatic experiences, separation from family, concerns about family and immigration status, the process of claiming asylum (including age assessment) and problems with social integration such as bullying at school and loneliness. Emotional well-being fluctuated during the course of placements. In some cases difficulties were also more visible at certain times when young people were less able to cope. Foster carers said that although some young people had appeared worried and upset in the early days of the placement, this had improved later on. Foster carers and social workers reported that young people nearing the point at which they applied for extensions to their leave to remain often became more anxious and preoccupied as they worried about the final outcome of their asylum claims. Furthermore, some social workers worried about the effects of a negative decision on young people's behaviour and therefore on the placement.

> *If a young person has a refusal then it will impact on their mood and some young people become frustrated, which is understand-able . . . So it has an impact on placement stability.* (Social worker, Area 2)

Meanwhile, emotional well-being could also fluctuate from time to time in general during the course of the placement.

> *Sometimes we have a couple of weeks of memories and another time we don't hear nothing for ages . . . He wakes up in the night*

where he can't get out of bed because everything's on top of him. (Andrew, Rafi's foster carer)

In the first week or first two weeks I was like, I didn't know where I was, and just like missing my family. (Ermir)

As we have seen, young people's emotional well-being was affected not only by issues relating to pre-migration experiences and anxieties about asylum claims. Foster carers also referred to young people's age and teenage life and the difficulties this could create as young people attempted to establish their own identities and form new relationships. Well-being was also affected by the quality of life in placement, the quality of relationships young people were able to forge with those in and around the home, and by their social experiences and relationships outside the placements, at school or with friends. Levels of well-being were therefore subject to the ebb and flow of everyday living, although uncertainties about the future figured more prominently as young people aged and the time for leaving care drew near.

Access to support

Guidance on promoting the health of looked after young people recommends that commissioners and providers of mental health services should ensure that unaccompanied asylum-seeking children have access to specialist psychological services. These services are expected to have the expertise to meet some of the particular health needs these young people may have, including stress related to the immigration process, dislocation from countries of origin and culture, separation from family, and physical and emotional trauma from war (National Institute for Health and Clinical Excellence, 2010).[64]

The managers of the asylum teams in our study were broadly satisfied with the quality of Child and Adolescent Mental Health Services (CAMHS) in their local authorities and felt that young people

---

64 The need for governments to ensure appropriate access to mental health care is also stated in EU Council Directive 2003/9/EC of 27 January 2003 laying down minimum standards for the reception of asylum seekers.

referred to these services had benefited from the provision. One team manager also noted the availability of two other counselling services locally for young people with psychological or emotional problems. Concerns were expressed in three of our areas about delays in access to CAMHS. Another team manager also highlighted the fact that the local CAMHS service operated within a fixed boundary and the asylum team therefore had less input over services provided to their young people placed outside the local authority.

While young people were said to feel sad or anxious at times, most foster carers said this was not at a level of severity that required specialist mental health interventions.

> *It doesn't look like he needs it. I mean he's quite stable and, you know, doesn't show any signs of trauma or anything like that.*
> (Elizabeth, Sabir's foster carer)

Only two young people in our interview and focus-group samples had received therapeutic support. One had regular appointments with a psychiatrist at a hospital.[65] In a focus group, the other young person spoke about his struggle to sleep and of his disturbed dreams, caused by thoughts about his family and past experiences. He had been visiting a counsellor but had stopped attending because his foster carer said it was too far away for him to travel. His social worker was at that time trying to find an alternative counselling service nearer to his home. Specialist support services are often only available in limited geographical areas and may not be easily accessible to all unaccompanied young people who wish to access them (Bhabha and Finch, 2006).

Even if access to therapeutic services is possible, some young people may be hesitant to attend for various reasons including, potentially, a lack of knowledge about the process of counselling and the stigma attached to mental health conditions.

> *One young person said: 'It's really bizarre. Why would I go and*

---

65 We were only able to interview the foster carer in this case as the young person did not wish to take part.

speak to an absolute stranger about my problems when, actually, they can't solve my problems because my problems are that I want to stay in this country and the Home Office don't want me to stay in this country? So, can this counsellor change the Home Office's mind?' (Senior social worker, Area 2)

One foster carer reported that a previous foster child had attended once, but decided not to continue. She thought this was because of the stigma attached to counselling. While some young people may be hesitant about attending counselling for the reasons described, young people we spoke to had valued the efforts made by foster carers to acknowledge difficult emotions they were contending with and provide companionship at this time. In a minority of cases, some wished that more effort had been made here.

You've got, like, so many things on your shoulders and you just think sometimes you just want [there] to be someone, you know, sensitive, so your emotions, it's emotional stuff . . . but at least just a hug. (Young men's focus group)

In the interviews, young people were asked who they talked to if they felt sad. Most young people said they turned to their foster carers or that their foster carer approached them if they sensed they were sad. A participant in one of the young men's focus groups said: 'When [foster carer] sees we are sad she talks to us, asks if we feel sad.'

Anything that I feel like talking about I would talk to her, so she's the person that I would . . . have . . . a good long conversation with . . . if something matters then I would speak to Eleanor [foster carer]. (Arian)

Rashid chose to speak to his foster carer about his feelings because he thought it was important not to keep such feelings contained inside him: 'When you keep it in your heart it's making you a problem.' Foster carers said that young people had spoken to them about some of their feelings and about aspects of their journeys and past experiences. Some young people were more open than others and some spoke on occasions about these experiences when they were feeling particularly sad, but did not raise these issues on a regular basis.

> *He wears his heart on his sleeve and he wants to get it out of his system and he tells me loads of things, the journey and everything. The others not so much, they're just different personalities.* (Ann, Abbas' foster carer)

Foster carers therefore tried to develop an organic understanding of each young person as an individual with particular needs and ways of responding. With some young people, foster carers were able to ask them directly about their feelings if they appeared sad. With others, carers felt it more appropriate to make sure the young people knew they were available to talk to, but resisted raising these matters themselves in case they caused upset and instead waited to respond to whatever the young person chose to discuss.

Summary

Young people were perceived by foster carers to be faring quite well especially in relation to their health, emotional well-being, friendships and ability to look after themselves in age-appropriate ways. Young people rated as "doing well" across these domains also scored highly on our Family Integration Measure.

However, variation was evident in some areas. Over one-quarter of young people were rated as faring "quite" or "very" poorly in relation to their education, their development of skills and interests, their emotional ties with adults and, to a lesser extent, their connections with homeland cultures and communities. There was also variation in overall progress according to young people's countries or regions of origin. Most young people in the survey sample originated from Afghanistan (69%). Young people from Afghanistan were tending to fare less well in comparison to other young people in the sample.

Most young people were in good physical health. In relation to the few reports of physical health conditions, these had existed for a limited period of time in the initial stages of the placement, shortly after the young person's arrival in the UK.

In overall statements about progress and well-being, foster carers often described young people as being cheerful, pleasant and easy to care for. Young people were frequently described as being resilient and were often admired for doing well in spite of the adversities they had faced. Although there were few reports of severe mental health conditions, comments indicated that, while young people had high emotional well-being, the full picture was rather more complex and multifaceted. While generally doing reasonably well in their everyday life in the UK, emotional well-being was undermined by the impact of past traumatic experiences, separation from and concerns about family, anxieties over immigration status, the process of claiming asylum (including age assessment) and problems with social integration such as bullying at school and loneliness. Emotional well-being fluctuated during the course of placements, with more tensions arising at the beginning and towards the end as the prospect of leaving care and final asylum decisions grew more sharply into focus.

11　Building social networks: social bonds and social bridges

This chapter explores the development of young people's social networks beyond the foster placement and identifies some of the factors that facilitated or inhibited networking. Levels of emotional well-being were influenced not only by pre-migration experiences and matters relating to asylum, but also by events and interactions in young people's social lives during the course of settlement in the UK. The chapter explores young people's experiences of social networks in the UK and considers ongoing contact with and feelings towards birth families.

Building social networks

A number of theories have been developed to categorise and explain the settlement experiences of migrants (Portes and Borocz, 1989; Berry, 1992; Castles and Miller, 1998). Berry (1992) identifies four potential outcomes of migrant settlement including "assimilation", "segregation", "marginalisation" and "integration". "Assimilation" requires immigrants to adapt or "assimilate" into the host society while institutions and the "host" population are not expected to change significantly (Castles *et al*, 2002; Modood, 2007). "Segregation" occurs when migrants' cultural roots and identities are maintained but there is little interaction with the host community. "Marginalisation" results from migrants losing their sense of identity and also remaining socially excluded from wider society. Finally, "integration" refers to a situation where migrants participate in wider society while maintaining their cultural roots and identities.

Establishing social networks has been recognised as an important aspect of experiences of settlement and processes of integration. Integration describes a two-way process requiring adaptation by migrants, but also by host communities and institutions (Castles *et al*, 2002). The concept of integration also denotes a greater degree of choice on behalf of the migrants rather than them being forced to assimilate into a host society (Van Hear, 1998). Acquiring leave to remain may be a key to integration, but integration also begins from a person's first day of arrival in the UK, and negative starts as asylum seekers can affect longer-term integration when they become refugees (Castles *et al*, 2002). It has been recognised that in order for asylum seekers, refugees and other migrants to experience integration rather than assimilation or segregation, it is important to establish networks that encompass both "social bonds" and "social bridges" (Agar and Strang, 2004; Rutter *et al*, 2007). Drawing on the concept of "social capital"[66] (Putnam, 1993; Portes, 1998), Agar and Strang (2004) have developed a framework for exploring integration pathways using the concepts "social bonds" and "social bridges". Social bonds refer to connections *within* communities defined by ethnic, national or religious identities; social bridges refer to connections *between* communities with different ethnic, national or religious identities.

Social bonds

What do social bonds provide?

In Chapter 6 we discussed the importance of creating safe and familiar environments in foster placements while also supporting young people to adapt to new experiences. "Cultures" and "communities" are fluid and evolve across different social contexts and interactions (Lewis, 2010). While certainly not a replication or continuation of culture and community from countries of origin, establishing contacts with people from young people's countries of origin and religions in UK neighbourhoods and building relationships here may contribute to creating initial feelings of comfort, security, companionship and familiarity, and ease transitions into life in a new country. This could help young people to settle in and feel less isolated. Nadir initially sought out contact with other Afghans by spending time in an area of

---

66 The term "social capital" describes connections in and between social networks and looks at how these non-monetary forms can become sources of power and productivity for individuals and societies.

town that had large Afghan and Asian populations. He began feeling less culturally isolated in the foster placement once he began attending school and made friends there with other Afghan young people. Foster carers also highlighted the shared experiences these young people had and the potential it provided for mutual understanding and support.

They need their peers. That's really important for them, 'cos they're all in the same boat and they need that. (Ann, Abbas' foster carer)

Coming from Afghanistan they've got no friends in England, so really their friends are their family. (Isobel, Majeed's foster carer)

Contact with people from their countries of origin also offered young people an opportunity to express themselves in their first language and communicate with ease, which could provide a welcome rest from the wider environment where they had to speak English. Friendships with other young people who spoke the same language could also help maintain language skills, although where young people had few friendships with young people from other ethnic groups, they had more limited opportunities to practise and develop their English language skills. In schools where there is greater ethnic diversity, there may be more opportunities for young people to develop skills in their first language. Majeed and Samir, who attended such schools, had been given the opportunity to study their first language at GCSE level. Young people who had not attended school, or had limited school experience, in their countries of origin were often unable to read and/or write in their first language when they arrived in the UK. Mahmud could not read or write in Pashtu. He pointed out that if he was told to return to Afghanistan he would not be able to write his name and address there. This could be an important area of development for schools. Not only would it help young people to maintain and develop skills in their first language, but it could also be an aspect of preparation in case they did return to their countries of origin.

As well as providing some familiarity, friendships with other refugee and asylum-seeking young people offered young people practical advice and support in negotiating their new surroundings. One foster carer described how older Afghan boys had looked after a younger Afghan boy she had fostered by taking him out with them to socialise and accompanying him home on the bus to ensure he arrived back safely. A young woman in the young people's focus group described how a friend at college, who was also in foster care, had advised her that she could speak to her social worker when she was unhappy with the way she was being treated in her foster placement.

Finally, in addition to shared language and shared experiences of migration and settlement, it was apparent that friendships were important for the maintenance and renewal of religious practice. Research on the role of religion in the lives of unaccompanied minors has illustrated how the social membership of religious institutions, but also faith in itself, can provide comfort and companionship (Wade *et al*, 2005; Ni Raghallaigh and Gilligan, 2010; Ni Raghallaigh, 2011). Contact with places of worships, but also informal friendships with others of the same faith, played an important part in helping young people practise and maintain this aspect of their identity. Foster carers could provide an environment in which young people could live according to their religious values by, for example, providing them with halal meat, prayer mats and religious books or by connecting them with mosques or churches. However, the shared communal aspects of religious activities were important to young people, in particular fasting and breaking fast during Ramadan and celebrating Eid. Afghan young people often chose to take part in these activities with other Afghans. Often they met at the houses of older young people who were living in semi-independent accommodation.

My mate's phoning me, 'Majeed, come, come, come, all the boys coming, going to be a celebration tonight, then we're gonna go, tomorrow we're gonna go to mosque together and we're gonna cook something. Then all the boys are gonna be here, we're gonna dance, everything.' (Majeed)

He's not lonely. 'Cos like, for instance, during Ramadan, you know, he'll spend a lot of time with his friend and they would

*share their evening meal together and that sort of thing, or go
off to the mosque together.* (Rachel, Nadir's foster carer)

Most young people shared this practice and celebrated with friends.
However, Mahmud chose to celebrate with his foster carer and foster
sibling:

*She [foster carer] go with me and [Afghan foster sibling] as well
in Eid time, to restaurant . . . One time we go to an Afghan
restaurant, yes. I show it to her, you know. I say to her: 'Excuse
me, Leena, this from Afghanistan, right?'* (Mahmud)

Abbas also celebrated with his Afghan foster brothers. Foster carers
arranged links to mosques and community organisations, but did not
generally attend community cultural or religious events with the
young people, although there were a few exceptions. One foster carer
commented that a previous foster child, who was a Coptic Christian,
was very religious and the foster carer had attended some services
with that young person. Another foster carer had gone to a service
with her foster child at a Catholic church, but he chose not to attend
regularly. A Ghanaian Christian in our young women's focus group
had recently moved to a new foster placement with foster carers who
were also Ghanaian Christians. She said that a positive aspect of the
placement was that she attended church every Sunday with her foster
carers.

Studies have illustrated how home-making practices can help to
create homely places of habitation within challenging circumstances
(Van Horst, 2004; Radley *et al*, 2005). Berger (1984) writes that
'practices, chosen and not imposed, offer in their repetition, transient
as they may be in themselves, more permanence, more shelter than
any lodging'. In our study it was apparent that young people's
friendships enabled them to share communal and social aspects of
religious practices and events that were import elements of their sense
of identity and home.

Young people's perspectives on developing social bonds

The previous section discussed some of the benefits described in developing social bonds. However, there was some variation among young people's attitudes towards and levels of interest in maintaining and developing their faith and other cultural practices and heritage. Some young people regularly attended places of worship, prayed at home and followed religious codes and practices. These included young people for whom faith was an important and central aspect of their life, but also others who fluctuated from time to time in the degree to which they adhered to these codes and practices. Although offered opportunities to engage in religious activities, a few made the decision not to continue to practise their faith in the UK.

Like, I love my religion but I'm not going to tell you, like I'm not lying, but sometime I'm praying, sometime I'm not. (Rashid)

I pray five times a day and because, like, now I've not got school, like there's no school on Friday, so I'm probably going to go to mosque on Friday. (Ayotunde)

I'm supposed to be a Muslim, but I don't really follow it, which is my choice . . . When I was in Afghanistan I didn't really, they just said Muslim, but I didn't really, I was a kid so I didn't really care the way or anything. (Rafi)

Places of worship, alongside school and college, were the most common places where young people met others from their countries of origin. Foster carers and young people did not report difficulties in accessing places of worship as such, although in some places this involved travel outside the local area. However, in some areas with more limited choices available, challenges sometimes arose in finding an appropriately matched and familiar place of worship where the young person felt comfortable, because of the heterogeneity within faith communities (Ni Raghallaigh, 2011).

He initially said that he was Catholic, but when I took him to a Catholic ceremony, although he took Communion, which he probably did when he was in Eritrea and Sudan, he . . . couldn't follow the service at all. Completely different to what he was used to, more sort of strict and very formal service, which he didn't really understand . . . When we talked to him he said that they're very informal services, a lot of singing . . . That's why . . . he goes to the Baptist church and he likes that because it's, it's more singing . . . We've offered to take him to [another area] to go to, to Tigrinyan services but he really isn't interested in going to it. (Susan, Abraham's foster carer)

We took him up there [mosque], I introduced him. He went a couple of times, didn't he? But they don't pray the same as him. They're not, though it's a mosque and it's for Muslims, it's a different form of Islam . . . So they didn't pray the same, he didn't understand it and he opted not to go. They did supply him with a Koran, which he couldn't read because he couldn't read his own language . . . He said: '. . . I don't want to go.' (Andrew, Rafi's foster carer)

Some foster carers and young people commented that interest fluctuated over time and depended on other aspects of young people's schedules. Abraham said he attended church occasionally, but did not attend regularly because he was busy playing football. Osman attended mosque, but not every week. His foster carer said: 'He goes on Fridays, some Fridays they will, but when they first come they're really keen to go, then afterward they relax when they're in education and doing other things.'

The extent to which young people sought out other cultural connections varied from case to case. Foster carers often commented on young people's friendship networks as indications of young people's attitudes towards "cultural connectedness". Some young people, particularly Afghan young people, had friends who were almost exclusively from their own ethnic background.

He's got lots of Afghan friends, but not very many English friends, and we always encourage him to make English friends.

He does say he does have a few at school, but never goes out with English friends, always Afghan friends. And there's quite a few Afghan boys at his school, so the minute they bump into anyone that's Afghan, they kind of stick together. So I think that's probably hindered him making English friends. (Elizabeth, Sabir's foster carer)

However, as mentioned in Chapter 9, others had friends across a whole range of ethnicities and countries of origin (including asylum seekers and refugees), usually reflecting the ethnic populations in their local area and school.

I've got black friends. I've got Asian. I've got Pakistani. I've got Iranian. I've got English . . . I've got 10 or 20 close friends. (Aarif)

Finally, some had very few or no friends of their own ethnicity and the majority of their friends were British-born young people, usually again from a range of ethnicities except in areas with predominantly white populations. Arian's foster carer had fostered Arian and another Albanian young person, Ylli, at the same time and compared their friendship pathways:

I don't know if [Arian] would say it like that but certainly his actions have, at various points when he's had decisions to make, he's always made the choice that's integrated him more and more fully . . . like choosing his friends. Most of the friends he spends time with now are white or African-Caribbean children who he plays football with either at college or socially . . . They're very different people and they've chosen a different path. Well, Ylli's much more, he still spends most of his weekend time with other Albanian speakers and he will be speaking Albanian a lot more than Arian. (Eleanor, Arian's foster carer)

While this explanation centres on choices made by the young person in a context where a range of options were available, it is possible that other choices might be being made in more complex circumstances.

For example, where young people live in an area with a predominantly white UK population, are decisions not to maintain cultural links made because these opportunities are not available, because young people want to fit in with others around them, or because these practices and values do not sit with their own evolving sense of identity?

While some young people developed close friendships with young people from their countries of origin, they also sought to establish more flexibility, limits and controls over their contact with the wider community from their countries of origin for various reasons. Rahim wanted to eventually move away from the area he currently lived in, which had a large Afghan population. He hoped to move to live near a friend in a particular area that happened to have a predominantly white population. Speaking about his current neighbourhood, Rahim said: 'When we meet each other we have to speak the same language so I don't like. I have to learn more English. I have to improve my English.' Nabil was also concerned that when he left foster care he may be offered accommodation in an area with a large Afghan population. His concern about living in close proximity to a large number of other Afghan young people related to some of the social pressures he anticipated might arise there:

I can't really go there. There are a lot of, like, same people and, like, if you don't like speak to them good they will tell you that you are . . . And they can ask, can they come to your house or you can go to their house and, like, some [are] friend like but actually is not good because they come every day to your house. They make you disrupt . . . It's not good to go there, I don't like to go there. (Nabil)

Some refugees and asylum seekers may also be cautious about establishing contact with people from their countries of origin in case information about them, or information that places their family at risk, is transmitted back to authorities in these countries (Sirriyeh, 2008; Bjornberg, 2011). Finally, being of the same nationality or ethnicity in itself alone is not necessarily a basis for feelings of affinity and friendship, and some young people simply wanted to choose. Osman's foster carer said: 'He wants to make his own choice of who from his country he wants.' There were some examples of contact set up by social workers or foster carers, particularly for young people who were isolated or in areas with limited cultural diversity. Some of these failed to develop because the young people had little else in common, although there was one example of a successful friendship that had developed between Osman and another Tigre young person introduced to him by his social worker.

In contrast, some young people sought greater links with their own ethnic group or, simply, greater ethnic diversity. On leaving foster care, Omid moved away from the area he had been living in and moved to an area with greater ethnic diversity, including a sizeable Afghan population. Aarif noted that most of his friends did not live in his predominantly white neighbourhood. Speaking about racism in the area he recommended that unaccompanied minors should be placed in foster placements in ethnically diverse neighbourhoods.

Overall, while young people may want different levels of contact, it was evident that most young people wanted and benefited from being given some opportunity to link with others from their own countries of origin. Even some young people like Arian, whose friendships were mainly with those from other backgrounds, often sought out some form of contact and links with aspects of culture from their country of origin.

Social bridges

Chapter 8 illustrated how within foster care placements it was helpful for young people to be able to find points of familiarity while also being supported through transitions to life in a new and less familiar environment. As mentioned in Chapter 6, for unaccompanied minors, transitions into foster care take place within the context of their wider transitions to life in a new country. In this wider environment, including, but also beyond, the foster home, social bridges where connections are developed with others beyond young people's own ethnic communities can have an important integrative function.

Much of the discussion on these themes has already taken place in Chapters 8 and 9. Therefore, this section focuses on young people's social relations and leisure activities outside school and the foster home.

Most of the young people had active social lives and took part in a number of activities with other young people beyond their own ethnic and religious communities. They took part in sports activities, attended youth clubs and spent time with friends playing computer games. Hobbies and leisure activities provided a number of benefits to young people. Participation in education has been highlighted as playing an important role in helping young people recover an ordinary "normal" routine in their lives and feel included and equal to their peers (Mosselson, 2007; Sirriyeh, 2010; Walker, 2011). Leisure activities provided a similar function and in the context of delays in access to education were an important route through which foster carers attempted to offset the social isolation such delays created.[67] A number of foster carers found out about their foster children's interests and made efforts to engage them in leisure activities very early on in the placement both through family leisure activities and also by taking them to clubs and sports centres where they would meet other people. Throughout the placements, hobbies and leisure activities played an important role in developing young people's social networks beyond the initial core sites of the foster home and school. This enabled young people to develop a range of networks and contacts which may be helpful for integration by developing social bridges as well as social bonds.

We asked young people how they found out about and accessed leisure activities. It was evident that foster carers, social workers and peers were key figures in facilitating access. Peers played an important role in informing young people about opportunities that were available in their area and recommending activities. For example,

---

67 While some young people attended mainstream school and college courses where they made friends with young people from a wide range of ethnic origins, other young people who were not in mainstream education or on ESOL courses may not have had this opportunity (Refugee Action, 2003).

some of the boys who played football at school found out about teams outside school from their school friends. Most foster carers responded to young people's expressions of interest in particular activities by helping to arrange them.

My mum helped me and I said to her, 'I want to do kickboxing'. And she's helped me and . . . she go with me and then I go two days in the week to kickboxing. (Abbas)

Some foster carers had asked young people what they were interested in. When Haaroon first arrived there was a period of delay before he could attend school. His foster carer asked him what hobbies he enjoyed and he told her that he used to play cricket in Afghanistan. She found him a cricket club, which he joined and continued to play for. Other foster carers suggested new activities that their foster children might like to consider. Sabir's foster carers introduced him to a boxing club where he was the only Afghan young person. Most of Sabir's friends were Afghan and his foster carers wanted him to also have the opportunity to meet young people from other backgrounds and to widen his social network. Finally, although foster carers were mentioned as the main figures who researched and arranged access to social activities, some social workers also became involved here. After Ban-hwa's friend told him about gymnastics he became interested in trying this out. He informed his social worker, who located a club for him and arranged the course fees and Ban-hwa attended the club for several months until his funding was withdrawn. Why this was the case was not clear.

In addition to the friendships which developed through these activities, foster carers and young people spoke of the successes a number of the young people had experienced here and the talent they demonstrated, for example, by gaining places on sports teams and winning competitions and medals. Young people were proud of their achievements and gained self-confidence in this process. For example, Rashid was a talented boxer and had received praise from his trainer. He said: 'I like working because he's [the trainer] given me hope. He said to me: "You'll be something and keep going and doing".' A social worker said that where foster carers were able to respond to young people's interests and helped them pursue these, young people did well because 'they meet people there, they actually start achieving. They build up their confidence and they start to build networks other than just in their own community.'

Racism, hostility and tensions

While many young people had developed positive relationships and contacts in their social lives outside school and the family home, there were also frequent reports of racism. Chapter 9 explored young people's experiences of racism at school. There were also a number of reports of racism encountered by young people in the neighbourhoods where they lived, particularly among those living in areas with little history of immigration or ethnic diversity (Robinson *et al*, 2007). Aarif explained how he chose to socialise outside the neighbourhood he lived in and spent as little time as possible in public spaces in his neighbourhood because of racism:

> *Some people don't like Asians. It's like it was really hard for me, but now I got used to it, so I'm not hanging around here that much. If I go gym, I come straight home and then I'll always go in town.* (Aarif)

Young people were generally able to be involved in social activities outside school. However, a minority reported experiences of racism which impeded these activities. In some areas incidents of racism at school seemed to reflect problems with racist attitudes and hostility in the wider community.

Hemmerman and colleagues (2007) undertook a study on racist victimisation in neighbourhoods in a city in the north of England. They found that young people were often on the front line, as both targets and perpetrators of racist violence and hostility in the neighbourhoods studied. In his study on refugee children and place, Spicer (2008) found asylum-seeking children and their parents to be fearful about threats and violence from white British children and young people. In the current study, two months into his foster care placement, Abbas began attending a local youth club and was involved in fights with white British boys who attended the club:

They take the piss because I was only – it was only me was in here my colour, is no one else. It was a bit hard. And then, they said to me, they said stuff like, 'What are you doing here? Go back your country, black', stuff like that. (Abbas)

Abbas agreed to walk away from fights after an attack on his foster carer's house by a group of people who had gathered outside. He said the situation improved once he was able to speak English and people became used to his presence:

When I learn a little bit English, and . . . now, it's – They know me, who I am, where I'm staying, what am I doing, what I'm not. And because . . . the first thing is, because when you not speak English, how can you even know someone, like, 'Who is him? Where he stay?' How, you know, like someone – you look at someone and they say to you: 'Why are you staring?' And you can't speak English, and so he think . . . he want the trouble, but you really don't want the trouble . . . And now it's everything is fine for me 'cos everything's – the boys know me, everyone know me, so I have peace, you know? (Abbas)

Abbas' comments indicate that initial hostilities expressed towards him appeared to have complex and intertwined motivations centring on his status at that point more broadly as an "unknown stranger" in the area, in addition to more racialised perceptions relating to his nationality and ethnicity. In research on racist attitudes and behaviour among young people, Lemos (2005) found that feelings of hostility often focused around three key themes, including: first, security fears and terrorism – 'Afghans – because they hijack planes and kill people'; second, too many incomers – 'asylum seekers – there's too many of them'; and, finally, preferential treatment – 'refugees – they get more than us'.

Foster carers and social workers often commented on the specific experience of Afghan young people. There may be a number of reasons why Afghan young people appeared to be targeted in particular. These may include perceptions of the war in Afghanistan where British soldiers are present, the size of the Afghan population as a proportion of the unaccompanied minors present in the area making them a particularly visible group, and attitudes about intersections between ethnicity, religion, masculinity and sexuality. One social work team commented on the difficulties they had found in locating foster placements for Afghan boys. One social worker said: 'Under the current climate of Afghanistan and people's views of Afghanistan, a lot of foster carers we've spoken to didn't want to take Afghan children.' It was thought that this was not always because foster carers did not want to foster these young people, but rather they were concerned that their family, friends or neighbours might not accept them, particularly in communities where neighbours had relatives or friends in the army. Commenting on bullying in school, Aarif's foster carer said:

This is bullying in a big way, whether it's to do with him being a Muslim, or the Afghanistan war, soldiers dying. And both my boys, they've only got to see it on television. If any soldiers die, they really get upset. (Aarif's foster carer)

Rashid was anxious about telling people that he was Afghan when he first arrived in the UK because he thought that there may be hostility directed towards him because of the war in Afghanistan. Other young people did not specify their Afghan identity as such, but spoke more broadly about being the target of racism because they were "outsiders" new to the area or because they were from ethnic minority populations living in a predominantly white neighbourhood.

Cases of racism and hostility created a challenge for some young people trying to expand their social networks in the wider community. However, there were also more mundane feelings and experiences of distance, lack of common values, interests or understandings of each other's lifestyle. Navid wanted to play football and had tried playing with a local team. However, he said he did not feel comfortable with the other team members because they smoked and drank alcohol. He wanted to join another team, but he and his foster carer were unsure where to find one.

He doesn't like other people who are a different culture because he doesn't know how to relate to them. (Amina, Housyar's foster carer)

It's easy if you find you like Afghan, but it's hard to find like English . . . I did have some friend in school . . . English people, they – all are not nasty. Some good, some bad . . . But it's quite hard to find a friend, good friend, like nice and to trust him to trust you. (Omid)

Others faced conflicting feelings between their religious and cultural values and some of the youth cultures they were exposed to in the UK and were uncertain which direction to take. Abbas' foster carer said: 'They're young boys, testosterone, they see these girls, but then their culture is no, no, no and it's very hard for them, 'cos they're torn.' Sexual behaviour in a few cases was also a source of tension in interactions with other young people in school and in the wider community.[68] In one case, the racist bullying and victimisation of an Afghan young person had incorporated accusations of sexual advances and inappropriate behaviour towards a female peer. While in another case, a young person and his foster carer were upset that the young person had been disciplined at school for what teachers perceived as inappropriate behaviour towards a female student, but which the young person and foster carer denied. These and other incidents suggest the existence of a complex mix of racialised stereotyping and perceptions of sexuality and masculinity, alongside divergent interpretations and misrecognition of culture and behaviour.

---

68 Although this was certainly not the experience for all young people and, as in other forms of friendships and relationships, there were also positive experiences of romantic relationships. Nabil was happy about his relationship with his girlfriend and said, 'It's a nice thing, a girlfriend. You feel you have, she cares and you care with her.'

Birth families

So far this chapter has explored the development of young people's social networks within the UK. This section moves on to look at young people's links with birth families.

In previous chapters we saw that the degree of information foster carers were able to build up about young people's backgrounds varied from case to case. Over time, some young people spoke quite openly to their foster carers about their experiences, including their birth family and the places they had lived. However, others were more reluctant to disclose information. There may be a number of reasons for this. Some young people did not know what had happened to their family and had not had contact since they were separated. For example, Nadir's foster carers said his father had fought in the conflict in his country and Nadir did not know if he was alive. Other young people did not talk about their family. Sabir had no contact with his birth family. When asked how that affected him, Sabir's foster carer said:

I couldn't tell you actually, 'cos he doesn't say anything about it. He doesn't really talk about his family, unless we mention it to him, but he doesn't say anything at all, really. (Sabir's foster carer)

Mahmud said that his social worker had attempted to ask him about his family, but he told her that he did not want to talk about them. However, he had built up a close relationship with his foster carer, whom he described as "like my mum", and said that he confided in her. As Kohli and Mather (2003) have highlighted, some young people may experience complex emotions in relation to thoughts of their family, with feelings of abandonment at being sent away to safety, or guilt at being sent to safety, while they are worried about family who may still be in a dangerous environment.

A few young people had regular contact with their families in their countries of origin although, as with their relationships in the UK, young people sometimes also felt the need to be careful and selective about the information they presented to birth families. Navid spoke to his mother and siblings in Iran every two days using the internet and a webcam. He found it a great comfort to be able to speak to and see his family on screen. However, he said he did not tell them that he was lonely because he did not want to worry them. Instead, he just told them that life in the UK was fine and that he was studying. Haaroon also had regular contact with his family in Afghanistan. His foster carer said that in these conversations Haaroon chose not to share certain information about his lifestyle in the UK with his family because he thought they would not understand and would not be happy. Other young people spoke to their family on the telephone, but did not indicate how frequent this contact was.

Young people were offered help in tracing family in countries of origin. Rafi's social worker had obtained contact details for his family in Afghanistan. Rafi (who was very young when he arrived in the UK) had then spoken to them on the telephone, although his foster carers said that he was reluctant to do this again as he struggled to understand what his family were saying and had not liked talking through an interpreter. His foster carers had also helped him to attempt contact through email, but there appeared to be technological problems with this. Some young people were less keen to establish or maintain contact. At each of his care review meetings, Sabir had been offered help to trace his family with the Red Cross, but had refused each time and his foster carer was unsure why. Osman and Samir said they chose not to speak to family on the telephone because they were aware that governments in their countries of origin may monitor telephone calls and they did not want to risk their families' safety (Yaya, 1998; Bjornberg, 2011).

Foster carers described some young people arriving with contact details for relatives. Some young people were disorientated and were trying to locate contacts they had been given for people from their country of origin in the UK. Haaroon's foster carer said: 'When they arrive here they may have a contact [for] other people. Normally they do come with contacts for people.' Some young people had arrived with contact details for extended family including cousins, uncles and aunts. These relatives had to be checked and verified by the social work team before young people were allowed contact. Social workers discussed some of the issues and dilemmas around confidentiality, trust and safeguarding with reference to sharing information between young people, foster carers and social workers about relatives and friends in the UK.

> *I had a young person who was very closed and didn't share information and their foster carer finally gained his trust and the young person shared information about family members he had in England. The foster carer didn't withhold that information and came and told me and the young person figured it out in a day and totally withdrew and denied it.* (Social worker, Area 4)

> *One foster carer was giving a weekly phone card to the young person and it became apparent that the phone card was being used to contact a family member who we thought was in a foreign country, but it transpires that they were in [the UK]. For me that is a significant piece of information but the foster carer didn't think it was any big deal.* (Social worker, Area 4)

Navid, Majeed and Abbas had contact with their cousins in the UK. Navid and Majeed lived relatively close to their cousins so they had regular contact, which they enjoyed, although Majeed's cousin had recently been deported to Afghanistan. Abbas' cousin lived in a different city, but his foster carer took him there for visits. Abraham had telephone contact with his aunt, although his foster carers said he expressed some reluctance to talk with her. Like Rafi (see above), Abraham had arrived in the UK when he was very young and had also not maintained his proficiency in his first language. His aunt wanted to speak in Tigrinya with him and he therefore struggled to communicate with her.

Finally, it is important to note that young people's attitudes and feelings about family relationships, bonds and contact were influenced by factors other than the process of migration to the UK. A few young people described more complex or ambiguous feelings about members of their family.

[Samir is] a happy, easy-going uncomplicated boy, whereas his older brother, who is the one who had it very hard at home with his parents, from what he's managed to tell us. You know, he was beaten and his father was harsh with him. He's a very nervous stammery boy who needs us more than the younger one does. (Laura, Samir's foster carer)

Ayotunde did not know what had happened to his father and missed him. However, his foster carer said that he expressed more complex feelings about his mother. His father had told him that his mother left him when he was five years old and he could not understand why she had done this. Two other young people had lived with their grandparents and did not have close relationships with their birth parents. The parents of one had died when he was a small child. His foster carer said: 'He never felt part of the family, he always felt an odd child. They [grandparents] had their own family and he was always the odd one.' The other young person had lived with his grandparents and he had only seen his mother intermittently when she returned on occasions to the home.

Summary

Establishing social networks has been recognised as an important aspect of settlement and of the process of integration. In order for asylum seekers, refugees and other migrants to experience integration rather than assimilation or segregation, it is important to establish networks that encompass both "social bonds" and "social bridges" (Agar and Strang, 2004; Rutter *et al*, 2007). Establishing contacts with people from young people's countries of origin and religions in UK neighbourhoods and building relationships here may contribute to creating initial feelings of comfort, security, companionship and familiarity and ease transitions into life in a new county. This could help young people to settle in and feel less isolated.

Meanwhile, for unaccompanied minors, transitions into foster care take place within the context of their wider transitions to life in a new country. In this wider environment including, but also beyond, the foster home, social bridges where connections are developed with others beyond young people's own ethnic communities play an important role in this transition. Most of the young people had active social lives and took part in a number of activities with other young people beyond their own ethnic and religious communities. However, while many young people had developed positive relationships and contacts in their social lives outside school and the family home, there were also frequent reports of experiences of racism. There were a number of reports of racism encountered by young people in the neighbourhoods where they lived, particularly among those living in areas with little history of immigration or ethnic diversity.

Some young people retained or had renewed connections with their own extended family network, both within the UK and overseas. Foster carers and social workers assisted young people to maintain regular communication or to trace family members where this was wanted. While some young people were happy to share information about their families over time, others were more reticent and kept their thoughts and feelings private. A few young people experienced some ambivalence towards their families and these feelings were often rooted in past experiences of abandonment or of abuse or neglect at the hands of family members.

12 Moving on from care: planning and immigration

Preceding chapters have identified some of the important principles that underpin good preparation for adulthood for young people in the looked after system, including: placement stability and the continuity in links and relationships it may afford; access to constructive educational pathways and the chance to acquire new skills; and, opportunities for young people to refashion their identities in new contexts and to develop close bonds and new networks of support. These are recognised as being important features of sound preparation for all young people (see Department of Health, 2001; Stein, 2004; Wade, 2006).

This chapter moves forward to anticipate young people moving on from care. Only a small minority of our survey sample of young people (n = 16) had left their foster placement at the time our fieldwork was conducted. Around one-half of these had moved on to live more independently and the remainder had moved to alternative placements. For most young people, therefore, the challenges of transition were in the future. This chapter considers the views of foster carers and young people about these transitions. In particular, we explore factors that might make moving on attractive to young people (pull factors), those that might propel them towards it (push factors), what kinds of obstacles they think may lie ahead, and issues arising from the support and resources available to assist them on their journey toward adulthood.

Most unaccompanied young people first arrive in the UK as teenagers. The time available to help them plan and prepare for the future is therefore frequently compressed. Planning is also profoundly affected by uncertainties arising from the asylum determination process. This chapter also explores issues related to immigration and the role of social workers and foster carers in supporting young people through the process of application and appeal and in preparing them for the likelihood of a negative final outcome.

We have previously described the through-care and after-care responsibilities of local authorities (see Chapters 1 and 3). The rising numbers of unaccompanied young people who are formally looked after has increased their eligibility for leaving care services in recent years. With respect to these services, their entitlement to support is the same as for citizen young people, although access to welfare benefits, housing, education and employment may be affected by their asylum status. Where a young person's asylum application is undecided as they approach 18 years of age, these services may continue until all asylum rights have been exhausted and they are classified as being 'unlawfully present in the UK' under Schedule 3 of the Nationality, Immigration and Asylum Act 2002 (Department for Education, 2010). Even at this stage, however, local authorities should be mindful about whether a withdrawal of services would breach a young person's rights under the European Convention on Human Rights (Dorling, 2009; Wade, 2011).

Preparation and planning for adulthood is therefore undertaken in circumstances that are complex and uncertain. Very few unaccompanied young people are granted refugee status (just 11% in 2009) and the majority are granted discretionary leave to remain for three years or until they reach 17.5 years of age (whichever comes soonest) or receive an outright refusal (17%).[69] For most young people, therefore, preparation and planning occur when their futures in the UK are undecided and need to take account of all possible outcomes of the asylum decision-making process, including the very real likelihood of an enforced or voluntary return to their countries of origin (Free, 2006; Department for Education, 2010).

Moving on: why and when

Most of the foster carers who responded to our survey had anticipated providing their young people with a longer-term placement of one year or more (83%) and almost two-thirds of young people (63%) had

---

69 Home Office (2010) *Control of Immigration: Statistics United Kingdom 2009.* Available: http://www.homeoffice.gov.uk/rds

been living there for more than one year. A similar proportion of young people (63%) were aged 16–18 years when our survey was conducted. Pathway planning was therefore at the forefront of people's minds. We asked foster carers to tell us at what age they anticipated their young people would move on from the placement (see Table 12.1).

Table 12.1
When did foster carers expect young people to leave this placement? (n = 132)[70]

	Per cent*	Number
After reaching 18	25.5	34
On reaching 18	28.5	38
When aged 16 or 17	22.5	30
Before age 16	1	1
As soon as a placement is found	1.5	2
Other	1.5	2
Not known	7	9
Young person had already left	12	16

* Column does not equal 100% due to rounding.

Further analysis identified that there was some variation in expected age of leaving by local authority.[71] In this respect, it may be that foster carers had tended to internalise the procedures and expectations of

---

70 "Other" included one child whose placement would be uncertain until the outcome of an age assessment was known. Explanation for the other case was missing. We also cannot comment on why the child expected to leave before age 16 would do so. The two young people expected to leave as soon as an alternative was found included one case where a move from a short-term to long-term placement was being planned. The other involved a boy who had not settled in placement, though we are not sure why.

71 Expected age at leaving was grouped into three categories for analysis: before 18 (16 or 17), at 18, after 18. Variation by local authority significant at p = 0.001, n = 102 (Fisher's Exact test). In Area 4, for example, 20% of young people were expected to leave before the age of 18, compared to 42% in Area 3.

these local authorities about the age at which young people generally move on. Where established cultures of moving on at an early age exist, it is highly likely to shape the thinking of foster carers and structure the kinds of conversations they have with young people in their care. The leaving care literature has consistently highlighted the early age at which young people are expected to leave care and assume adult responsibilities (see, for example, Biehal *et al*, 1995; Dixon and Stein, 2005; Wade, 2006). The intention to delay young people's transitions has consequently formed a central strand of leaving care legislation and, more recently, of government initiatives to safeguard against early leaving, such as the Right2BCared4 and Staying Put pilots, and there is now some emerging evidence of its effect on professional cultures (see Munro *et al*, 2010; Munro *et al*, 2011).

However, foster carers also thought that young people would leave at a later age where the relationship between them was perceived as being stronger. They tended to anticipate young people leaving later where they had scored more highly on our Family Integration Measure, where young people were thought to have no or few emotional or behavioural difficulties, where they had higher self-care and interpersonal skills and higher levels of emotional well-being. Put simply, foster carers were more likely to want young people to stay where things were generally going well and where there was a strong sense of social connectedness.[72] This is also consistent with wider research on leaving care that has tended to find that young people with unsettled care careers and with more complex needs, who frequently present behavioural management problems in placements, tend to leave earlier than those who settle and do well (Dixon *et al*, 2006; Munro *et al*, 2011).

Table 12.1 shows that foster carers expected almost one-quarter of young people to move on before reaching 18 years of age. Moving on before age 18 appeared to involve a variety of push and pull factors. Some young people seemed to be making relatively early moves toward

---

72 Kruskal-Wallis tests for expected age at leaving and Family Integration Measure ($p = 0.004$, $n = 100$), emotional and behavioural difficulties ($p<0.001$), self-care skills ($p = 0.006$) and emotional well-being ($p = 0.026$). See Table 7.2 for an explanation of the Family Integration Measure.

greater independence, either as part of their agreed care plan or because they had been assessed as having the skills for independent living.

He will move on to semi-independence, possibly this summer. This will be a planned move. His age will be 16.5 years.

This was discussed in his last review. He has demonstrated sufficient skills to live semi-independently. He also wants to move to (a different area). This is consistent with the care plan.[73]

In some instances, a relatively early departure seemed to have been agreed so that young people could move to semi-independent living together or that closer relationships with relatives could be achieved.

The care plan is for him to move just before his 18th birthday. He may leave, however, at 17-and-a-half due to his wish to share a flat with another foster boy living with me who is five months older, as they have always been together. A two-bed flat/house will be offered locally with semi-independent support.

His brother has arrived in the UK and now lives locally. They want to live together and are hoping to live together when my child becomes 16.

Other pull factors were also present. In particular, foster carers reported on the attraction that was derived from having friends who had already achieved independence or from a refusal on the part of young people to bend to the rules and rhythms of the foster home. In one instance, there was also a somewhat stereotypical assumption expressed about the presumed early readiness of these young people for independence.

This lad is very independent and will probably push for an independent placement himself. He has friends who have achieved this.

---

73 Unattributed quotes relate to comments provided by foster carers on questionnaires. All attributed quotes derive from individual or focus-group interviews.

Because he wants his independence, he doesn't like to be told what to do and doesn't like our house rules.

They tend to be very independent and want to move on very quickly.

Although some foster carers were reluctant to let young people go and worried whether they really had the maturity and skills to manage independently, most tended to acquiesce when faced with young people's desire to try. Even where foster carers thought young people would stay longer, they were mindful from past experience of how young people's minds can change.

He is quite an independent young man . . . He's got a wide range of friends in different areas. So he got to see how the other boys were living in shared housing . . . I think obviously he liked the idea that they had far more freedom than he had when he was here . . . I would have imagined him staying here until at least 18, him being in education . . . I didn't want him to go . . . But now, I would say for any unaccompanied minor who came here, I would say you're looking at 16, 'cos I think they all like to follow suit and they'd all want to be living independently. (Stephanie, Omid's foster carer)

The other girl that we had before, she was just like a daughter . . . We never thought she'd leave us, but she says: 'I really want to try and live independently.' (Ann, Abbas' foster carer)

Amongst young people preparing to move on in the near future, views were mixed. While some felt it was the right time for them to move, others experienced considerable apprehension, but had come to be persuaded that this was an inevitable pathway that they had to accept. A few were very anxious and worried about how they would cope.

Actually, before I like to stay here but now I have a girlfriend, I am ready. Before, I wasn't fit to go. (Nabil)

They give you, like, in a plan . . . like a pathway plan. They come and they ask you . . . they give you a choice to do what you want. But I say to them: 'I want to live up to 18. I'm not moving from here when I'm 18.' My [foster carers] they don't want me to move. They said to me: 'If you want, you can stay with us.' (Samuel)

They told me you're 18 now, but I don't accept that. I said I'm now 15, supposed to be 15. They said you have to move from this house. I said no. I want to stay here, because I can't live alone. I'm scared. (Rahim)

There was considerable evidence of pressure on local authority social workers to move young people on, especially as they approached 18 years of age. Moving on at (or shortly before) 18 was frequently cited by foster carers as normal procedure for these local authorities. This was what was expected to happen.

Our foster son will be compelled to move when he turns 18, as the local authority will not allow him to stay longer.

They tend to move on when they're 18. Some have stayed in their placement, but not many . . . They tend to move on . . . 'cos that's the arrangements . . . It's mainly about policy and resources. (Team manager, Area 4)

Foster placements were always in short supply. Heavy use was being made of fostering agencies in the independent sector, where placement costs were considered to be higher. Most local authorities were also facing a squeeze on spending and the grants provided by the Home Office to fund work with unaccompanied minors were being reduced. In consequence, there was growing evidence of pressure to release foster placements earlier.[74] Referring to the Special Grant, one team

---

74 See Pemberton, C. (2011) 'Protests against cuts to services for child asylum-seekers', *Community Care*, 8 April; Cooper, J. (2011) 'Asylum-seeking children and family support suffer most cuts', *Community Care*, 28 September. The latter suggests a potential 29 per cent cut in local council budgets for 2011/12 for asylum-seeking children compared to 2010/11.

manager highlighted its potential implications; a view also reflected by some foster carers.

So it's going to be straitened circumstances and one of the issues will be whether we can sustain 16- and 17-year-olds in foster care, given the money that UKBA is going to give us . . . For a 16-year-old they're only going to give us £71 per day and that's got to cover everything. So there's not much scope there really. (Team manager, Area 3)

The reality is that all services are cutting budgets . . . so social workers need to work really hard to take as many as possible out of foster care because it's too expensive . . . That's the reality. It's not because they don't like it, it's that they can't. It's not up to them, because they work within the system too. (Eva, Haroon's foster carer)

As Table 12.1 suggested, some young people were likely to remain in foster care beyond their 18th birthday. The likelihood of staying on varied by local authority and was more likely where the quality of relationship between young person and foster carer was good. Where young people appeared reluctant to leave, some foster carers seemed to be willing to press for them to stay longer, to act as their advocates with children's services.

My child does not want to move out until he is 21.

She wants to go to university. She does not want to move away from home with us. She will stay until she is ready.

As the last comment suggests, the potential for staying on was closely linked to young people being in education (see also Munro *et al*, 2010). In some instances, this had been achieved by recasting the placement as supported lodgings. Staying on, therefore, was very much time limited and, as one team manager made clear, these arrangements were likely to come under strain in the new spending environment:

I can only speak for the three cases where people have wanted to stay on post-18 and they have been allowed to, but there has been a cutting-off point and that is when they finish their college and move on. (Team manager, Area 2)

We have got some staying-on arrangements . . . But I think the reality is that there aren't going to be that many . . . because there aren't enough foster placements to go round . . . While the legislative impetus was to get young people to stay on longer in foster care . . . the realities are that we need to try and find attractive alternatives to that because the resources simply aren't there . . . We're now into this situation where we've got a problem with grant funding as well. (Team manager, Area 3)

Social workers were also mindful of the tensions between local authority policies and resources and their desire not to see young people move on too early. In some instances, not bringing things to the attention of managers could help. In others, the presence of supportive management could help to reduce the pressure on individual social workers.

She gets an awful lot of support from the family and I don't think it's appropriate to take her out of that . . . It hasn't come up on the radar yet, so I'm just not mentioning it to anybody. (Social worker, Area 1)

I think that we can be flexible in our pathway planning . . . and management allow you to do that . . . I think it is really crucial to planning that you've got somebody at the top who is flexible and realises that you might have to have more money or we might need a different plan. (Social worker, Area 3)

Despite recent government initiatives designed to extend young people's stay in foster care beyond 18, these experiences are fairly typical of those reported in the leaving care literature. Although practitioners are frequently aware of the need for flexibility and for young people to leave care when they are ready to do so, it has not commonly been the case that fostering has provided young people with a stable home base into early adulthood (see, for example, Dixon *et al*, 2006; Wade, 2008). As we shall see further for this group, uncertainties that derive from the immigration system only serve to compound these problems.

Accommodation resources for young people moving on

Since staying on was not an option for a majority of young people preparing to leave care, the development of "attractive alternative" forms of supported accommodation takes on greater significance. At the time of data collection, however, the range of accommodation options that was available in our local authorities appeared quite limited.

Leaving care services have had success in improving young people's access to permanent tenancies with councils and housing associations through the development of corporate housing strategies and formal agreements with housing providers covering needs assessments and allocations. Studies also show that most care leavers receive accommodation that is suitable for their needs on leaving care and have relatively good housing outcomes some time later (Dixon and Stein, 2005; Wade and Dixon, 2006; Cameron *et al*, 2007; Simon, 2008; Stein, 2009). Only two of our local authorities reported having reasonable access to council and housing association tenancies for unaccompanied young people leaving care. Furthermore, access was circumscribed by young people's immigration status:

> *If a young person has refugee status and/or leave to remain beyond 18 years, then they will have access to housing and benefits . . . If young people do not have substantial leave to remain then they will be supported in shared housing and receive financial support until their individual circumstances have been confirmed by UKBA.* (Team manager, Area 4)

Previous research has highlighted the heavy reliance of local authorities on private sector shared housing for unaccompanied young people, the variable quality of much of this accommodation, and the support provided to young people while living in this sector of the housing market (Humphries and Mynott, 2001; Stanley, 2001; Chase *et al*, 2008; Brownlees and Finch, 2010). In two local authority areas that lacked good access to social housing, this still formed the bulk of the accommodation provision open to young people. Some social workers noted variations in quality and support dependent on the nature of the housing provider.

> *I think it depends on which housing provider. Some accommodation is quite nice and young people like to stay there, but some . . . is of a very poor standard . . . Some providers have good support for young people when they move into shared accommodation [and] regularly support them with accessing education, health and integration into the local area, while some other key workers provided by housing agencies do not.* (Social worker, Area 3)

The choice available to young people was also constrained by the scarcity of these housing resources and some complained about the quality of housing offered and, more particularly, about its location, frequently at some distance from their current social networks.

> *They tell me you have to apply to [Area A] but I don't want to apply to there. If you put me outside on the street I will accept that, but not [Area A].* (Nabil)

> *They wanted me to go to [Area B], which I don't want to 'cos I don't know anyone. I have friends, my own friends in [Area C]. I'm going to college in [Area C] . . . I don't want to be . . . sad every day 'cos I don't know anyone . . . I don't want to be like that. So I refused. And now they say that because you turned down that house . . . we don't want to move you. They're saying that I don't have a good enough reason.* (Omid)

The availability of supported housing options to help young people prepare for greater independence also varied from area to area.

Although practitioners acknowledged the benefits of young people making a stepped transition, the resources were frequently not there to support it. Only one area had access to a range of supported accommodation that included a supported lodgings scheme, access to supported hostels and floating support arrangements for young people living independently, where regular support was provided directly by the asylum team. Two areas had access to some aspects of this provision, but often on a very small scale, and one area relied almost exclusively on private sector shared housing. Young people leaving care (including unaccompanied young people) have different needs. While some are able to manage quite well in the independent housing sector with a relatively small amount of support, others need time to develop confidence in the practical and interpersonal skills they will need to make a successful transition. Since many are not able to stay on longer in foster care, opportunities to spend time in appropriate and well-supported sheltered settings are likely to be beneficial. Although the current resource climate is not propitious, further investment in these areas, perhaps drawing on the lengthy experience of wider leaving care services, will be needed (see Stein, 2009).

Resources provided by foster carers

As we have seen, Omid was most worried about the risk of loneliness and social isolation. Other young people were worried about whether they possessed the practical and social skills they needed to live independently.

> *I need help [to] know how to cook, how to make food and clean clothes and washing.* (Sabir)

> *Learn how to cook, how to shop, how to go to a bank, how to go to a doctor, how to make an appointment with a doctor, you know.* (Nadir)

Foster carers, sometimes in combination with social workers, had a pivotal role in helping young people to acquire practical skills for independent living. Some young people, like Aarif below, were able to spend some time in trainer flats designed to help them practise their independent living skills whilst having a safety net of support should mistakes be made. Lisa, Aarif's foster carer, reflected on the persistence required to bring about changes in young people and on the challenges that confronted them when they had to take responsibility for themselves:

> *He's quite capable in running a home. He might not be able to budget well, but he can cook, he can clean, he can wash clothes. He looks after himself. He knows about paying for water. He knows about the cost of electricity; only because I've drummed it into him. 'Turn some of them lights off!', 'Turn this off!' and so on. And actually, the first week he was in the [training] flat, he says he put £5 in the electric and it had gone in a day and he got up and he had no shower. It was cold.*

As young people were preparing to move on, foster carers provided practical, emotional and companionable support to ease the transition to their own accommodation. They helped young people to move and settle into their new homes. They helped them to acquire furniture and furnishings, to decorate their homes and, usually in conjunction with social workers, to arrange the financial aspects of these transitions. For example, one foster carer described how he had been helping a previous foster child: 'She's going into a lovely little flat . . . so we've painted it and we've made sure everything's gone in and that it's nice for her.' Another foster carer, Eleanor, described how she had furnished a flat attached to her house for Arian to live in so that he would not have to leave the area and could stay close to his college and friendship network. Arian had relied heavily on Eleanor for support throughout this move as he felt his social worker had not proved to be very reliable:

> *It's, just before me leaving, they're meant to do a pathway plan about six months before . . . But they didn't really follow up with anything and so everything came out last minute . . . So they're not, they weren't really helpful. (Arian)*

Although most young people were unable to stay on in foster care, stability and continuity in these relationships may also be provided through continuing contact with foster carers and their families once young people leave. This is important for the practical and emotional support foster carers may provide but also for young people's symbolic connection to family through involvement in key family rituals and events. Research on leaving care has tended to emphasise the gradual erosion of these connections in the period after leaving care. For example, Dixon and colleagues' (2006) study of 106 young people leaving care found that more than over two-fifths (46%) of those who had left care from foster placements were still in contact with their carers some 12–15 months later. However, frequency of contact had declined from 42 per cent in at least monthly contact at the outset to just 14 per cent at follow-up. Of course, some reduction in frequency of contact is to be expected once young people leave care. Returning for infrequent visits or to mark special occasions are part of the fabric of family life (as is contact through telephone and text) and can provide considerable emotional support and reassurance for young people when they leave home. However, it would appear that support of this kind is still not available to the majority of young people leaving foster families and that the support that does take place often occurs informally, without recompense or formal integration into the pathway planning process. Contact is largely dependent on the goodwill of foster carers (Fry, 1992; Wade, 2008).

The foster carers we interviewed expressed a willingness to stay in touch with young people and to be active members of their social networks. While they could not predict that young people would want to stay in touch, they expressed hope that they would and gave examples of previous foster children who continued to visit and were actively involved in family occasions.

She comes over. She'll come over and stay over here. I mean we've got a spare bedroom, we can do it, no problem. (Michael)

I expect him here every other day [laughter], which is no problem at all. He's very welcome ... I'm sure they'll keep in touch, I mean with each other as well as with me. (Leena, Mahmood's foster carer)

The few young people we were able to talk to who had moved on had also remained in touch with their foster families and were invited to all family events.

They treat me like a son when I was living in the family, but now they call me if they have a party. They call me and I come. (Young person focus group)

These connections appeared to be highly valued by young people and helped to reduce the feelings of isolation experienced by many care leavers who lack strong social networks. Given that most still faced considerable uncertainty as they waited for a final decision on their asylum claims, they also provided an important source of emotional support and practical advice to help young people think into and plan for the future.

Immigration and pathway planning

The approach of adulthood brings uncertainties that derive from the asylum determination process to the fore. Only one in nine (11%) of young people in our survey sample had been granted refugee status. Amongst those aged 17 or over, more than a quarter were still seeking an initial asylum decision (28%), over half (56%) had been granted discretionary leave and were therefore making or were soon to make an application to extend that leave, and a small number (6%) had been refused asylum. Uncertainty about their prospects for remaining in the UK, therefore, figured prominently in the lives of the vast majority of young people (see Broad and Robbins, 2005 and Wade *et al*, 2005 for similar findings).

Planning

Pathway planning, premised on helping young people to develop plans for the future, is complicated by these uncertainties. Where young people had received a positive decision, the planning process could be more certain. Young people were able to think ahead and plan their futures in the UK, at least for the next five years. Their entitlements to housing, benefits, work and education were clear and social workers and foster carers could work together to develop support plans consistent with young people's skills and aspirations. Where this was not the case, the future was foreshortened and crowded with uncertainty. Planning could not stretch much beyond the immediate horizon. Decisions about whether to go to college or university or to plan a holiday with their foster family the next year became difficult to contemplate without magnifying young people's feelings of precariousness.

> It's hard for him now because he doesn't have the same sort of security. Can you plan? If you say to him: 'Oh, we're thinking of going to such-and-such a place for a holiday next year, would you like to come with us?' You get this shrug . . . It takes a certain kind of mental toughness to deal with it. (Eleanor, Arian's foster carer)

Young people coped with uncertainty and the long wait for an asylum decision in different ways. Some busied themselves in the present and tried to avoid looking too far ahead, while others found it more difficult to be purposeful in the here and now, the uncertainty they felt creating a form of stasis that could have negative effects on their health and well-being.

> How does it affect them? Well, some are great. Some will just say, right, well, I'll get on with it. Other people cannot move past that barrier . . . It's like a brick wall to them and they just cannot move on with their lives. Other guys . . . they're just getting on with things, but others are just sitting, waiting. (Social worker, Area 3)

Social workers conveyed a strong sense of changing times that had definite effects on planning. The government had become clearer in its intention to speed up asylum decision-making and to return failed asylum seekers to their countries of origin. It was no longer possible to develop plans based on the assumption that young people would most likely not be returned on reaching adulthood.

> *It's difficult, you know, because for the last two years we've seen the way that the Home Office is working . . . Decisions are being made . . . [and] young people are being sent back a lot more swiftly . . . but you've still got to plan . . . We're still trying with pathway plans and we're looking at: right, if you stayed here what would the plans be here? If you returned home what would your plans be there? We're doing that more and more.* (Social worker, Area 2)

This changing context has made it imperative for social workers to develop a parallel or triple planning approach to pathway planning that takes account of all potential outcomes of the asylum process (Free, 2006; Dorling, 2009; Department for Education, 2010). Where young people do not have a final decision, these would include:

- a long-term plan to prepare young people for life in the UK should they receive indefinite leave to remain;
- a transitional plan with short-term achievable goals while young people are in the UK without a permanent immigration status;
- a return plan to prepare young people for return to their country of origin should all rights of appeal be exhausted or they decide to return of their own accord.

There may also be a need to arrange help for young people who become failed asylum seekers, are no longer officially eligible for local authority support, and are at risk of destitution, but who are unable to leave the country immediately (Dorling, 2009). These cases present local authorities with problems, not least because there is no funding stream to support work undertaken with them. Before local authorities withdraw support, they need to be mindful of not breaching young people's rights under human rights legislation. Although this is very much a grey area, there was evidence in our local authorities of social work teams continuing to provide baseline support to young people until they received explicit directions from the Home Office to leave the country.

> *Well, that limbo situation is happening for people. For example, some young people from Iran [have been] refused outright and classed as "all rights exhausted", but because of the difficulties in Iran, they can't be returned. So they remain with social care and have done for the last couple of years.* (Team manager, Area 2)

> *We are supporting a number of "appeal rights exhausted" people in ... what will increasingly be ... [due to funding constraints] ... bargain-basement accommodation with a limited range of support. We will carry on doing that until they get removal directions.* (Team manager, Area 3)

Representation
Planning must also address young people's need for consistent legal representation through the asylum process. Concerns about the availability of good legal advice and of the quality of decision-making by UKBA have been consistently raised in the literature (Crawley, 2007; Nandy, 2007; Refugee Council, 2010). While unaccompanied young people may be involved in a range of legal proceedings related to their care and immigration status, the latter stands out as having the least formal and specialised provision for young people, including a lack of formal procedures to ensure legal representation (Crawley, 2004). In recent years, reductions made to Legal Aid budgets and in the availability of legal representatives with specialist knowledge of both the asylum system and children's welfare may be exacerbating these problems (Nandy, 2007; Brownlees and Smith, 2011).

The young people we interviewed generally found the asylum process daunting, confusing and exhausting. Meetings and interviews linked to their asylum application frequently merged with a plethora of meetings designed to assess and meet their welfare needs. In their early months in the UK, before most young people had command of English, the presence of many different professionals in their lives was bewildering. Young people remembered being asked a multitude of specific questions by solicitors and immigration officials. They sometimes found the details, the particular timing and course of events, and details of all the people involved difficult to recall. Some aspects of the past that had suddenly gained significance were simply unknown to them. Just understanding what was being asked of him was challenging for Ayotunde, when he was seeking to extend his leave to remain:

Sometimes they would ask you the questions, like: what are you talking about? Just say it the way it's supposed to be, but they just complicate the questions.

Young people were often reliant on interpreters during these meetings. A number of concerns about the availability and quality of interpreting services have been highlighted in research studies. These have included young people arriving for important interviews or meetings with no interpreter present, providing interpreters who do not match the young person's language and interpreters who intervene in meetings beyond their formal role (Rutter, 2003a; Brownlees and Smith, 2011). Omid, for example, who was from Afghanistan, had found it very difficult to understand his Pakistani interpreter during his screening interview, causing him great anxiety in case it had adverse effects on his claim:

I had a problem with the interpreter [who] was speaking a [particular] kind of Pashto. In Pakistan they speak a bit of Pashto, which the accent is different and you find it hard to understand . . . So I said: 'If I answer anything wrong it's not my fault because I can't understand [him] hardly, you know.'

It is extremely difficult for young people to decipher the complexities of the asylum process. It is also difficult for them to judge whether their legal representatives are working effectively on their behalf

(Wade *et al*, 2005; Chase *et al*, 2008). Representatives may change, as legal practices close or solicitors withdraw from individual cases, and claims may be subject to delay for a variety of reasons, including the inefficiency of solicitors or of the immigration service. Although social workers and foster carers should not give legal advice, they have an important role to play in helping young people to arrange solicitors, in monitoring the progress of claims, supporting young people through these encounters and advocating on their behalf.

Immigration support

The interviews revealed much about the emotional and practical support provided by foster carers, often in conjunction with young people's social workers. Some foster carers commented on the highly stressful nature of immigration interviews, both for them and their young people, as very painful aspects of young people's lives had to be relived and retold in environments that were cold and sometimes hostile: 'We've been his shoulder to cry on sometimes . . . He talks to us and we support him' (Isobel, Majeed's foster carer). Eva tried to lessen the emotional upset through her efforts to turn these meetings into a day out in London:

> And this is the way I do it . . . I go bouncing to town with them and I say: 'Let's go, I will take you as a day out. We're going to the Home Office today' [she laughs]. On the way back, if the children take too long we will stay in London. We drag ourselves all together... and I must say to you that the interviews are very frightening. They drain you emotionally, so you need to switch off . . . They need to take out all that and to clean their minds. Some of them come out with a real headache because the process is so long-winded, very long. (Eva, Haaroon's foster carer)

There were, however, differing perspectives about the appropriate balance of responsibilities between social workers and foster carers when it came to managing young people's asylum claims. Some social workers (and rather more foster carers) thought that social workers should have lead responsibility for accompanying young people to official meetings, liaising with solicitors and UKBA officials and monitoring the progress of claims. In contrast, some foster carers (and rather more social workers) felt that this was an important feature of the fostering task. Some foster carers took on this work willingly. Those who did so, spoke about the close bond they had formed with their young person, and how they were therefore best placed to provide the support the young person needed, out of recognition of its importance to their young person's overall well-being.

I mean, it's better me, really, than anyone else because, I mean, we bonded. He's like my own son now. (Leena, Mahmood's foster carer)

Because I knew him much better I decided, with his immigration solicitor, that I would do his statement . . . We had a three-hour session, with some breaks, where we literally went through the whole thing . . . We kind of prepared for it and we did it and it was difficult, but he was OK with it. And I think it means [that] I've got that level of knowledge now that you wouldn't normally have. (Eleanor, Arian's foster carer)

Although Eleanor's commitment to listen to all of Arian's experiences and write them down may not have been common, other foster carers became active advocates for their young people, sometimes in consort with social workers. This was perhaps clearest in connection with a number of attempted Third Party removals where social workers and foster carers worked jointly to advocate with UKBA on behalf of young people and, in one instance, to secure the return of a young person who had been forcibly sent back to Italy.[75] The basis of the claim rested on the apparent failure of that country to provide the

---

75 Safe third country removals (or Dublin 11 cases) involve cases where young people are deemed to have come through what is described as an EU "safe third country" on route to the UK. Under EU law, the country into which the person first arrived must take responsibility for their asylum claim. In such instances, the person concerned can be returned to that country.

reception arrangements for young people that had been agreed. The information collected and relayed to solicitors enabled successful challenges against these transfers to be made.

The [social worker's] been great . . . The last meeting that we had with the solicitor . . . she brought a colleague of hers . . . It was this particular social worker who'd experienced this situation with young children being returned to Italy. She was the one who brought the evidence for the solicitor, who was very interested in it, and understood how things were not working over in Italy. He had the proof. He knew things weren't like they should be. (Michael, Samuel's foster carer)

Even where foster carers were willing to take on an active role in this way, it was time intensive, often involved juggling their other childcare responsibilities, and back-up was needed from time to time.

There's been lots of meetings . . . It was sort of left down to us really . . . The asylum team were pretty good . . . and . . . when I couldn't go to interviews at the Home Office, then the company I work for would take them. So that was quite good, because I still had to be here for my own children, as well, so I couldn't be everywhere. (Stephanie, Omid's foster carer)

As Stephanie implies, taking a large share of responsibility for supporting young people through the asylum process involves considerable pressure. Some foster carers took on this work more reluctantly because social workers had expected it of them, even though they felt it should not necessarily have been part of their remit. While they were willing to provide support, they were more likely to feel that they had been taken for granted and frequently felt that they lacked sufficient understanding of the asylum process (at least at first) to support young people effectively. These foster carers described their induction as a steep learning curve undertaken with limited support other than the advice provided by legal representatives. Some had received support from their supervising social workers, but these workers had also frequently lacked specific knowledge on asylum issues.

One social worker, in the past, wanted us to do all the immigration appointments and, I'm sorry, but we were unaware of all the rules at that time . . . and I didn't know what the legal issues were . . . Basically we were being made to do them all . . . We were being forced into it; that was part of our job, apparently. Well, I thought as a foster carer your job is to feed them, look after them, take them for medical appointments, make sure you go to parents' evenings, like you do your own kids. Immigration isn't really to do with us, although we like to know what's happening. (Isobel, Majeed's foster carer)

I've been to the solicitors with them quite a few times . . . Personally I think that is not my job. It's not my job to accompany a young person to a solicitor's and to sit there listening to stuff I'll not fully understand, although I do now. (Lisa, Aarif's foster carer)

Getting the right balance for foster carers is clearly important. In part, their worries about taking on this work stem from a lack of confidence that might be addressed through improved preparation and training opportunities before young people are placed with them. Our next chapter considers these issues further and also identifies that, for many foster carers, the training and support given in relation to asylum issues appeared weaker than that given in relation to core fostering skills. This may need to be adjusted. However, it is also a matter for negotiation in individual cases. It is clear that foster carers have different perceptions about where the boundaries of the fostering role should lie. Careful negotiation may therefore help to reduce resentment and increase the potential for fruitful collaboration.

Return

There is a realistic prospect that many young people will eventually have to return to their countries of origin. Preparation for return should therefore form an important strand of pathway planning (Department for Education, 2010). At present, government policy is to return failed asylum seekers once they have exhausted all their rights to appeal. Unaccompanied young people (below the age of 18) face return only if adequate reception and care arrangements exist in their country of origin. However, the majority will be expected to return as young adults and, prior to return, young people may be subject to regular reporting requirements or detention (Nandy, 2007; Dorling, 2009).

Facing up to the prospect of return is difficult for young people, foster carers and social workers. Very few young people want to return. Most, having lived in the UK for some years, want to settle here. Questions of identity and belonging are complicated by young people's physical and emotional distance from their countries of origin. Some will have been exiled for several years or moved between countries from an early age. For some young people, therefore, defining where they belong or to where they should return is difficult (Chase *et al*, 2008). The period of time they have spent in the UK may have been the safest and most stable period of their lives. The roots they have put down and the relationships they have formed may have been amongst the most sustaining they have known. It is not surprising that the threat of losing these connections is a source of great anxiety to young people.

Our interviews with young people and foster carers highlighted how difficult it can be to find a suitable vocabulary through which these issues can be discussed. Young people appeared generally resistant. Foster carers were frequently hesitant about upsetting young people when the final outcome was not yet known. When asked if she spoke to her foster child about his asylum claim, Marion said it was only discussed '. . . when he talks about it . . . I try not to unless I've got something positive to say' (Osman's foster carer). Foster carers generally tried to keep young people in a positive frame of mind, to keep them occupied in the present and encouraged them to do the right things in the hope that this might help their asylum claims.

I keep trying to reassure him that it'll be alright. It's not good worrying about it. That's not going to change anything, you know, and don't get into trouble. (Leena, Mahmood's foster carer)

The caution exercised by foster carers demonstrates the difficulty of retaining a balance between providing young people with care and security, while also supporting them to prepare effectively for potentially difficult future circumstances. Where foster carers endeavour to raise these issues, discussions need to be managed with great care. One young person who had left care spoke of the unsettling experience she had had when her foster carer had lacked sensitivity in the way she spoke about the risk of return:

She always told me in this country you have to be careful. She scared me. Always I was worried. She said they are not going to accept you. They are going to deport you and always she is telling me that. I don't know anyone. I just know her and I don't know anything. She said she been in this country more than 30 years . . . I was the 14th person living there and five of them were being deported. (Sophia, Young women's focus group)

Where social workers tried to encourage young people to consider the potential for different immigration outcomes and the pathways that might flow from these, the challenges that this involved were evident in some cases:

We haven't started thinking about it yet . . . We have talked about it a little bit. My social worker tried to talk to me about it, and one thing she was talking about was: what is plan B and C? I was like, no plan B and C [he laughs], I want to stick to this one, and if this gets ruined, [then] everything gets ruined . . . so we didn't look. If I have a back up, what would it be? I'm not sure. But if this happens, then what I've done, like, for the past three years, everything will be ruined . . . I'm not going to need it . . . You've got to live life as you go. (Haroon, aged 17.5 years)

Social workers did, however, convey a sense of how practice is changing. The determination of government to speed up asylum decision-making and return more failed asylum seekers has brought a new focus to questions of preparation and planning for return:

I think it [practice] has had to change and, certainly, we now see it very differently in this team. In the past, we didn't look at that [return] and we felt, I'll put my hand up, we felt uncomfortable talking about that because your social work role is that you want to protect and safeguard the young person . . . So it was almost a conflict, really, at times, but now, because of the number of young people who are being deported, we have to look at it . . . I don't think we'd be doing our job if we didn't do that because it's about preparation for that young person. (Social worker, Area 2)

It was this discomfort felt by practitioners that had led to quite high levels of planning drift in the past (Wade *et al*, 2005). The tensions with child welfare principles also contribute to social workers' feelings of powerlessness when confronted by the imperatives of the immigration system, since they are unable to greatly influence the course of events and can only generally intervene at the margins on behalf of young people (Dunkerley *et al*, 2005). However difficult this area of work may be, it is of vital importance that social workers and foster carers help to raise young people's awareness of the likelihood of a negative outcome and help them prepare for this eventually.

Work undertaken in partnership with other groups and organisations may also prove helpful. For instance, there were examples of social work teams working alongside refugee groups and the International Organisation for Migration (IOM) in an effort to raise young people's awareness, provide them with realistic information and consider the option of voluntary assisted return packages.

Until they get that paper, they don't think they have to do anything and it's really hard . . . I've got this big thing about raising young people's consciousness and their understanding of things . . . I've started using this group which is run by refugees and I take them there and then they get advice from them and it does seem to help, 'cos they're getting it from people in a similar situation. (Social worker, Area 3)

What we also do now is run a monthly drop-in with the IOM. We get young people to come down and IOM talk to them about voluntary return. If you are to be sent back, this is another option and it can be a supported move. That's really difficult for young people to hear. Some choose to act on it and listen, whereas some can't bear to hear it because the thought of going back to Afghanistan . . . they just don't want to hear that, especially if they've been settled here for two or three years. (Social worker, Area 2)

However resistant young people may be to the idea of return, it is important that this eventuality forms an integral part of pathway planning. It is important for planning to be realistic, for it to take place over an extended period of time, to weigh all the options and pathways open to young people, and to provide them with the maximum opportunity to make informed decisions for the future, even where this future is unlikely to be in the UK.

Summary

This chapter moved forward to look at preparation and planning for adulthood, in circumstances where young people's futures in the UK were often uncertain. Foster carers expected young people to move on from their placements later (at or after 18) when relationships between them were positive and young people were perceived to be doing well. Where young people lacked skills or presented behavioural challenges it was anticipated that they would move on earlier.

Young people were considered to be attracted to independence by a number of "pull" factors, especially by the experience of older peers who had already done so. However, when approaching 18, the policies, procedures and expectations of local authorities about the appropriate time for young people to move on came much more sharply into play.

These "push" factors are likely to be accelerated by current pressures on placement supply and on the financial resources available to support young people. Staying on beyond 18 was linked to being in education and tended to be time limited. Foster care, therefore, continues not to provide young people with a stable home base into adulthood, and access to other supported accommodation options continues to be relatively limited. Foster carers have a pivotal role in helping to maintain contact and continuity for young people through transition and most appeared to welcome that role.

Pathway planning is profoundly affected by the immigration process. A majority of young people were still awaiting a final asylum decision. Pathway planning therefore needs to take account of the range of likely outcomes for young people, including the increasingly realistic prospect that they will have to return to their countries of origin. Young people had great difficulty understanding the meaning of their encounters with a wide range of legal and immigration professionals, especially at first, and depended on the consistent practical and emotional support and advocacy provided by foster carers and/or social workers, even though some foster carers felt that this should not be a core feature of the fostering task.

13 Supporting foster carers

This chapter will focus on the background experience of foster carers. It will consider their perceptions of the preparation and training they have received both as foster carers and, more specifically, as foster carers of unaccompanied children and young people. It will describe the impact that fostering has had on them and their families, their overall satisfaction with fostering and their perceptions of the professional support they have received from social workers and, more informally, from other foster carers, relatives and family friends.

As we saw in Chapter 4, most foster carers in our sample had considerable experience of fostering. Only six per cent had fostered for one year or less and almost two-thirds (62%) had fostered for at least three years. Most had also fostered a number of children in the past (median number of five) and only four carers reported that this was the first young person they had fostered. Most (71%) had also fostered a wider range of young people than just unaccompanied minors.

Preparation for fostering an unaccompanied child

Although most foster carers had garnered considerable fostering experience by the time of data collection for this study, they were asked to rate the extent to which they had felt prepared to foster their first unaccompanied child. Around one-third of foster carers (34%) reported that they had felt "well" prepared, and almost one-half that they had felt prepared "to some extent" (48%). But small minorities of carers reported not being "very well" (13%) or "not at all" prepared (5%).

Some groups of foster carers were more likely to have reported that they had been "well" prepared and many provided a brief note to explain why this was the case. In particular, foster carers were more positive about their readiness to foster an unaccompanied child where:

- they had been born outside of the UK (p = 0.001, 0.295, n = 130);[76]
- they had only ever fostered unaccompanied young people (p<0.001, 0.345, n = 131);[77]
- the index young person fostered with them was matched by religion and/or country of origin (p<0.001, n = 130);[78]
- to a lesser extent, they had been fostering for a shorter period of time (p = 0.028, t 0.154, n = 127).[79]

These findings suggest that carers were more likely to have felt ready to foster where they themselves had prior experience of migration and of the challenges of making a new home in the UK. It is likely that these experiences had helped to prepare them for the challenges that lay ahead and had motivated them to foster these young people in particular. It may also be the case that children's services had recognised the potential in these carers, sought to recruit them for a specialist role and therefore had greater scope to match young people and carers more closely.

In contrast, carers had tended to feel less ready to foster an unaccompanied child where they had fostered for longer, had fostered a broader range of young people and where there was no match by religion or country of origin. Despite their greater overall experience, the challenges of caring for this group of young people were new. Although these carers had evidently felt less confident and less well prepared, it may be the case that their social workers had felt that this transition could be made with relative ease, given their greater experience, and that their potential need for further specialist training and support may have been overlooked or given insufficient emphasis.

The brief comments made by foster carers in the survey help to clarify their views on readiness. Amongst those who reported having

---

76 Mann Whitney U Exact test
77 Mann Whitney U Exact test
78 Kruskal Wallis test. This is an admittedly crude proxy for matching and was compared to placement with a) minority ethnic carers (not sharing country of origin or religion) and b) white foster carers. There was no difference between these latter groups in paired tests.
79 Kendall's tau-b test

felt "well" prepared, some highlighted the quality of preparation and training they had received from children's services. Even where the experiences of carers had been positive, however, much still needed to be learned gradually over time.

> I had lots of training and support; I trained for six months before becoming a foster parent.

> The social work team were very informative and professional . . . We had training courses, tasks and questions to complete and [learned from] other experienced foster carers.

> Because it was my first placement, preparation was given in the sense of support and training and guidelines. The rest had to be experienced and learnt. You can never be totally prepared as you learn more and more as you do this job.

Alongside provision of advice, information and training, some foster carers highlighted their motivation to foster, prior experiences of parenting or fostering within the family and a motivation for self-directed learning and discovery about fostering regulations and about the needs of asylum seekers and refugees.

> I always wanted to look after a child and give them a loving home. As my own children had grown up I thought that this was a good time to do it.

> My family had been fostering, so I had some experience beforehand. I had also cared for my nieces and nephews.

> I read information about [fostering] legislation, read books and articles on fostering, on different cultures and all about asylum seekers.

> Several of my relatives were approved foster carers, caring for unaccompanied minors. However, caring for a child whose language and culture was different to mine required some adjustment in the first few months.

Some also made reference to their past careers in teaching, youth and social care work, sometimes working alongside refugee children, or they referenced their own experiences of migration to the UK as having provided them with a relevant foundation for fostering and a sense of connectedness to the young people in their care.

> *I understand the child's situation as I moved here from Zimbabwe and had to settle all over again.*

> *My father's and mother's families came here under similar circumstances and I also did research through the Refugee Council after my child came to live with me.*

> *Both myself and my partner (an EAL teacher) have worked extensively with children from a wide variety of cultures and backgrounds, including asylum seekers and refugees. We have also worked in South Asia and travelled in Afghanistan.*

As we have seen, however, many foster carers had felt less well prepared to foster their first unaccompanied young person. Where these first placements had been made in an emergency, a number of carers noted that there had been no time to think through how the needs of these young people might differ to those of other looked after children. In these circumstances, it was not surprising to find that some carers were anxious about the challenges that lay ahead. These feelings tended to be accentuated where carers were inexperienced or were unused to interacting closely with people from other cultures.

> *It was an emergency placement with one hour's notice. I knew very little about the country and culture of the young person who was arriving at the time. I didn't know of the existence of Eritrea prior to this.*

> *I had no experience (and) no way of knowing what to expect . . . I was apprehensive about knowing how to meet (his) "unknown" cultural needs.*

Other foster carers also mentioned this uncertainty and the challenges of working with the "unknown". Considerable anxiety was evident where foster carers were not or could not be provided with information about young people's family backgrounds, the reasons for them being in the UK, their past educational experiences, and about their physical and emotional health needs, which became known only with the passage of time. Others mentioned difficulties associated with communication, dietary and religious needs and, in particular, with their lack of knowledge about immigration procedures. Even where preparation and support were provided, foster carers had to feel their way into these relationships over time. Some foster carers, however, suggested that more appropriate training before starting to foster might have helped.

Appropriate training before caring for asylum seekers would have prepared me for the complex task of working with them.

Although I had diversity training, I had no knowledge of official procedures (visas, leave to remain, processes, the Home Office, etc) or about particular cultures and religions.

Where constructive support was promptly provided by supervising and children's social workers, these difficulties appeared to be overcome, sometimes with relative ease. Where this was not the case, foster carers had to be more self-reliant.

We learnt as we went along at first. My company has since brought specialist training on unaccompanied minors into their training programme.

I had attended training but I had no first-hand experience. I was very nervous and often called my supervisor for advice.

My supervising social worker and social worker were very supportive. They helped and answered questions as they arose – about halal food, religion, official papers and appointments.

Ongoing training, information and advice

Training, of course, should not end with the first placement. We were therefore interested in exploring the training, information and advice that foster carers had subsequently received. All reported that they had received some formal training during the course of their fostering careers. The majority (82%) felt that this had been broadly sufficient for their needs, although a further 16 per cent would have liked some more.[80]

We also asked foster carers to rate their satisfaction with (a) the amount, (b) the quality and (c) the relevance of the training and advice they had received over time. In each case, between 52 and 58 per cent reported being "very satisfied" and a further 33 to 39 per cent were "quite satisfied". Only a small minority (between 7% and 9%) were dissatisfied. These questions replicated those used by Sinclair and colleagues in their earlier survey of 944 foster carers. Our findings provide a slightly more positive appreciation of the training provided since, in that study, one-quarter to one-third of foster carers expressed themselves "very" satisfied in these respects and a further 60 per cent were broadly satisfied. In that study, satisfaction with training rose with the number of hours of training reported by foster carers. In this study, similar to our findings on initial preparation, appreciation of training and advice was higher where foster carers had only ever specialised in fostering unaccompanied minors and had fostered a smaller number of children in the past.[81] Although these findings are not strong (and would need to be corroborated by a larger study) they do point to the need for close attention to be given to the particular training needs of more experienced foster carers who may transition to fostering unaccompanied young people later in their fostering careers. Generic fostering experience may not always prepare them

---

80 Three foster carers (2%) failed to answer this question.
81 Mann Whitney U Exact tests for whether carers had only fostered unaccompanied minors or not (amount of training p = 0.01, n = 131; quality p = 0.01, n = 131; relevance p = 0.14). Kendall's tau-b tests for number of children fostered (amount p = 0.05, t 0.141, n = 126; quality p = 0.07; relevance p = 0.036, t 0.152, n = 127)

sufficiently to meet the specific needs of this group of young people.

In order to gather more detail about the specific training, advice and support provided to foster carers, we asked them to report the extent to which they had received advice and support in a total of 16 discrete areas. These areas could be clustered into three broad groupings. These included items addressing: (a) core fostering skills (important to the care of all young people); (b) cultural skills; and (c) skills related to the more specific asylum needs of unaccompanied young people. The distribution is presented in Table 13.1.

In overall terms, foster carers reported a good degree of coverage, with a majority having received advice and support, at least to "some degree", in all areas. Some areas, in particular those addressing what might be called the core fostering skills, rated more highly. For example, areas such as support for education (72%), developing life skills (61%), managing challenging behaviour (56%) and understanding young people's physical and emotional health needs (55.5%) were "very much" at the centre of the informal advice and training that had been provided.

In contrast, some areas more specific to unaccompanied young people appeared not to have been so well covered, at least in the estimation of foster carers. Substantial numbers of carers reported a lack of support in relation to dealing with legal and immigration officials (24.5%), young people's dietary needs (22%), making cultural connections for young people (21%), working with an uncertain future for the child (24.5%) and, to a slightly lesser extent, in the area of language and communication (18.5%). In a context of broadly positive findings, therefore, evidence about the particular skills needed to care for this group of young people is rather more mixed. The findings also point to areas of support that, especially in relation to the cultural and immigration needs of young people, local authorities should seek to strengthen.

Foster carers certainly expressed more uncertainty about their knowledge in these areas, their capacity at first to grasp the meanings that underlay cultural differences and their ability to empathise with the emotional impact that young people's experiences had on their day-to-day lives.

Table 13.1

Ongoing training, advice and support provided to foster carers – per cent

To what extent have you received training, advice and support in the following areas:	Very much so	To some degree	Not at all
Core skills			
Understanding physical/emotional health needs (n = 131)	55.5	37	7.5
Understanding anxiety/depression in children (n = 130)	49	41	10
How to work with children who are distant/unaffectionate (n = 129)	44	43	13
Helping children to develop practical, social and life skills (n = 130)	61	35	4
Providing support for children's education (n = 131)	72	26	2
Handling disobedient/difficult behaviour in children (n = 129)	56	41.5	2.5
Cultural skills			
Dietary needs and food preparation (n = 132)	37	41	22
Children's religious needs (n = 130)	43.5	43.5	13
Working with cultural differences in the home (n = 130)	42	45	13
Helping children cope with racism (n = 130)	44	44	12
Connecting children to "home" country activities/groups (n = 128)	26	53	21
Asylum-related skills			
Language and communication (n = 130)	34.5	47	18.5
Working with interpreters (n = 128)	49	36.5	14.5
Support for children through asylum process (n = 132)	45	40	15
Dealing with solicitors/immigration officials (n = 130)	42	33.5	24.5
Working with child's uncertain future in the UK (n = 129)	31	44.5	24.5

Poor old thing; when I look back now, because I didn't really understand what they had been through on the journey here . . . A lot of things I didn't really understand. I remember taking this (official) letter up to him and he said, 'Stay with me Mum,' because he was scared . . . and I didn't really realise; now I do. Perhaps a bit more understanding of the emotional side of it and what they've been through would be helpful, their hopes and fears, just so I could have had a little more empathy. (Ann, Abbas' foster carer)

A fact sheet, anything like that would have been helpful. Something that you could refer back to or you could look at . . . Instead of asking the boys for information about Ramadan or Eid . . . What happens for that and what do you do for this? You have to ask them. Surely you should at least have that, shouldn't you? (Stephanie, Omid's foster carer)

Although, as these comments suggest, specific information and knowledge was gradually built up over time, we need to be mindful that migration patterns change, the cultures from which young people arrive differ over time and therefore knowledge needs to be continuously updated. We should also be wary of treating particular cultures and religions as in some way static and homogeneous since, as Leena pointed out, interpretations and meanings may vary considerably:

I think it may be helpful if social workers could maybe have short courses on Islam and culture, because there is a lot of culture mixed in with Islam according to the country. I mean in every Islamic country they practise Islam in a different way because it's mixed with the culture of that country and people need to be aware of this. (Leena, Mahmud's foster carer)

I think it's appropriate for foster carers to have training from time to time on orientation to different cultures . . . We've got so many children from different countries and most of them are different in their culture. So I think if foster carers can receive training to update their knowledge of cultural backgrounds for different groups of young people, this would help. (Social worker, Area 2)

Where some supervising social workers felt foster carers were inexperienced and might struggle to adjust to these challenges, an important part of early ongoing placement support was directed at brokering the relationship between children's social workers and foster carers to prevent difficulties arising that might jeopardise the placement. Some social workers also recognised that a key part of their role lay in educating foster carers about the significance and meaning of cultural differences.

A huge amount of our work when we start with a new foster placement, especially if the foster carers have not had asylum-seeking children before, is about educating the foster carer. (Social worker, Area 1)

Professional contact and support

Foster carers were also asked for their views on the professional contact and support that had been provided to them and the young person in their care. These questions covered the support provided by social workers in the children's asylum teams and from supervising social workers linked to the carers' fostering agencies.

Childcare social workers

The frequency of social work contact with young people was broadly in line with statutory visiting requirements. Two-fifths of childcare social workers (41%) were reported to have visited at least monthly over the course of the placement and well over one-third (38%), while visiting less frequently, were doing so at least bi-monthly.[82] Frequency of contact was higher for younger children and for young people who

---

82 Only a small minority of social workers were in touch on a weekly basis (8%) and 12 per cent less often than bi-monthly. Only in one case was there reported to be no contact at all.

had been in placement for a shorter period of time.[83] While the majority of young people aged below 16 years were in at least monthly contact with their social workers (62%), this applied to just over one-quarter (28%) of those aged 16 or over. Equally, where young people had been in placement for 12 months or less, the proportion in at least monthly contact was 60 per cent, compared to 44 per cent of those placed for two years or more.

There was also some evidence that contact tended to be higher where young people had been placed through an independent fostering agency. Where this was the case, over half (54%) of young people were in at least monthly contact with their social workers compared to less than one-quarter (22%) of those placed through the local authority.[84] Unfortunately, it is not possible to explain this finding adequately from the data available to us. It is possible that these patterns of contact may relate to the contractual relationship between local authorities and IFAs when placing young people in the independent sector, to the responsibilities of IFAs to ensure statutory visiting and review requirements are met or, alternatively, it could perhaps relate to the monitoring arrangements set by local authorities when placing young people in this sector.[85] However, while social work contact with the young person tended to be higher when placed through an IFA, it was no more likely to be rated by foster carers as being particularly helpful to them or the young people in their care. In other words, the lower level of contact in local authority placements was just as likely to be viewed as helpful.

Overall, the vast majority of foster carers considered contact with

---

83 Kendall's tau-b tests for frequency of social work contact and age of young person (p = 0.018, t –0.181, n = 125); length of time in placement (p = 0.011, t –0.186, n = 116)

84 Mann Whitney U test (p = 0.023, n = 127). It is important to be mindful that only a small minority of young people (n = 19) were placed through the local authority in this study.

85 IFAs have a responsibility under National Minimum Standard 31.6 to remind social workers of the need to meet statutory visiting and review requirements specified in the Planning Regulations 2010 and these duties are considered in inspections (Personal communication, The Fostering Network).

the young person's social worker to be reasonably helpful, as shown in Table 13.2. Only a small minority had found this contact unhelpful.

Table 13.2
Foster carer rating of the helpfulness of contact with childcare social workers – per cent

Is social work contact	Very helpful	Some help	Not very helpful	Very unhelpful
Helpful for the child (n = 132)	52	37	9	2
Helpful for the foster carer (n = 126)	54	33	11	2

In Chapter 10, we saw that where the young person's contact with their social worker was rated as helpful this was one of the factors associated with them "doing well" across a number of key life domains.[86] A majority of young people who were considered by foster carers to be making "above average" progress (61%) were also receiving support from social workers that was rated as being "very helpful". This compares to less than one-third of young people (30%) where social work support was considered to be of "some help", seven per cent where it was "not very helpful" and just two per cent where it was rated "very unhelpful".[87]

Foster carers were asked to comment on the kinds of support from social workers that, in their opinion, were likely to have been most helpful to the young people in their care. A key role of social workers, beyond their responsibilities for care planning and review, rested in their access to networks and resources. Access to financial resources was important, including payment of allowances, travel costs and additional money for social or sports activities and provision of laptops, cameras or other items that young people needed and foster carers could not resource themselves. Curbing or moderating young

---

86 See Table 10.1 for a description of these nine domains.
87 The progress scale ranged from 9–36, with a high score as positive (mean 29.52; median 30).

people's desire for extra resources was also considered to be an important feature of the social work role, backing up messages given by foster carers, and expressed succinctly by one carer as: 'Don't be a candy store'.

Facilitating young people's access to education, arranging additional educational support where this was needed and providing resources to assist English language development and communication (interpreters, extra tuition and so on) also figured prominently. Alongside these, mention was made of advice and guidance, emotional encouragement, support around healthy lifestyles and practical life skills, and support directed at connecting young people to religious and cultural networks. Finally, especially for many foster carers lacking knowledge of the asylum process, social workers had a central role in monitoring claims, arranging legal representation and providing or facilitating access to advice on the application process.

Foster carers understandably tended to view their own role as pivotal in helping young people to settle into family life, build relationships of trust and respect, and facilitate transition into new social and educational networks. Given the pattern of social work contact described above, the social work role was generally more distant. However, excessive distance and a perceived preoccupation with bureaucratic routines brought sharp criticism from some foster carers and placed a brake on the concept of corporate parenting.

Social services, they say that they are parents, but they are not . . . because they see them only . . . once in a month. Have you ever seen a parent see their kids only once a month? So the real parents are foster carers . . . I don't have a problem in that regard and I think social workers cannot be involved because of too much bureaucracy. (Sanaz, Rahim's foster carer)

In our survey, more frequent contact with social workers was associated with a perception amongst foster carers of this support being more helpful to young people.[88] The importance of frequent and

---

88 Kendall's tau-b test (p = 0.007, t 0.215, n = 130)

regular contact was also echoed by young people as an important sign that social workers were genuinely interested in their well-being. Nabil reflected on this in relation to two social workers, one current and one in the past, although he hesitated to criticise too strongly:

She's nice, she respects me. But the only problem is that she doesn't come down much, she doesn't ask me anything . . . Before it was OK, because he was coming down when I asked him . . . She's alright, maybe she's busy, maybe she don't see any problems for me. That's maybe why she doesn't visit me. (Nabil)

As we have seen, the early stages of placement were often challenging. This especially tended to be the case where language and communication were difficult or where foster carers were inexperienced in looking after unaccompanied young people. In these circumstances, foster carers emphasised the need for more intensive support from social workers to provide reassurance and practical help.

I think what I would like or what would probably be helpful in the future was if someone could be there to work with you in those early days. Even just to pop in once a week to see how you're getting on and whether there are any practical things they could help with. (Rachel, Nadir's foster carer)

Where social workers were accessible, responsive and predictable in the support they provided, however, this was greatly appreciated. In these circumstances, there was potential for all parties to work as a team with and on behalf of young people.

I feel the combination of parental support and guidance from me with regular visits and communication from the social worker for information and guidance has worked really well. (Survey)

My experience has been quite positive, with all professionals you need to link and work with working well together. It's been extremely positive. (Eva, Haaroon's foster carer)

In contrast, criticism was evident where foster carers felt excluded from consultation, planning and decision-making. At the extreme, some foster carers had felt marginalised and de-valued. Not only did they have limited power to affect the course of events for the young person in their care but they also felt that, overall, their contribution had gone unrecognised.

You don't hear from (the social worker) from one meeting to the next and then, a lot of the time, they will go and meet them at the school so you don't know what's been said, what's gone on. You don't feel confident in anything. You're left out of the cycle really. But then you're told later on that something happened. (Stephanie, Omid's foster carer)

The social workers don't recognise or appreciate anything we've done for our children particularly. The Independent Reviewing Officer does, but that's because she's seen them over the whole three years and she's seen what's happened. (Eleanor, Arian's foster carer)

Clearly, not all foster carers felt this way, since most responding to the survey were broadly satisfied with the support provided by children's social workers. However, the comments do highlight the discouragement and divisions that can occur when communication, contact and relationships with foster carers and young people are not properly fostered. Feeling part of a team, where information is shared, being valued as a colleague, and being included in planning and decision-making have been identified as being of considerable importance to foster carers (Triseliotis *et al*, 2000; Farmer *et al*, 2004; Kirton *et al*, 2004; Sinclair *et al*, 2004). Alongside this, access to training and good support and supervision of foster carers have been associated with increased satisfaction and competence to manage the challenging behaviour of children (Macdonald and Turner, 2005; Sellick, 2006; Whenan *et al*, 2009).

The last comment above also raises the issue of continuity. The importance of continuity in relationships between young people and their social workers is recognised in the care literature, as are the challenges of providing it as social workers too frequently come and go in the lives of young people (Biehal *et al*, 1995; Jackson, 2002). Some of our young people had been supported by different social workers during their time in the care system and reflected on differences in their relationship with each social worker; some considered very helpful, others less so. Changes of social worker frequently meant that painful stories had to be retold and new relationships had to be forged in circumstances where the transitory nature of these relationships became gradually more apparent. Failure to properly manage these transitions was a source of great frustration to young people and foster carers alike. In these scenarios, important information about the young person's history, interests, progress and needs could become lost or insufficiently considered before first meeting. In the mind of one foster carer, this was read as disinterest:

> *They are just not interested . . . I'll give you this as an example. One of the social workers turned up, a new one yet again . . . and they asked him basic questions. He said, not unreasonably: 'Have you not read my file?' And I thought: that's good, because you haven't read the file. Go back and sit in your car and read it.* (Eleanor, Arian's foster carer)

Handling these transitions, where they become necessary, with care and sensitivity is important. First impressions set the tone for a future relationship and may provide a platform for productive working relationships between social workers, young people and foster carers.

These relationships may also become subject to strain where the boundaries between what properly constitutes the respective roles of foster carers and social workers are not carefully negotiated in each case. As we saw in Chapter 12, the tensions that may arise around this boundary were most readily apparent in relation to immigration work. Some foster carers were happy to embrace an active role in dealing with the Home Office, solicitors and other officials, while others either felt less confident in these areas or that this should not really be their province. In these cases, foster carers perceived that they were being asked to adopt what was properly a social work role. In some instances, where foster carers appeared confident and able, their skills were relied upon and support from children's social workers was sometimes reduced accordingly. This could give rise to tensions.

It is sometimes difficult. We need to be very careful because there is a very thin line and I must say there are some social workers that need to do their job properly. I need to be very aware of that. I am capable of doing it; I have the ability to do it; I have the knowledge to do it but, excuse me, that's not my role. (Eva, Haaroon's foster carer)

Positive working relationships are therefore more likely to be built and sustained successfully where there is a clear and negotiated understanding of where this boundary lies in individual cases and where it is respected over the course of time.

Supervising social workers

Research with foster carers has tended to find that they are generally more appreciative of the support provided by supervising social workers than is the case for that offered by children's social workers (Triseliotis et al, 2000; Farmer et al, 2004; Sinclair et al, 2004; Murray et al, 2011). Most foster carers in our survey were employed by independent fostering providers and evidence suggests that they are generally satisfied with the support and services they receive from their agencies (Kirton et al, 2004; Sellick, 2006; Selwyn et al, 2010). The role of supervising social workers is to provide a link between foster carers and the fostering agency, to provide direct support to the foster family (rather than the child per se) and to broker relationships with the local authority. Given their role, the findings are therefore not surprising.

This was certainly the case for foster carers in our survey. Most foster carers (82%) reported receiving at least monthly visits from supervising social workers and a further 18 per cent had less frequent contact. Monthly contact appeared most common, as contact was only more frequent than monthly for 13 per cent of the sample. Supervising social workers who were in more frequent contact were rated as being more supportive.[89] In contrast, contact tended to be less frequent for foster carers with more extensive fostering experience and, although not reaching the threshold for significance, these foster carers tended to view the support provided as less helpful.[90]

Overall, however, foster carers were very satisfied with the support that was being provided. The vast majority (83%) reported that the support provided was "very helpful" and a further 14 per cent that contact provided "some help". Only four foster carers found contact with their supervising social workers to be unhelpful. This reflects a higher level of satisfaction than that found in Sinclair and colleagues' (2004) earlier study of foster care, in which 55 per cent felt that the support provided by their link workers had helped them "a lot".

More detailed questions were asked to enable foster carers to specify more clearly the areas in which they valued this support. Over-whelmingly, foster carers "strongly agreed" with a number of state-ments: that their supervising social workers visited them frequently enough (69%); that they were sufficiently available by telephone, text or email between visits (78%); and, that when in contact they listened carefully (75%), responded promptly to requests (70%) and did what they promised (65%). For most, there was also "strong" agreement that these workers appreciated the work done by foster carers (74%); offered good advice (69%); sorted out practical problems (60%) and had a good understanding of the needs of unaccompanied children (57%).

Eight of these items were included in a scale measuring the overall support provided by supervising social workers.[91] There was some evidence of variation according to the ethnicity of foster carers that

---

89 Kendall's tau-b test for frequency of contact by whether support viewed as helpful (p = 0.019, t 0.193, n = 133)

90 Kendall's tau-b test for frequency of contact by length of fostering experience (p = 0.018, t 0.168, n = 129); for helpfulness of support (p = 0.09)

91 'S(he) sorts out practical problems' was dropped. Factor analysis suggested that it would not combine well with the other eight items. Reliability analysis also suggested that while these eight items made for a very reliable measure (Cronbach's alpha 0.938), 'sorts out practical problems' was the only item that (if included) reduced this score – and did so substantially. This created a scale from 8–32, with a higher score being positive.

applied to all dimensions of support, apart from having an understanding of the specific needs of unaccompanied young people. White foster carers were generally more appreciative of the role played by their supervising social workers than were either black or Asian foster carers.[92] To give just two examples, a higher proportion of white carers "strongly agreed" with the propositions that their workers visited frequently enough (81%) and that they responded promptly to requests (83%) than was the case for black (67% and 64% respectively) or Asian carers (56% and 60% respectively). Unfortunately, it is not possible to explain these differences, although they do prompt questions about the respective quality of these working relationships and about the degree to which the support provided by social workers is delivered in appropriate and culturally sensitive ways to minority ethnic carers.

It was not surprising to find some association between satisfaction with this worker and overall satisfaction with the support and planning role of specialist children's social workers. Where foster carers felt that childcare planning and support for the young person had been positive, they were also more likely to be very satisfied with the performance of their supervising social worker. In this respect, it reflects satisfaction with the overall package of support provided by all professionals working together constructively.[93]

Our interviews with foster carers also highlighted the high quality of relationships that had often been forged with supervising social workers, emphasising their availability, responsiveness and, in some instances, their place within the fabric of family life.

She's part of our family really . . . If I ever have a problem I know I can rely on an instant reaction from her. If she can't give me an answer, she'd be on to the agency. (Michael, Samuel's foster carer)

---

92 Kruskal Wallis exact test (p=0.016, n=119). Paired tests showed that this difference applied to both Black (p=0.05) and Asian carers (p=0.006).

93 Kendall's tau-b tests for supervising social worker support scale by planning score (p = 0.027, t 0.187, n = 106) and rating of helpfulness of social worker support for the child (p = 0.001, t 0.262, n = 119)

I can always pick up the phone to her and she's always willing to listen to me, even if I just want to have a moan, to get something off my chest . . . And when she comes she's always very encouraging you know. (Jasmine, Ban-hwa's foster carer)

In some instances, the support provided by fostering social workers was contrasted to that available from children's social workers, although the strains placed upon these practitioners were acknowledged.

I think they're very understaffed . . . To be fair to social workers, I don't think they've got enough manpower . . . Whereas our fostering team has been very supportive. If they know we've been going through a hard time, they will make sure they contact us a lot more regularly, keep in weekly touch or, at points, in daily touch. (Mark, Abraham's foster carer)

Criticisms of supervising social workers were extremely rare, although two carers felt they had received more prompt assistance from the children's social work team and, in some instances, that the fostering agency's knowledge of immigration and asylum issues was rudimentary.

I think sometimes they could have been more supportive. I'm not knocking the agency, it's not their fault, they've probably never dealt with these issues before. (Isobel, Majeed's foster carer)

My supervising social worker is really good, not because she knows loads about immigration, because she doesn't, but she's really supportive. (Eleanor, Arian's foster carer)

Informal support networks

Although the support provided by professionals is highly valued by foster carers, it forms part of a potential network of support that may include other foster carers, relatives, friends and members of the local community. Fostering agencies and local authorities often provide groups, newsletters, social activities and events that include foster carers and their children. Foster carers are known to value these groups, even though they do not suit all (Kirton *et al*, 2004; Sinclair *et al*, 2004). As is the case with training, foster carers tend to value the support available from other foster carers who really understand the rewards and challenges of fostering and the potential in communal gatherings to engender a sense of professional identity (Sinclair, 2005; Schofield *et al*, 2008). They may also help to reduce strain on carers and play a part in enhancing their commitment to fostering (Sinclair *et al*, 2004).

Almost all of our foster carers (94%) acknowledged that their local authority or fostering agency provided generic support groups for foster carers. Only eight carers suggested that this was not the case. Groups specifically designed for foster carers caring for unaccompanied young people were, however, less common. Amongst those who responded to this question (n = 99), just over one-third (36%) suggested that this specialist provision existed locally, the same proportion that it did not (36%) and the remainder were uncertain. Foster carers also made quite good use of these groups, with over half attending regularly (56%) and one-third (35%) from time to time. Where foster carers reported not attending regularly, their reasons included: the timing of groups clashing with work, education or childcare commitments; the difficulties of arranging childcare; difficulties with travel arrangements; or, that the group setting did not particularly appeal. As one carer expressed it: 'It wasn't our scene!'

Groups played a valuable role in introducing foster carers to others caring for unaccompanied young people. Individual links and connections were also very helpful, especially in the early days when foster carers lacked experience of caring for this group of young people.

We found out through a friend, that a friends of hers had two Afghan boys and so ... we got those boys and Nadir together ... We chat to her about food, the cultural ways and background [of Afghan boys] and about their expectations. (Rachel, Nadir's foster carer)

I had a friend who is a foster carer that took an asylum seeker about two months before we took Sabir, so she helped me a lot. I got a lot of information from her . . . Maybe that's why I felt that I didn't need more help, because she was feeding me all this information about what she was going through. (Elizabeth, Sabir's foster carer)

Where groups had not been available, some foster carers felt the need for specific support to be provided by experienced foster carers who had fostered unaccompanied minors. There was also a sense of loss amongst some carers where groups that had existed had withered on the vine or disappeared altogether.

I didn't have anyone to talk to. I think maybe if foster carers had more contact with each other that might help. (Amina, Housyar's foster carer)

There's no real support group for foster carers. There used to be [one] but it disintegrated through lack of interest and, basically, we didn't have anywhere to meet. We did have an office at social services, but they took that off us. There's no real support group for foster carers looking after unaccompanied boys or girls. (Lisa, Aarif's foster carer)

Table 13.3 provides an overall rating of the support foster carers received from their informal and professional networks. The findings show that, although support was conjured from a wide and interlocking network of people, the support upon which foster carers most relied was generally quite narrow. The crucial role of the supervising social worker was highlighted, followed quite closely by immediate family members (partners, sons and daughters) and, to a lesser extent, from specialist children's social workers. Others had their part to play in the overall picture and some, such as other foster carers, friends or relatives, were commonly relied upon quite heavily.

Always our family; they're always there. At the beginning they wanted to learn about Rafi, they wanted to interact with him.

Even when it was hard work they still wanted to try and encourage him. They've always been a hundred per cent behind what we do. (Andrew, Rafi's foster carer)

I just talk to my friends mostly and sometimes my ex-mother-in-law. She's my support. (Amina, Housyar's foster carer)

Table 13.3
Rating of practical and emotional support foster carers received from professional and informal networks (per cent)

	A lot of help	Some help	No help
Immediate family (n = 130)	63	25	12
Other relatives (n = 129)	26	43	30
Friends (n = 128)	29	52	20
Neighbours (n = 125)	8	30	62
Members of child's community of origin (n = 127)	7	22	71
Other foster carers (n = 129)	30	53	18
Child's social worker (n = 129)	47	46	7
Supervising social worker (n = 132)	77	21	2
Other professionals (n = 125)	17	62	21

Overall satisfaction with fostering

The foster carers who took part in our study overwhelmingly showed a very high degree of commitment to the young people in their care. They obviously liked them immensely, took great pride in the progress they were making and, despite the obvious challenges that arose along the way, felt a strong sense of reward for the contribution they had made to their successful resettlement in a new and initially strange land. The vast majority (95%) got a lot of satisfaction from fostering and felt that fostering had enriched their lives (90%). For most (83%), the experience had been more or less what they had expected and similar proportions felt that most members of their own family and friends had supported them in this venture. In this vein, only one foster carer reported not feeling satisfied overall with the support they had received as a foster family.

Fostering unaccompanied young people was therefore felt to be highly rewarding work. The ways in which foster carers expressed these rewards and their affection for their young people are indicated below. These are just small fragments of the large number of comments made by the foster carers we surveyed, but through their own voices they provide a flavour of the satisfaction and mutual learning that had been experienced by many.

I find it very rewarding to see a child who is so far away from their birth country and family blossom and grow in confidence and knowing how much they appreciate what my family is offering. This young lady has decided to call me auntie, which I don't mind as it only shows how comfortable she is in my home.

Being able to help a child settle and feel secure and safe. Giving them time to talk and helping them to learn everything from the language onwards . . . Seeing them mature and grow into a confident and well-rounded person who can take care of themselves.

Supporting a young person to integrate into a new culture and seeing the development in their grasp of the language, culture and norms. Meeting and having such close interactions with people from Afghanistan and Iran, hearing about their different cultures I find fascinating. I get exposed to a different world view and gain different perspectives on issues such as diversity.

Watching them grasp the English language, make friends, grow in confidence and become integrated into our family and community. Above all, watching the fear and bewilderment fade. They are generally polite and grateful for the help they receive.

The rewarding thing is when the young person has built their trust in you and is able to confide in you about their family and how they had felt through their journey to this country. They start regarding the family home as their home and start seeing themselves as part of the family.

When they come to me they are frightened. We have to be so careful and take them in (in) a kind and friendly way. Show them what I am cooking so I can give them the food they like. If they don't speak much English, get books to teach them, watch their body language and listening. Have the family round often so they feel part of the family ... I involve them in everything and everywhere we go. Sometimes they will be challenging, but we know what to do and how to handle it ... They run to me for everything. We laugh and tell jokes. They will tell me about growing up in their country and all the history. I know they are my children; we are very close and when they leave they always visit and phone. We always invite them to birthdays and Christmas. I feed. I provide.

As we have seen in previous chapters, the challenges involved in fostering were many. The experience of forced migration was often underpinned by the death and persecution of family members or by the traumatic experiences of young people themselves, and many foster carers found listening to these stories extremely painful, once young people had felt able to tell them. Many young people presented behavioural challenges and resisted the boundaries and discipline of foster homes. Others pressed for access to greater material resources, causing strain within the household and with other foster or birth children. Tensions were also evident at cultural borders and emerged in relation to gender roles, developing sexual identities, accepted customs and norms of behaviour. However, only one foster carer made a distinctively destructive comment that sat within an overarching negative discourse on asylum seeking:

I find it difficult knowing they are just using the system. They have admitted (to me) that they are older than the age they gave the Home Office. They don't always respect or try to understand other cultures and don't integrate. I feel they want adult privileges but child responsibilities. They want money and accommodation and feel that they are entitled to it, even though they have never contributed anything to the country.

Although this view seemed to be extreme, elements of this discourse (especially in relation to materialism) were expressed by other foster carers. A number of foster carers also felt the weight of this negative discourse about asylum more directly. Although most foster carers had found their neighbours and local community to be reasonably supportive, around one-fifth (20%) admitted that they had encountered varying degrees of hostility and criticism when others realised they were caring for asylum seekers. This hostility was often directed to carers of children from Afghanistan.

Some people say: 'How can you let these children into your home and you don't know anything about them or what they carry with them?' We always say: 'If you were lost and didn't know where to go, wouldn't you like someone to help you?' You should see their faces. They are children, lost and hungry. (Survey)

Some people no longer speak to me. Some will not give me eye contact. I must say that others have been very supportive. (Survey)

We still get looks in the street and everything, but you know I walk down the street with my arm round him. (Mark, Abraham's foster carer)

Occasionally, hostility took the form of racist attacks on the homes of foster carers and their children.

We've had a lot of problems with racism and fighting and with his bike getting smashed up. One day we had a really big problem. There were about 17 of them, boys and girls, chasing after him and we had a big five-gallon beer keg thrown through the window. (Ann, Abbas' foster carer)

Fostering also impacted on family life in other ways. Although most foster carers were reasonably satisfied with the financial allowances paid to them, only one-fifth (19%) "strongly" agreed that these met the real costs of care, one-half (55%) thought the it did so "more or less", but over one-quarter (26%) thought the allowances were inadequate. Their comments highlighted steep increases in the cost of living and the fact that the job was 24:7 without breaks, reducing the hourly rate to way below minimum wage levels. In this respect, fostering was still perceived to be a vocation rather than a profession: 'I never really thought about the money, it was the job I wanted to do, but it seems quite low for what you actually do.' The older age of many unaccompanied young people also served to increase costs and insufficient account was taken of their need for sport and leisure activities, teenage clothing requirements, the cost of meeting their dietary and religious needs, or the level of travel required to official appointments such as screening interviews or with solicitors.

Fostering also had some effect on the employment prospects of many foster carers and their partners (44% had thought so). Some fostering agencies required one carer to be at home and, as indicated above, many others found fostering to be a full-time job. This inevitably depressed overall family earning power. While two-thirds of partners were in paid external employment, the majority full-time, this was only the case for just over two-fifths (42%) of primary carers who returned our questionnaires. Well over half saw fostering as a full-time job (58%). This was often a requirement of fostering agencies. Where primary carers did work, like many parents they often worked flexible hours, worked from home, organised their working life around school hours or used this "free" time to study.

When considering the practical challenges of fostering, a sizeable minority of carers reported that a range factors had created strain for them and their families, at least "to some degree". These included overcrowding or lack of privacy (22%), financial strain on family resources (40%), the impact of fostering on the family as a whole (48%), the impact of children's behaviour (56%) and, of greatest concern, coping with a lack of leisure time, loss of social life and the limited availability of respite (73%). While foster carers therefore found fostering rewarding and fostering unaccompanied children, in particular, a generally positive and personally enriching experience, fostering also involved considerable compromise for carers and their families. This led some, as we have seen, to question the culture of vocationalism that continues to pervade fostering. These feelings of frustration appeared to be at their most acute when the professionalism of foster carers was insufficiently appreciated by social work and fostering agencies and where their contribution was insufficiently recognised in planning and decision-making.

> *It should be a salaried job now. It's got to the point now where it's like a job and I think we should get paid a salary for it . . . We should get holiday pay and a few weeks holiday break. I don't think they appreciate the work we put into it and that it's 24:7. You can't just log off . . . even when you go to bed at night. You're still responsible for them even when they're asleep . . . We're not appreciated; we're not valued and sometimes we're not listened to.* (Lisa, Aarif's foster carer)

Ian Sinclair's (2005) review of findings from 16 fostering studies summarised some of the key requirements and expectations of foster carers that had emerged from these studies:

> *Carers want respect; efficiency; reliable, warm support from social workers; good information on foster children; responsive out-of-hours services; relief breaks when they need them; information on entitlements; fair remuneration; appropriate training and an absence of avoidable hassles.* (p.107)

These are perfectly consistent with the views expressed by foster carers in this study. However, as the Fostering Network's periodic surveys of the support requirements of foster carers reveal, there is still some distance to go before foster carers are fully recognised as equal members of the childcare team and are adequately resourced and supported in their efforts to provide the high-quality care that children and young people need and deserve (see, for example, Clarke, 2009, p.10).

Summary

This chapter has reviewed evidence on the preparation, training and support available to our foster carers. Around one-third felt "well" prepared and one-half "to some extent" prepared to receive their first unaccompanied child. Feeling ready was associated with good preparation packages, carers' own experiences of migration and resettlement or of relationships with members of refugee communities and/ or a willingness to engage in self-directed learning about the cultural and religious needs of young people. There may be a tendency for the preparation and support needs of established foster carers who have not previously cared for unaccompanied minors to be underestimated. They tended to feel less well prepared.

Information, support and training needs to be ongoing. Migration patterns and immigration policies change. Cultural and religious practices are dynamic, not homogenous, and require a subtle and nuanced understanding. Foster carers valued the chance to update their skills and knowledge and, while findings on ongoing support and training were generally positive, satisfaction was higher in relation to core fostering skills than was the case for culture and immigration, about which carers often lacked confidence.

Foster carers drew on a wide range of professional and informal support. Support from supervising social workers was pivotal and highly rated, although black and Asian foster carers appeared to be rather more ambivalent about this role than were white foster carers. Satisfaction was also higher where the supervising social worker and the child's social worker were able to work in harmony to support the family as a whole. Where professional support was reliable, predictable and responsive, foster carers felt that they and the young people in their care benefited considerably. This supplemented the crucial support available from immediate and extended family members and to a more limited (but no less important) extent from other foster carers who had faced (and overcome) similar challenges and who could exchange information about the particular needs of unaccompanied young people.

14   Conclusion

Introduction

Children and young people over many generations have left their homelands to seek asylum and safety alone in countries far from their own. However, it is only in recent years that UK research studies have begun to systematically explore the contours of their experiences, including the strategies they employ to cope with the challenges of resettlement, and to examine the support provided by foster carers, social workers and others to help them navigate a successful pathway. This study has made a contribution to this developing evidence base.

Once young people arrive in the UK without the support of their parents or other customary caregivers, it is the responsibility of local authority children's social care services to assess and meet their needs for safety and protection under duties provided by the Children Act 1989 and its subsequent amendments (and under equivalent legislation in other parts of the UK). Most unaccompanied children and young people are now supported in the looked after system and those who are younger, most often those below the age of 16 at arrival, are placed in foster care. This report has explored their experiences of fostering and examined the ways in which foster carers and social workers can, and frequently do, make an important positive imprint on their lives.

This study is also quite timely. While the evidence base on fostering for the wider population of looked after children and young people has been steadily growing, the needs and experiences of this group of young people has been largely excluded from mainstream fostering literature. This is not surprising, since their numbers are relatively small in comparison to citizen children in the care system. The purpose of this study has been to bring their needs and experiences to the research table and to provide some important messages about the kinds of support and services that appear helpful to them as they try to find their feet and move forward with their lives. This final chapter draws together some of our main findings and review these messages. In doing so, we hope the findings will have considerable relevance for our understanding of the relationships that are forged between young people and foster carers more generally.

The study

The study took place in four geographically disparate local authorities catering for proportionately different numbers of unaccompanied minors. Our large census study used administrative data to provide a basic profile of all 2,113 unaccompanied young people being supported by the authorities on 31 March 2009, including those being supported as care leavers, and a description of all placements that were being used to accommodate them at that time. The census enabled us to answer questions about changes that have taken place in the legal status and placement pathways of this group of young people in recent years.

Our *survey sample* included 133 foster carers who were looking after an unaccompanied child or young person on 31 December 2009. A postal survey provided information on the history and progress of young people, the characteristics and fostering experiences of foster carers, the support being provided to young people and the placements from all sources (professional and informal) and on the foster carers' perceptions of the fostering task and the preparation, training and support they had received during their fostering careers. The survey was supplemented by 23 *case studies*, comprising semi-structured interviews with 23 foster carers and 21 young people, which provided a depth understanding of the fostering experience, three *focus groups* with young people and a detailed *policy study*, including focus groups and key informant interviews with social workers and managers in the children's asylum teams.

Most of the foster carers that participated in the study had considerable experience of fostering and many had fostered a wide range of children and teenagers. They were much more likely to come from minority ethnic backgrounds and to have been born overseas than would be the case with general fostering samples. For some, therefore, experiences of migration and resettlement prefigured their involvement in fostering unaccompanied young people and perhaps attracted them to it. The young people in our survey sample were relatively young on entering the UK (almost all under 16), were mostly male, and a disproportionate majority had arrived from Afghanistan (69%). They had mostly arrived alone, rather than as part of a sibling group, and had entered foster placements that contained partners or other adults and a number of birth, fostered or adopted children. As such, they needed to find their place within a broad network of pre-existing relationships, which most foster carers thought they had managed to achieve quite successfully. Most young people had been living in these placements for more than one year at the time of the study and most were expected to remain until they left care for independence.

Care pathways

Chapter 3 described important changes that have taken place in the legal care status of unaccompanied young people and the implications this has had for their pathways through care and beyond. Earlier studies had found that only a small proportion of unaccompanied young people had been formally looked after through *Section 20* of the Children Act 1989 and that the majority (especially those aged 16 and over at arrival) had been supported as children "in need" under *Section 17*. This distinction was important, since those supported in this way had no legal entitlement to allocated social work support, to care planning and review procedures nor, as they aged, to pathway planning and after-care support (Stone, 2000; Stanley, 2001; Dennis, 2002; Wade *et al*, 2005). For most young people who had taken a *Section 17* pathway in the past, all social work support had ended when they reached 18 years of age (Dixon and Wade, 2007).

Findings from our large census study demonstrated the extent to which this had changed. The vast majority of young people below the age of 18 were being formally looked after by these local authorities on our census date, very few (2%) were being supported in the community as children "in need", and most would therefore have eligibility for after-care support on leaving care. These developments should be welcomed and reflect changes over the past decade in the legal and policy framework governing services for this group.[94]

However, changes in legal status had not led to profound changes in the *placement pathways* of young people. Patterns of accommodation were broadly similar to those identified in earlier studies (cited above). Age continues to be a key driver of placement, with younger children (below 16 years at referral) accessing foster or (to a much lesser extent) residential placements and most older young people moving straight to supported or independent accommodation, with the vast majority being placed in private sector shared housing with (or without) floating support. Other supported options, such as supported lodgings, hostels and training flats continue to be in short supply. These age-related pathways have been reinforced by variations in the level of Home Office Special Grant for those aged under or over 16, the grant local authorities rely upon to provide services to unaccompanied minors (Audit Commission, 2000; Stone, 2000; Wade, 2011).

There is a risk that these pathways may become more (rather than less) divergent in the future. We found some evidence from practitioners that a combination of limited accommodation supply, pressure on foster placements, overall resource shortages in local authorities, and reductions in the level of Special Grant could further constrain young people's access to supportive environments and create pressure to move young people on from foster placements earlier (well before reaching 18). This would run counter to the direction of leaving care legislation and guidance, which has been towards delaying young people's transitions from care beyond 18

---

94 In particular, government clarification in 2003 of the appropriate use of Section 17 and Section 20 of the Children Act 1989 for lone children (Department of Health, LAC(2003)13), including asylum seekers, and the findings of the Hillingdon Judicial Review in 2003 have been influential in gradually increasing the numbers of unaccompanied minors looked after and therefore entitled to receive leaving care services [R. (Beher and others) v Hillingdon Borough Council (2003) EWHC 2075 (Admin)].

(Department for Education, 2010; Munro *et al*, 2010; Munro *et al*, 2011). It would also run counter to recent research identifying the potential protective effects of supportive living environments (in foster care or small group homes) for positive mental health and trauma recovery amongst unaccompanied children (Bean *et al*, 2007a; Hodes *et al*, 2008). It would also act to reverse the direction of travel of the children's asylum teams in this study towards strengthening support and services for the unaccompanied young people in their care. For all of these reasons, these developments would be unwelcome.

Initial assessment

Age therefore acts as an important marker of eligibility for receipt of children's services (being under 18) and for young people's subsequent placement pathways. Age determination has consequently assumed an important place in assessment, although the priority given to it within the assessment process (relative to young people's needs) varies from area to area (Crawley, 2007; Mitchell, 2007). The conduct of age assessments is known to be challenging and local authority approaches have evolved through practice development, the emergence of practice guidelines and developing case law (Levenson and Sharma, 1999; Crawley, 2007; Walker, 2011).[95] All social work teams in this study acknowledged these challenges, including the need to consider young people's different life histories and experiences, cultural perceptions of age-related behaviours, the potential effects of traumatic and flight-related experiences, and the approximate nature of the age-assessment process. Holistic approaches predominated, with particular attention paid to young people's appearance, behaviour and interaction, their social and family history (where known), and their health, capabilities and developmental trajectories.

Practitioners frequently felt constrained by time. Decisions were often needed quickly, but social workers were aware that account also needed to be taken of changes over time. Once provided with a secure base in foster care, some young people blossomed, while others no

---

95 *B v The London Borough of Merton [2003] EWHC 1689 (Admin) (14 July 2003)*

longer felt a self-protective need to act older than they really were. In contrast, some foster carers harboured suspicions that young people were older than their official age. This was sometimes troubling when these young people were placed with younger children or resisted the house rules and a small number of foster carers conducted their own unofficial enquiries through dental or doctors' appointments. Age assessment should therefore be a process, rather than a single event, and (as current guidance suggests) it should adopt a holistic approach over time when reviewing markers of age. However, continuing suspicions were found to have negative effects on relationships of trust between young people and foster carers and tended to act as a barrier to young people becoming fully integrated into family life.

Many social workers and foster carers were able to set aside these concerns and maintain a focus on the needs of children and young people as individuals. These initial encounters were frequently marked by young people's sense of confusion, suspicion and anxiety and were generally conducted through interpreters (see also Kohli and Mather, 2003; Chase, 2010). Young people had taken flight from countries where mistrust of official figures and caution about what information should be revealed was important to safety and survival and therefore affected the potential for trust (Hynes, 2009). Social workers generally understood these worries and the silences that sometimes resulted (Kohli, 2006a). Initial assessment therefore centred on young people's immediate health, placement and educational needs. Social workers sought to reassure young people about their role, as distinct from those of other professionals (medical, immigration, lawyers) who would orbit around them and seek information during this early period, and were alert to signs of particular vulnerabilities in young people. More detailed questions about young people's family backgrounds, their past experiences, reasons for flight and the emotional legacy these had left tended to be postponed until young people were more settled in placement. Time was also often taken at this stage to help reassure young people about what lay ahead and to explain where they would live and what it would be like.

Preparation for foster care

None of the young people in this study had understood the meaning of foster care before they first experienced it. While some had lived with relatives in their countries of origin after becoming separated from their parents, none had lived with non-relatives. As others have found, fostering was an unfamiliar and confusing concept that some young people justifiably associate with a risk of exploitation or less favourable treatment within the home (see Abdullai *et al*, 2002; Mann and Tolfree, 2003; Hek, 2007). An important initial social work task was therefore to explain in simple terms why young people were going to live in foster care, what it would be like living with a family and what kinds of help foster families would provide. This was reassuring to young people, although none remembered being told about the characteristics, composition or lifestyle interests of their foster families or who else would be living in the household, including other foster children. These things matter greatly to young people and help to reduce the obvious anxieties that are linked to moving into territory that is unknown (Farmer *et al*, 2004; Mitchell *et al*, 2010).

The time available for such preparation is usually short. A large proportion of unaccompanied young people require immediate placement on the day of referral to children's services (Wade *et al*, 2005). In keeping with other looked after children, placement-making in these circumstances is heavily constrained by available resources and young people may then need to wait for more durable solutions to be found (Farmer *et al*, 2004; Sinclair *et al*, 2005b). Placements for unaccompanied young people are very often found in the independent fostering sector and, to a lesser extent, outside the boundaries of the responsible authority. In consequence, opportunities for matching young people to foster carers are frequently limited (Sinclair, 2005; Schofield and Beek, 2006) and these constraints were felt keenly by social workers in this study.

Pressure for placement also affected the time available for foster carers to prepare themselves to receive young people into their homes. Most foster carers were only given a few hours notice of a young person's arrival and only very basic information about them. Lack of information at this stage is a matter of wider concern for foster carers (Farmer *et al*, 2004). For most citizen young people entering care, however, children's services have a track record of involvement with the family and with associated professionals and access to documentary evidence about children's needs and experiences. For unaccompanied young people, this is rarely the case. The child is often the sole keeper of their story and information important to care planning can only be garnered slowly over time. In these circumstances, foster carers busied themselves with the generic practical preparations they would make for any young person. Those with prior experience of fostering unaccompanied young people adapted their mental checklists based on their understanding of the unique stresses and pressures on young people at this time. In the early stages of placement, the evolving relationship between foster carer and young person was central to gaining a rounded understanding of each young person's particular needs and experiences that could then, in turn, inform the process of assessment.

Some foster carers had felt better prepared to receive their first unaccompanied young person than were others. Only one-third (34%) of foster carers had felt "well" prepared. Feeling prepared was more likely where foster carers had been born outside of the UK, where the young person was matched to them by religion and/or country of origin, and where they had only ever fostered unaccompanied refugee children. Carers were therefore more likely to have felt ready to foster where they themselves had experiences of migration and of the challenges of making a new home in the UK. It is likely that these experiences drew them towards fostering this group of young people. It may also have led children's services to recognise their potential, to recruit them for this specialist role and therefore have had greater scope to match young people to them.

In contrast, foster carers were less likely to have felt ready where they had fostered for longer, fostered a wider range of young people and where there was no match by religion or country of origin. Despite their greater experience, the challenge of caring for this group of young people was new. These foster carers were more likely to report that, at that time, they had only a very limited understanding of other cultures and of immigration procedures and that they had received only limited (if any) preparation prior to this first placement. It is important, therefore, that social workers are mindful of the additional support needs of experienced foster carers coming to foster this group of young people for the first time. Although these carers had evidently felt less confident, it may be that their social workers had felt that this transition could be made with relative ease, given their greater experience, and that their potential need for specialist training was given insufficient emphasis.

Settling into foster care

Foster care has been described as the coming together of strangers in circumstances where new understandings of intimacy and together-ness have to be co-authored in a short space of time (Rees and Pithouse, 2008). Making an offer of hospitality represents an import-ant first step. By itself, however, it is insufficient. Hosts welcome strangers into the home but tend to retain control, including control over when strangers should leave, and power generally continues to reside with the host, so it is a conditional welcome (Derrida, 2000). An extended period of hospitality may therefore act as a barrier to the development of more intimate relationships. Relationships need to become reciprocal and permit young people to help shape aspects of the culture and practices within the family. In this way, relationships and bonds between young people and their foster carers and young people's sense of belonging are likely to be strengthened (Sirriyeh, forthcoming). A central purpose of this study was to understand how, from very uncertain beginnings as strangers coming together in contexts where they were frequently separated by language, culture, experience and custom, these young people and foster carers were able (in the main) to co-construct positive family-like relationships that helped young people to (re)settle and (re)fashion their lives successfully in what was for them very new and uncertain territory.

As indicated above, many young people first arrived at short notice and frequently late at night. A first action by foster carers was to provide hospitality, to welcome young people into their homes and to provide rest and refuge from what had often been arduous journeys. The transition into foster care is stressful for all young people (Wilson *et al*, 2004; Sinclair, 2005). Most young people had experienced adversity and loss, felt a degree of uncertainty about starting life in new families, starting new schools and settling into life in a new country where their right to citizenship was uncertain (Kohli and Connolly, 2009). Some foster carers were very aware of these pressures and their emotional effects and sought to calm and reassure young people, aware that they needed time to adjust and re-establish a more ordinary rhythm to their lives.

Young people appreciated the efforts of foster carers to make them feel welcome and at home. Where language, religion and customs were shared, this process was made easier. Given the challenges of communication that often existed, however, familiar points of reference were comforting. Welcome signs in the young person's language, the use of a few words of greeting or provision of a welcome pack were interpreted symbolically by young people as signs of inclusion. Young people also appreciated more creative strategies used by foster carers through sign language, joint practical tasks, their attempts to find shared interests and through enquiries into the dietary customs, likes and dislikes of young people. These represented the foundations of relationship-building and were remembered as significant by young people some time later. In similar vein, some foster carers used the internet and libraries to develop their knowledge of young people's countries, cultures and religions in order to educate themselves and to provide familiar reference points for young people, to help them bridge the old and the new. Some social workers and foster carers were mindful that religious and cultural identities are not homogeneous nor are they practised in uniform ways (see Hall, 1996). Some foster carers, therefore, went beyond a simple "cultural checklist" in order to engage in an interactive process of refinement with young people through which they were able to understand and create an experience that took proper account of young people's histories, needs and wishes.

Food had a central place in the accounts of young people and foster carers. In addition to being necessary for survival, comfort and well-being, food and food practices hold a wider symbolic significance for feelings of inclusion and belonging. Food could therefore provide a "first refuge" for young people and an initial psychological fix that would help them to find their bearings (Kohli *et al*, 2010). Many Afghan young people who lived with Afghan, Pakistani or Iranian foster carers mentioned their pleasure at having the scents and tastes of familiar food. However, young people also appreciated the efforts made by foster carers in trans-cultural placements where they demonstrated early on that they were prepared to discover the food that young people liked and to source and prepare it. Preparing meals and eating together helped to cement relationships and involved reciprocal journeys of discovery. Taking young people on shopping expeditions could help to overcome language barriers and provide reassurance that the food purchased met young people's religious needs. Some foster carers delighted in exploring new cuisines that might otherwise have remained closed to them. While this sense of familiarity was important to young people, so too was the exercise of choice and control, which helped to move relationships beyond the limits of hospitality and enabled them to have an influence on the shape of family cultures and practices and, through this, to have stronger feelings of being "at home" (Van Horst, 2004; Sirriyeh, 2010a).

Feeling at home: family integration

Most young people were living in longer-term foster placements. What they wanted from these placements bore considerable similarity to the hopes and expectations of other looked after children (Sinclair, 2005; Hek, 2007; Selwyn *et al*, 2010). They wanted normality, to feel safe and protected and to have a chance to reconstruct an ordinary life after the extraordinary events they had lived through. They wanted to be treated equally to others within the household, to feel that they belonged (to the extent that they needed to) and to have support to resume their education. They also wanted respect for their origins and culture and to have opportunities to reacquaint themselves with cultural practices and connections that were important to them. Of course, some young people wanted to maintain these relationships at a more respectful distance; others found family life more challenging; and many young people acknowledged obstacles to them achieving a "normal" life arising from their social and legal position as asylum seekers and the sense of impermanence to which this gave rise.

From the perspective of foster carers, most of these placements seemed to be working out successfully. Over three-quarters of foster carers felt that the placement had gone "very well", both for them and their young person, and most young people were perceived to have carved out positive relationships with other birth, fostered or adopted children in (and around) the household. A majority of young people were thought to have become quite well integrated into the structure and rhythm of family life. However, foster carers indicated that sizeable minorities of young people had more equivocal feelings about their place within the family and their ability to trust and confide in foster carers, and they suggested that more than one-third had expressed a desire to leave, if not immediately, at some point in the future.

While our findings on family integration are therefore generally positive, it is clear that life together could be challenging. Associations with family integration were not surprising. Young people were perceived to be more integrated into the family when they had lived there longer and where they were not rated as having emotional or behavioural problems. Tensions existed in some placements where young people failed to meet the expectations of foster carers with respect to boundaries and house rules, where they were perceived to be consistently demanding more money and resources than was considered appropriate or where foster carers continued to be troubled by doubts about the authenticity of young people's assessed ages or asylum narratives. These kinds of factors had continuing corrosive effects on relationship-building.

For most young people, therefore, the passage of time had helped to create conditions in which confidence, trust and communication could grow, provided relationships were not unduly troubled by other doubts and behavioural challenges. As wider research has shown, coping with persistent challenging behaviour is a source of great difficulty for foster carers that may create strain, reduce their responsiveness to children and signal a risk of placement breakdown (Quinton *et al*, 1998; Farmer *et al*, 2004; Sinclair *et al*, 2005b).

Family practices: making relationships work

Recent research on family and kinship has tended to turn its gaze from a focus on biological connectedness ("being" family) to a focus on family practices ("doing" family). Family practices describe how kinship relationships and feelings of intimacy and belonging are actively created and reproduced through the regular routines and interactions that are embedded in everyday family life (Morgan, 1996; Finch, 2007; Mason and Tipper, 2008). Family-making is therefore dynamic, relationships are fluid and activities need to be "displayed" so that their meaning is understood by its members before they become embedded as family practices (Finch, 2007). Although this approach has not previously been applied to foster care, it has a clear relevance to young people as new family members learning about existing family practices but also, where it works well, contributing to the creation of new practices as families adjust to their presence. It is this sense of reciprocity in relationships that helps to create a strong feeling of security and belonging and to reduce the feeling of dislocation that can be a legacy of forced migration.

Young people's place and relationships in foster families evolved over time. In many cases these relationships became enriching and sustaining, while some others were unable to flourish. In general terms, three broad types of relationships could be identified:

- *Family-like relationships* – where young people and foster carers established new family-like connections and bonds which were expected to endure beyond the life of the placement.
- *Temporary home bases* – where relationships between young people and foster carers worked well, but where a continuing emotional

distance persisted that delimited the relationship to the period of placement.

- *Lodgings* – where foster carers delivered the contracted service as they saw it, but where young people never felt at home and understood themselves to be lodgers in their homes.

Many foster carers and young people emphasised the importance of displaying family-like behaviour. Showing empathy, care and a willingness to nurture the relationship helped to establish a secure base for young people within the family. Displays of trust were also important to the development of successful relationships (Schofield and Beek, 2006), especially as many young people had come from societies where mistrust was commonplace. Being given responsibility, being entrusted with valuables, having access to space within the home and its resources, being invited to family events and being able to invite friends to visit were all seen as important markers of inclusion within the family. In these circumstances, trust was often reciprocated and young people would gradually begin to confide in their foster carers and perhaps other members of the family, share stories about their past and their dreams and anxieties about the present and future. Foster carers became important witnesses to young people's earlier experiences, holding and containing their emotions and (in some instances) acting as advocates for young people in their dealings with social workers, schools, lawyers and immigration officials. All of these actions served to strengthen the emotional bonds between them and demonstrated to young people that their foster carers were on their side.

Many young people were also able to contribute to the emergence of new family cultures and practices. Flexibility, negotiation and being open to new experiences were recognised as important attributes amongst foster carers willing to make adaptations to their own family lifestyles. Young people also made adjustments, learning to fit into culturally distinctive family practices in ways that paralleled the two-way integration model recommended in much literature on the resettlement of refugees (Castles *et al*, 2002). As we have seen, a willingness to incorporate young people's cuisines, to celebrate their religious and cultural events and to share in young people's particular hobbies and interests was socially inclusive. Time spent on shared activities both reflected and reinforced the quality of family relationships. While not all activities were directly associated with greater family integration, the association was clearest where time was spent on activities that might be expected to improve communication, create closeness and a sense of belonging. These included having friends to visit, preparing meals and eating together, talking to young people about their own families or homelands and listening to their worries and fears. Fun activities, such as picnics in the park or going to sporting events, were also positively associated with greater family integration.

Where young people were matched to foster carers by religion and/or country of origin, joint involvement in religious and cultural activities was higher than was the case for placements not matched in these ways. Despite these patterns of difference, however, there was no association between this kind of matching and whether young people were perceived to be integrated into the family network. They were as likely to feel part of the family, to trust and confide in their carer, to share their personal feelings or, conversely, to feel excluded irrespective of the type of placement. While a matched placement (in these restricted terms) may help young people to develop or reconstruct a sense of cultural connectedness, all placements appeared to have a similar potential to be inclusive and nurturing.

This potential was less likely to be realised where young people felt like they were lodging or the placement was viewed only as a temporary arrangement. Some of these placements exhibited less flexibility and were more rigid in outlook. Adjustments tended to be one way, with young people being required to fit into the household regime. Young people recognised their exclusion and felt sad or angry about their position outside the family unit. Markers of exclusion included separate mealtime arrangements, locked cupboards or rooms, not being entrusted with a key to the house or, in extreme cases, not being allowed in the house if the foster carer was not present. Other markers included their exclusion from family activities or from family holidays and not feeling comfortable about inviting friends to the house. While the willingness of foster carers to demonstrate their care was highly prized by young people, the meaning that underlay overt and covert demonstrations of separateness was also keenly understood.

Supporting educational progress

Schools and colleges represent major sites through which refugee young people are able to re-establish an ordinary rhythm to their lives, learn English, gain qualifications and develop important peer relationships. Foster carers and social workers have important roles to play in assessing young people's skills and interests, facilitating their access to good-quality education, supporting their progress and advocating on their behalf (Candappa, 2000; Wade *et al*, 2005; Kohli, 2007). Refugee young people have diverse educational backgrounds, making careful assessment essential, and the difficulties encountered by many in accessing appropriate education are well documented (Candappa and Egharevba, 2000; Rutter, 2006). Around one-third of young people in this study encountered problems accessing education that was most helpfully resolved (in some cases at least) by social workers, fosters carers and education departments working together to arrange appropriate school places. Where this was not the case, foster carers were sometimes the sole advocates for young people and actions directed at finding the best available solutions also helped to cement their relationships with young people, who valued and remembered the efforts that had been made.

Learning English quickly is important not just to allow young people to take full advantage of mainstream academic courses but also to build confidence and encourage everyday social interactions. Many young people were in need of English language support. Around two-fifths of young people in mainstream schools were receiving additional classroom-based language support and a further fifth were accessing help in community settings, through private or home tuition or through community education centres. Social workers and foster carers were often active in brokering these arrangements and caregivers supplemented this formal tuition by supporting young people's development through everyday family routines using dictionaries, flash cards and the resources of the internet.

Education is generally given a high priority by unaccompanied asylum-seeking young people as part of their journey towards future success and citizenship (Kohli, 2007; Brownlees and Finch, 2010). Sometimes their aspirations could be viewed as unrealistic, given their limited past education experiences and English language skills and the relatively short period of time they have to accomplish these tasks (Kohli, 2007; Watters, 2008). However, the dedication of many young people, sometimes to the exclusion of other aspects of their lives, drew considerable admiration from adults supporting them.

From the perspective of foster carers, most young people were making "quite" (46%) or "very" good progress (25%), but well over one-quarter (29%) were either struggling to catch up or to engage with education. Good progress was more likely where young people had made fewer placement moves in the past, where they had a wider range of hobbies and interests outside school and where they had received positive social work planning and support. However, the two factors that contributed most to young people's educational progress were the absence of emotional and behavioural difficulties and attending courses that were appropriate to their abilities at that time. The former reinforces what is known about risks of poor educational attainment for those with continuing emotional and behavioural problems in adolescence (Farmer *et al*, 2004) and of poor overall outcomes on leaving care (Wade and Dixon, 2006). The latter brings the question of assessment and matching to the fore as a prelude to placing young people on courses appropriate to their abilities, interests and aspirations. Some young people were caught in a cycle of part-time English language tuition or engaged on low-level courses that failed to match their needs. In these circumstances, it is not surprising that young people's motivation tended to suffer and that they went on to do less well. The association between educational progress and social work support is likely to reflect the activities of social workers and foster carers directed at helping young people to access and manage courses that were reasonably well matched to their interests and abilities, liaising with teachers and providing the nurture, equipment and materials needed for successful study.

Linking and bridging: social life beyond the placement

Foster carers and social workers have an important role to play in helping young people to make social connections outside of the placement. The development of social networks has been recognised as an important aspect of successful resettlement. In order for asylum seekers, refugees and other migrants to experience integration, it is important to establish networks that encompass both "social bonds" and "social bridges" (Agar and Strang, 2004; Rutter *et al*, 2007). Social bonds refer to connections within communities defined by ethnic, national or religious identities; social bridges refer to connections *between* communities with different ethnic, national or religious identities.

Helping young people to make religious and cultural connections with others from their countries of origin may help to create initial feelings of comfort, security and companionship and may ease young people's transitions into life in a new country. The development of social bonds may reduce the feelings of dislocation and isolation associated with migration. Opportunities were more common in areas with greater ethnic diversity, although some foster carers living in more mono-cultural areas helped young people to make these connections outside the area of placement. However, some young people who expressed a desire to leave their current placement did so because they were prompted by the need to live in areas that were more ethnically diverse or to be closer to siblings, cousins or other relatives who shared their cultural heritage.

Friendships with other young refugees provided a welcome source of practical advice and support in the early period after arrival and could increase feelings of safety by accompanying young people to social activities. These friendships were also important to the maintenance and renewal of religious practice that helped to centre young people's lives and provide opportunities for companionship and cultural exchange (Ni Raghallaigh, 2011). Many foster carers tried to create environments in which young people could live according to their religious values. However, unless they or other fostered children shared a common faith, the sense of communality associated with religious activities often needed to be found outside the placement and there were many examples of young people communally sharing the rituals surrounding religious and cultural festivals.

Not all young people wanted to create these social bonds to the same degree. While some regularly attended places of worship, prayed at home and followed religious codes and practices, others chose not to or expressed reluctance. Some fluctuated over time in the extent to which they sought out religious or cultural connections. While some young people developed friendship networks that were almost exclusively confined to others from the same ethnic background, others went on to construct social bridges to young people from a wider ethnic range or concentrated almost exclusively on cross-cultural relationships (through choice or lack of a local alternative). It is therefore important to consider the choices that young people make, why they are making them and the constraints on choice that form the context for young people's decision-making. It is also important to be mindful that young people's concepts of religion, culture and identity are fluid; they may evolve and develop over time. Generalising assumptions are therefore not helpful and paying careful attention to what individual young people want, think and say is perhaps the best way to help them retain aspects of their identities that are important to them while simultaneously helping them to move forward in their new lives.

Social bridges to wider networks of young people were commonly created through schools, colleges or involvement in youth, leisure or sporting activities. Schools that provided good welcome and induction procedures, and that had developed peer mentoring arrangements or after-school clubs, tended to create relatively safe and contained environments in which young people could begin to explore relationships with young people from other ethnic backgrounds (see also Hek,

2005a; Beirens and *et al*, 2007). Most young people also led active social lives outside school that introduced them to young people from other backgrounds and helped them to re-establish the routines of everyday life. They recognised the importance of foster carers and their families in sharing these activities with them and linking them into activities they liked that also introduced them to other young people with similar interests. Successful involvement in hobbies and leisure pursuits were also a source of pride to young people, improved their confidence and self-esteem, and could provide a sense of purpose and hope for the future.

Experiences of bullying and racism, however, were not uncommon and acted as a barrier to social integration. These experiences were more common in schools and localities that were culturally homogenous. School responses were variable. While some schools had strong anti-bullying and racist harassment policies and acted quickly in response to complaints from young people and their foster families, others did not. This led some young people to develop self-protective strategies with other refugee or minority ethnic young people as a defence against verbal and physical abuse that could in turn expose them to negative responses from schools.

Within communities, some young people took measures to avoid threats, by socialising in different areas or withdrawing from particular social activities. Foster carers and social workers commented on the particular experiences of young Afghan males, who were often targeted for racist hostility, linking these experiences to the war in Afghanistan and the presence of British soldiers, their visibility as the largest group of unaccompanied minors currently in the UK and on the community pressures experienced by some foster carers to dissuade them from fostering this group of children. Some Afghan young people mentioned that they had initially concealed their identities (as Afghans and as asylum seekers) as best they could, while others spoke less about their ethnic origin and more about their position as community outsiders, a position that sometimes eased as their presence became more familiar and as their grasp of English enabled them to communicate with local peers more readily. Some found these social bridges too difficult to cross, the differences in cultural and religious values too great a divide, and chose to socialise only with young people who shared a common value base. Whatever response to these difficulties young people adopt, helping them to negotiate pathways into the wider world involves foster carers in a range of complex tasks that require understanding, empathy, guidance and a willingness to take young people's side and advocate on their behalf when tensions do arise.

Preparing for the future: transition and immigration

Most unaccompanied young people first arrive in the UK as teenagers. The time available to help them prepare for adulthood is therefore frequently compressed and should provide a focus to the work of foster carers and social workers. Thinking about the future is often unwelcome, as it brings to young people's minds the uncertainties that arise from the immigration and asylum process. As looked after children, most unaccompanied young people are protected by the provisions of the Children (Leaving Care) Act 2000. Social workers, in partnership with foster carers, have duties to prepare young people for adult life, to prepare pathway plans and provide ongoing support at least to the point where young people become "unlawfully present in the UK" (Department for Education, 2010).

Foster carers and social workers had a key role in helping to equip young people with the practical and interpersonal life skills they would need once they had moved on, in providing emotional and companionable support to ease young people's transitions to their own accommodation, to help them move and settle in, and to provide stability and continuity in these relationships through patterns of continuing contact once this transition had been made. Continuing links are important not just for the practical and emotional support they provide but also for young people's symbolic connection to family through involvement in key family events and rituals. Research on leaving care has pointed to the gradual erosion of these connections over time (Fry, 1992; Wade, 2008). Most foster carers in this study expressed a willingness to stay involved in the young people's lives.

Some also expected their young people to stay with them beyond the formal age of leaving (at 18) and were prepared to advocate with children's services on their behalf. This was more likely where young people were perceived to be strongly integrated within the family, where things were going well and where young people exhibited few behaviour problems. This is consistent with wider findings on leaving care, which suggest that young people with more complex needs are more likely to leave care earlier than those who settle and do well (Dixon *et al*, 2006; Munro *et al*, 2011).

Many young people were approaching adulthood without a settled asylum status. Pathway planning was profoundly affected by uncertainties arising from the asylum determination process. Lack of status created great anxiety for young people that, for some, profoundly affected their mental and emotional health. The fact that, in today's political climate, most young people will be forced to return to their countries of origin on reaching adulthood has reinforced the need for planning to simultaneously take account of all potential outcomes of the asylum process and for plans to be adjusted as young people's pathways (within the UK or in their countries of origin) become clearer (see also Dorling, 2009; Department for Education, 2010). Preparation for young people to return to their countries of origin should therefore form an important strand of pathway planning. Facing up to this prospect was difficult for young people, foster carers and social workers. Although communication about the future was often difficult, it is important to avoid drift, for planning to be realistic, and for it to take account of all the options and pathways open to young people to enable them to make informed decisions about the future, even where this is unlikely to be in the UK.

Most young people found the asylum process bewildering. They were generally reliant on interpreters, who they sometimes found difficult to understand. They needed good legal representation, which recent cuts to Legal Aid budgets and a reduction in specialist legal firms has made more challenging to find (Nandy, 2007; Brownlees and Smith, 2011). As the adults who have formed the closest bonds with young people, social workers and foster carers have an important support role. Young people needed their help to arrange solicitors, monitor the progress of their claims, help them to understand the meanings conveyed in these encounters and to provide emotional support and advocacy. There were some tensions between foster carers and social workers in interpreting their respective roles. While some foster carers took on this work willingly, feeling they were best placed to provide the help young people needed, others felt less confident, more reluctant, and that social workers were sometimes abdicating their responsibilities. Getting this balance right for individual foster carers is clearly important. While improved training for foster carers may help to increase confidence, it is clear that foster carers have differing perceptions about where the boundaries of the fostering role lie and requests for them to take on this work should therefore be a matter of careful negotiation.

Supporting foster carers

Foster carers need opportunities to access ongoing training and advice and they depend upon consistent predictable support from social workers to help them perform their role successfully. Most foster carers (82%) felt that the training and advice that had been provided for them had been broadly sufficient for their needs. However, foster carer satisfaction was higher in relation to what might be termed the core set of fostering skills, those required to look after any foster child, and somewhat lower in relation to the specific skills needed to care for unaccompanied young people. For example, around one-fifth to one-quarter of foster carers felt they had lacked support in dealing with legal and immigration officials, in meeting young people's dietary needs, helping them to make cultural connections, working with uncertainty about the future, and also in relation to help with language and communication. These findings help to explain the lack of confidence on immigration matters described by some foster carers and, as discussed earlier, the lack of readiness amongst some foster carers, especially amongst those who had no previous experience of migration, to receive their first unaccompanied child. Further attention should therefore be given to the specific training needs of this group of foster carers and for these skills to be reviewed and updated on a regular basis.

Although foster carers received support from a wide and inter-locking network of people, the support upon which they most relied was generally quite narrow. The crucial role of the supervising social worker was highlighted, followed quite closely by immediate family members and, to a lesser extent, specialist children's social workers. This order of priorities is consistent with wider research showing that foster carers are generally more appreciative of the support provided by supervising social workers when compared to children's social workers (Farmer et al, 2004; Sinclair et al, 2004; Murray et al, 2011). Other people also had their part to play and some, such as other foster carers (individually and in support groups), relatives and friends were relied upon quite heavily at times.

Foster carers appreciated social work support where social workers visited regularly, were accessible outside of visits (by telephone, text or email), listened carefully, were responsive and did what they said they would do, and treated foster carers with respect, valued the work they did and included them in planning and decision-making (see also Triseliotis et al, 2000; Kirton et al, 2004; Sinclair et al, 2004). Not surprisingly, satisfaction with support from supervising social workers correlated with that from children's social workers. In other words, foster carers were most satisfied where professionals worked with them and with each other in relative harmony to provide a constructive overall package of support for the young person and the foster family.

Young people appreciated frequent and regular contact from their social workers as a sign that they were genuinely interested in their well-being. Frequent contact was also associated with young people doing well overall. Beyond their role in care planning and review, foster carers viewed the key role of children's social workers to lie in their access to networks and resources (financial resources, access to education and language support, health information and service access) and in relation to the asylum process. However, they also highlighted the advice, guidance and emotional support and encouragement that good social workers consistently offered to young people. Social workers drew criticism where they were physically or emotionally distant, where they were overly preoccupied with bureaucratic procedures and routines, or where foster carers felt excluded by them from consultation and decision-making.

A last word . . .

Despite these elements of frustration, the overall findings from this study are broadly positive. The foster carers who took part overwhelmingly expressed satisfaction with their experience of fostering and felt that it had enriched their lives. Most showed a very high degree of commitment to the young people in their care. They obviously liked them immensely, took considerable pride in the progress they had made and, despite the obvious challenges that had arisen along the way, felt a strong sense of reward for the contribution they had made to their successful resettlement.

Not only had foster carers opened their homes to young people, in many cases they had allowed young people to make an imprint on the routines and practices of family life, to make changes to the cultural life of their families. By being adaptive, flexible and willing to negotiate, many foster carers and young people had managed to create a network of family-like relationships that provided young people with a secure and supportive home base from which to explore life beyond the boundary of the home. Of course, not all young people were this fortunate, and where they lived only as lodgers or as temporary members of families, the relationships between young people and their foster carers were less likely to have flourished. Although these placements may have worked, in the sense of providing a period of stability, young people were more likely to have experienced placement life as outsiders in the home or as temporary residents without realising the warm and empathic relationships that were evident in other foster families.

Even though many young people were described as being easy to care for, foster carers were nonetheless presented with many challenges. The experience of forced migration was often underpinned by the death or persecution of family members or by young people's own experiences of threat or exploitation. Inevitably, foster carers found listening to these stories and, in some instances, helping young people to record them in support of their asylum claims, difficult to witness. Where foster carers were able to ease the emotional burden that young people carried with them, this was highly valued and helped to strengthen the bonds between them. Not infrequently, young people also presented behavioural challenges and resisted the boundaries and discipline of foster homes. Others pressed for access to greater material resources, causing strain within the household and with other foster or birth children living there. Tensions were also evident at cultural borders, emerging in relation to gender roles, social customs and norms of behaviour. Not all foster carers managed these tensions successfully. Where they did (and had sufficient support to help them at difficult moments) young people tended to settle, thrive and develop new feelings of belonging. In these circumstances, foster carers were viewed as parent figures, companions and confidantes, contributing towards young people's new and emerging sense of citizenship.

It is also important, however, for us to be mindful of the wider context to this study. Only a minority of unaccompanied children and young people ever get to experience foster care. As we have seen, most young people move straight to semi-independent or independent living, especially those aged 16 or 17 years at referral. The range of supported accommodation continues to be quite restricted. Most young people move on to private sector shared housing, the quality of which we know is highly variable. The pressures on fostering resources are also intensifying. As local authorities receive increasing numbers of children into the care system, as they have done in recent years, these pressures are likely to grow and opportunities to choose placements that are well suited to the needs of young people will become more restricted, at least for the foreseeable future.[96] Reductions in the resources available to local authorities and,

---

96 See, for example, Taylor J. and Lakhani, N. 'Foster system at breaking point as 10,000 children go into care', *The Independent*, 12 April 2012.

specifically, in the Home Office Special Grant that funds work with unaccompanied minors, will add to these difficulties. Foster care is relatively expensive, when compared to other housing options, and the children's asylum teams in this study were experiencing pressure to reduce the numbers in foster care and/or to move young people on to independent living at an earlier age, even though this is at odds with the direction of child welfare and leaving care policies for citizen young people.

There is no doubt that good foster care can make a positive difference to the lives of many unaccompanied young people, even though some may not choose it or adapt to it successfully. We know that it can be protective of the mental health and emotional well-being of young refugees, many of whom benefit from its shelter as they recover from past traumas and orient themselves to everyday life in the UK. We now know that, at its best, it provides for warm family-like relationships that can be transformative for young people and foster families alike. Whether it can deliver the grounded and continuous relationships that will support young people through the transition to adulthood could not be assessed through this study, although the initial signs offered some encouragement. There is therefore a strong case for more of it to be available to refugee young people. However, today's economic and policy environment is not encouraging. Local authorities are experiencing a period of retrenchment and have to prioritise their services carefully. The extent to which resource restrictions will fall disproportionately on asylum-seeking children and young people will provide an important test of our understanding of citizenship and of the needs of one of the most marginalised groups of young people in our society.

Today's policies on asylum and immigration give weight and emphasis to exclusion. However we may feel about these policies, many asylum-seeking young people will be forced to return to their countries of origin as young adults (if not before) and some may eventually choose to do so. It is therefore important that preparation for return is properly included as one strand of pathway planning. For young people who may eventually face deportation, it is important that the time they do spend in the UK helps to prepare them properly for the journey that their lives will take, provides them with a range of qualifications and skills that will help them to thrive, ensures that they are able to participate in all the decisions that affect them, and properly prepares them for adult life, whether that proves ultimately to be within the UK or elsewhere.

References

Abdullai M., Dorbor E. and Tolfree D. (2002) *Case Study of the Care and Protection of Separated Children in the Sinje Refugee Camp, Liberia*, London: Save the Children

Agar A. and Strang A. (2004) *Indicators of Integration: Final report*, Home Office Development and Practice Report, London: Home Office

Ahearn F. L. (ed) (2000) *Psychological Wellness of Refugees: Issues of qualitative and quantitative research*, New York, NY: Berghahn Books

Aitkin S. C. (2001) 'Global crises of childhood: rights, justice and the unchild-like child', *Area*, 33, pp 119–127

Anthias F. (2006) 'Belongings in a globalising and unequal world: rethinking translocations', in Yuval-Davis N., Kannabiran K. and Vieten U. (eds) *The Situated Politics of Belonging*, London: Sage, pp 17–31

Audit Commission (2000) *Another Country: Implementing dispersal under the Immigration and Asylum Act 1999*, London: Audit Commission for Local Authorities and the National Health Service in England and Wales

Ayotte W. (1999) *Supporting Unaccompanied Children in the Asylum Process*, London: Save the Children

Ayotte W. (2000) *Separated Children Coming to Western Europe: Why they travel and how they arrive*, London: Save the Children

Ayotte W. and Williamson L. (2001) *Separated Children in the UK: An overview of the current situation*, London: Save the Children

Barrie L. and Mendes P. (2011) 'The experiences of unaccompanied asylum-seeking children in and leaving the out-of-home care system in the UK and Australia: a critical review of the literature', *International Social Work*, 54:4, pp 485–503

Bean T., Derluyn I., Eurelings-Bontekoe E., Broekaert E. and Spinhoven P. (2007a) 'Comparing psychological distress, traumatic stress reactions, and experiences of unaccompanied refugee minors with experiences of adolescents accompanied by parents', *The Journal of Nervous and Mental Disease*, 195:4, pp 288–97

Bean T., Eurelings-Bontekoe E. and Spinhoven P. (2007b) 'Course and predictors of mental health of unaccompanied refugee minors in the Netherlands: one year follow-up', *Social Science and Medicine*, 64, pp 1204–15

Bebbington A. and Miles J. (1990) 'The supply of foster families for children in care', *British Journal of Social Work*, 20:4, pp 283–307

Beek M. and Schofield G. (2004) *Providing A Secure Base in Long-term Foster Care*, London: BAAF

Beirens H., Mason P., Spicer N., Hughes N. and Hek R. (2006) *Preventative Services for Asylum Seeking Children: A final report to the national evaluation of the Children's Fund*, London: Department for Education and Skills

Beirens H., Hughes N., Hek R. and Spicer N. (2007) 'Preventing social exclusion of refugee and asylum seeking children: building new networks', *Social Policy and Society*, 6:2, pp 219–29

Berger J. (1984) *And Our Faces, My Heart, Brief as Photos*, London: Bloomsbury Publishing

Berridge D. (2007) 'Theory and explanation in child welfare: education and looked-after children', *Child and Family Social Work*, 12, pp 1–10

Berridge D. and Brodie I. (1998) *Children's Homes Revisited*, London: Jessica Kingsley Publishers

Berridge D. and Saunders H. (2009) 'The education of fostered and adopted children', in Schofield G. and Simmonds J. (eds), *The Child Placement Handbook*, London: BAAF, pp 327–44

Berry J. (1992) 'Acculturation and adaptation in a new society', *International Migration*, 30, pp 69–85

Bhabha J. and Finch N. (2006) *Seeking Asylum Alone: Unaccompanied and separated children and refugee protection in the UK*, Harvard, MA: Harvard University Committee on Human Rights Studies

Biehal N. (2009) 'Foster care for adolescents', in Schofield G. and Simmonds J. (eds), *The Child Placement Handbook*. London: BAAF, pp 159–77

Biehal N., Clayden J., Stein M. and Wade J. (1995) *Moving On: Young people and leaving care schemes*, London: HMSO

Biehal N., Ellison S., Baker C. and Sinclair I. (eds) (2009) *Characteristics, Outcomes and Meanings of Three Types of Permanent Placement*, London: Department for Children, Schools and Families

Biehal N., Ellison S., Sinclair I. and Baker C. (2010) *Belonging and Permanence: Outcomes in long-term foster care and adoption*, London: BAAF

Bjornberg U. (2011) 'Social relationships and trust in asylum seeking families in Sweden', *Sociological Research Online*, 16:1, available at: www.socresonline.org.uk/16/1/5.html

Blackwell D. (1997) 'Holding, containing and bearing witness: the problem of helpfulness in encounters with torture survivors', *Journal of Social Work*, 11:2, pp 81–89

Bourdieu P. (1984) *Distinction: A social critique of the judgement of taste*, London: Routledge

Boyden J. and de Berry J. (2004) *Children and Youth on the Front Line: Ethnography, armed conflict and displacement*, New York, NY: Berghan Books

Broad B. and Robbins I. (2005) 'The wellbeing of unaccompanied asylum seekers leaving care', *Diversity in Health and Social Care*, 2:4, pp 271–77

Bronstein I. and Montgomery P. (2011) 'Psychological distress in refugee children: a systematic review', *Clinical Child and Family Psychology Review*, 14:1, pp 44–56

Brown J., Sintzel J., George N. and Arnault D. (2010) 'Benefits of transcultural fostering', *Child and Family Social Work*, 15, pp 276–85

Brownlees L. and Finch N. (2010) *Levelling the Playing Field*, London: UNICEF

Brownlees L. and Smith T. (2011) *Lives in the Balance: The quality of immigration legal advice given to separated children seeking asylum*, London: Refugee Council

Cameron C., Bennert K., Simon A. and Wigfall V. (2007) *Using Health Education, Housing and Other Services: A study of care leavers and young people in difficulty (Research Brief)*, London: Thomas Coram Research Institute, Institute of Education, London and University of London

Candappa M. (2000) 'The right to education and an adequate standard of living: refugee children in the UK', *International Journal of Children's Rights*, 8:3, pp 261–70

Candappa M. and Egharevba I. (2000) *Extraordinary Childhoods: The social lives of refugee children*, Children 5–16 Research Briefing, Hull: ESRC Children 5–16 Research Programme

Carsten J. (ed) (2000) *Cultures of Relatedness: New approaches to the study of kinship*, Cambridge: Cambridge University Press

Castles S., Korac M., Vasta E. and Vertovec S. (2002) *Integration: Mapping the field*, London: Home Office Immigration Research and Statistics Service

Castles S. and Miller M. (1998) *The Age of Migration*, New York, NY: Guilford Press

Chase E. (2010) 'Agency and silence: young people seeking asylum alone in the UK', *British Journal of Social Work*, 40:7, pp 2050–68

Chase E., Knight A. and Statham J. (2008) *The Emotional Well-Being of Unaccompanied Young People Seeking Asylum in the UK*, London: BAAF

Clarke H. (2009) *Getting the Support they Need: Findings of a survey of foster carers in the UK*, London: The Fostering Network

Cleaver H. (2000) *Fostering Family Contact*, London: The Stationery Office

Council of the European Union (2003) *Laying Down Minimum Standards for the Reception of Asylum Seekers, Council Directive 2003/9/EC*, Brussels: European Council on Refugees and Exiles (ECRE)

Courtney M., Dworsky A., Ruth G., Keller T., Havlicek J. and Bost N. (2005) *Midwest Evaluation of the Adult Functioning of Former Foster Youth: Outcomes at age 19*, Chicago, IL: Chapin Hall Centre for Children, University of Chicago

Crawley H. (2004) *Working with Children and Young People Subject to Immigration Control: Guidelines for best practice*, London: Immigration Law Practitioners' Association

Crawley H. (2007) *When is a Child Not a Child? Asylum, age disputes and the process of age assessment*, London: Immigration Law Practitioners Association

Crawley H. (2010) *Chance or Choice? Understanding why asylum seekers come to the UK*, London: Refugee Council

Dando I. and Minty B. (1987) 'What makes good foster parents?', *British Journal of Social Work*, 17, pp 383–400

Davidson A. (2008) 'The play of identity, memory and belonging: Chinese migrants in Sydney', in Kwah-Pearce K. and Davidson A. (eds) *At Home in the Chinese Diaspora: Memories, identities and belongings*, Basingstoke: Palgrave Macmillan, pp 12–32

Davis N., Kannabirān K. and Vieten U. (eds) *The Situated Politics of Belonging*, London: Sage

Dennis J. (2002) *A Case for Change: How refugee children in England are missing out*, London: The Children's Society, Refugee Council and Save the Children

Dennis J. (2005) *Ringing the Changes: The impact of guidelines on the use of sections 17 and 20 of the Children Act 1989 to support unaccompanied asylum seeking children*, London: Refugee Council

Department for Children, Schools and Families (2009) *Statistical First Release, Children Looked After in England (Including Adoption and Care Leavers) Year Ending 31st March 2009*, London: Department for Children, Schools and Families

Department for Education (2010) *The Children Act 1989 Guidance and Regulations Volume 3: Planning transition to adulthood for care leavers*, London: Department for Education

Department of Health (1995) *Unaccompanied Asylum Seeking Children: Training pack*, London: Department of Health

Department of Health (2000) *Framework for the Assessment of Children in Need and their Families*, London: The Stationery Office

Department of Health (2001) *Children (Leaving Care) Act 2000: Regulations and Guidance*, London: Department of Health

Department of Health (2003) *Guidance on Accommodating Children in Need and their Families, LAC(2003)13*, London: Department of Health

Derrida J. (2000) 'Hospitality', *Angelaki*, 5:3, pp 3–18

Dixon J. and Stein M. (2005) *Leaving Care: Throughcare and aftercare in Scotland*, London: Jessica Kingsley Publishers

Dixon J., Wade J., Byford S., Weatherly H. and Lee J. (2006) *Young People Leaving Care: A study of costs and outcomes. Final Report to the Department for Education and Skills*, York: University of York

Dixon J. and Wade J. (2007) 'Leaving "care"? Transition planning and support for unaccompanied young people', in Kohli R. and Mitchell F. (eds) *Working with Unaccompanied Asylum Seeking Children*, Basingstoke: Palgrave Macmillan, pp 125–40

Dona G. (2001) *The Rwandan Experience of Fostering Separated Children*, Stockholm: Save the Children Sweden

Dorling K. (2009) *Seeking Support: A guide to the rights and entitlements of separated refugee and asylum seeking children*, London: Children's Legal Centre

Dunkerley D., Scourfield T., Maegusuku-Hewett T. and Smalley N. (2005) 'The experiences of frontline staff working with children seeking asylum', *Social Policy and Administration*, 39:6, pp 640–52

Farmer E., Moyers S. and Lipscombe S. (2004) *Fostering Adolescents*, London: Jessica Kingsley Publishers

Farmer T. W., Estell D. B., Hall C. M., Pearl R., Van Acker R. and Rodkin P. C. (2008) 'Interpsersonal competence configurations, behaviour problems and social adjustment in preadolescence', *Journal of Emotional and Behavioural Disorders*, 16, pp 195–212

Free E. (2006) *Unaccompanied Refugees and Asylum Seekers Turning 18: A guide for social workers and other professionals*, London: Save the Children

Finch J. (2007) 'Displaying families', *Sociology*, 41:1, pp 65–81

Fink C. (2001) *Living Silence: Myanmar under military rule*, London: Zed Books

Fry E. (1992) *After Care: Making the most of foster care*, London: National Foster Care Association

Geenen S. and Powers L. E. (2007) '"Tomorrow is another problem": the experiences of youth in foster care during their transition into adulthood', *Children and Youth Service Review*, 29:8, pp 1085–1101

Ghorashi H. (2007) 'Giving silence a chance: the importance of life stories for research on refugees', *Journal of Refugee Studies*, 21:1, pp 117–32

Giddens A. (1991) *Modernity and Self Identity: Self and society in the Late Modern Age*, Cambridge: Polity

Gifford S., Bakopanos C., Kaplan I. and Correa-Velez I. (2007) 'Meaning or measurement? Researching the social contexts of health and settlement among newly-arrived refugee youth in Melbourne, Australia', *Journal of Refugee Studies*, 20:3, pp 414–440

Gilbert A. and Koser K. (2006) 'Coming to the UK: what do asylum-seekers know about the UK before arrival?', *Journal of Ethnic and Migration Studies*, 32:7, pp 1209–25

Gilligan R. (2001) *Promoting Resilience: a resource guide on working with children in the care system*, London: BAAF

Gilligan R. (2007a) 'Adversity, resilience and the educational progress of young people in public care', *Emotional and Behavioural Difficulties*, 12:2, pp 135–45

Gilligan R. (2007b) 'Spare time activities for young people in care: what can they contribute to educational progress?', *Adoption & Fostering*, 31:1, pp 93–99

Gilroy P. (1993a) *There Ain't No Black in the Union Jack*, London: Hutchinson

Gilroy P. (1993b) *The Black Atlantic: Modernity and double consciousness*, London: Verso

Goodman J. H. (2004) 'Coping with trauma and hardship among unaccompanied refugee youth from Sudan', *Quality Health Research*, 14, pp 1177–96

Groark C., Sclare I. and Raval H. (2011) 'Understanding the experiences and emotional needs of unaccompanied asylum-seeking adolescents in the UK', *Clinical Child Psychology and Psychiatry*, 16:3, pp 421–42

Hage G. (1997) 'At home in the entrails of the west: multiculturalism, ethnic food and migrant home-building', in Grace H., Hage G., Johnson L., Langsworth J. and Symonds M. (eds), *Home/World: Space, community and marginality in Sydney's West*, Melbourne: Pluto Press

Hall S. (1996) 'Who needs "identity"?', in Hall S. and Du Gay P. (eds) *Questions of Cultural Identity*, London: Sage, pp 1–17

Harris M. J. and Openheimer D. (2001) *Into the Arms of Strangers: Stories of the Kindertransport*, London: Bloomsbury

Hek R. (2005a) *The Experiences and Needs of Refugees and Asylum Seeking Children in the UK: A literature review*, London: Department for Work and Pensions

Hek R. (2005b) 'The role of education in the settlement of young refugees in the UK: the experiences of young refugees', *Practice*, 17:3, pp 157–71

Hek R. (2007) 'Using foster placements for the care and resettlement of unaccompanied children', in Kohli R. and Mitchell F. (eds), *Social Work with Unaccompanied Asylum Seeking Children*, Basingstoke: Palgrave Macmillan

Hemmerman L., Law I., Simms J. and Sirriyeh A. (2007) *Situating Racist Hostility and Understanding the Impact of Racist Victimisation in Leeds*, Leeds: Centre for Ethnicity and Racism Studies

Hodes M., Jagdev D., Chandra N. and Cunniff A. (2008) 'Risk and resilience for psychological distress amongst unacccompanined asylum seeking adolescents', *The Journal of Child Psychology and Psychiatry*, 49:7, pp 723–32

Home Office (2000) *Policy Bulletin 33: Age disputes*, London: The Home Office, Immigration and Nationality Directorate

Home Office (2002) *Unaccompanied Asylum Seeking Children Information Note*, London: Home Office

Home Office (2010) *Control of Immigration: Statistics United Kingdom 2009*, Home Office Statistical Bulletin, London: Home Office

Hopkins P. and Hill M. (2008) 'Pre-flight experiences and migration stories: the accounts of unaccompanied asylum-seeking children', *Children's Geographies*, 6:3, pp 257–68

Hubbard P. (2005) 'Accomodating otherness: anti-asylum centre protest and the maintenance of white privilege', *Transactions of the Institute of British Geographers*, 30:1, pp 52–65

Humphries B. and Mynott E. (2001) *Young Separated Refugees in Greater Manchester*, London: Save the Children

Hynes P. (2003) *The Issue of 'Trust' or 'Mistrust' in Research with Refugees: Choices, caveats and considerations for researchers, new issues in refugee research*, Evaluation and Policy Analysis Unit, Geneva: UNHCR

Hynes P. (2009) 'Contemporary compulsory dispersal and the absense of space for the restoration of trust', *Journal of Refugee Studies*, 22:1, pp 97–121

Jackson S. (2002) 'Promoting stability and continuity in care away from home', in McNeish D., Newman T. and Roberts R. (eds), *What Works for Children?*, Buckingham: Open University Press

Jackson S., Ajayi S. and Quigley M. (2005) *Going to University from Care*, Institute of Education, London: University of London

Jenkins R. (2008) *Social Identity*, London: Routledge

Jones C. (1998) 'The educational needs of refugee children', in Rutter J. and Jones C. (eds), *Refugee Education: Mapping the field*, Stoke-on-Trent: Trentham Books

Jones C. and Hackett S. (2011) 'The role of "family practices" and "displays of family" in the creation of adoptive kinship', *British Journal of Social Work*, 41:1, pp 40–56

Judge R. (2010) 'Refugee advocacy and the biopolitics of asylum in Britain: the precarious position of young male asylum seekers and refugees', *Refugee Studies Centre Working Papers*, Oxford: Refugee Studies Centre

Kearney M. (2007) 'Friends and family care of unaccompanied children: recognising the possible and the potential', in Kohli R. and Mitchell F. (eds), *Working with Unaccompanied Asylum Seeking Children: Issues for policy and practice*, Basingstoke: Palgrave Macmillan

Khan P. (2000) 'Asylum-seekers in the UK: implications for social service involvement', *Social Work and Social Science Review*, 8:2, pp 116–29

Kidane S. (2001a) *Food, Shelter and Half a Chance: Assessing the needs of unaccompanied asylum seeking and refugee children*, London: BAAF

Kidane S. (2001b) *I Did Not Choose to Come Here: Listening to refugee children*, London: BAAF

Kidane S. and Amarena P. (2004) *Fostering Unaccompanied Asylum Seeking Children: A training course for foster carers*, London: BAAF

Kidane S. and Amarena P. (2005) *Looking After Unaccompanied Asylum Seeking and Refugee Children: A training course for social care professionals*, London: BAAF

Kirton D., Beecham J. and Ogilvie K. (2004) *Remuneration and Performance in Foster Care: Report to the Department for Education and Skills*, Canterbury: University of Kent

Kohli R. K. S. (2006a) 'The sound of silence: listening to what unaccompanied asylum-seeking children say and do not say', *British Journal of Social Work*, 36:5, pp 707–21

Kohli R. K. S. (2006b) 'The comfort of strangers: social work practice with unaccompanied asylum-seeking children and young people in the UK', *Child & Family Social Work*, 11:1, pp 1–10

Kohli R. K. S. (2007) *Social Work with Unaccompanied Asylum Seeking Children*, Basingstoke: Palgrave Macmillan

Kohli R. K. S. and Connolly H. (2009) 'Transitions for young people seeking asylum', in Petch A. (ed), *Managing Transitions: Support for individuals at key points of change*, Bristol: The Policy Press

Kohli R. K. S., Connolly H. and Warman A. (2010) 'Food and its meaning for asylum seeking children and young people in foster care', *Children's Geographies*, 8:3, pp 233–45

Kohli R. K. S. and Mather R. (2003) 'Promoting psychosocial well-being in unaccompanied asylum seeking young people in the United Kingdom', *Child and Family Social Work*, 8:3, pp 201–12

Kramer A.-M. (2011) 'Kinship, affinity and connectedness: exploring the role of genealogy in personal lives', *Sociology*, 45:3, pp 379–94

Kunz E. (1981) 'Exile and resettlement: refugee theory', *International Migration Review*, 15:1, pp 42–51

Lawler S. (2008) *Identity: Sociological perspectives*, Cambridge: Polity Press

Lemos G. (2005) *The Search for Tolerance: Challenging and changing racist attitudes and behaviour among young people*, York: Joseph Rowntree Foundation

Levenson R. and Sharma A. (1999) *The Health of Refugee Children: Guidelines for paediatricians*, London: Royal College of Paediatrics and Child Health

Lewis H. (2010) 'Community moments: integration and transnationalism at "refugee" parties and events', *Journal of Refugee Studies*, 23:4, pp 571–88

Lewis J. D. and Weigert A. J. (1981) 'The structures and meanings of social time', *Social Forces*, 60:2, pp 432–62

Linowitz J. and Boothby N. (1988) 'Cross-cultural placements', in Ressler E., Boothby N. and Steinbock D. (eds), *Unaccompanied Children: Care and protection in wars*, Oxford: Natural Disasters and Refugee Movements, Oxford University Press

Luster T., Qin D., Bates L., Rana M. and Lee J. A. (2010) 'Successful adaptation among Sudanese unaccompanied minors: perspectives of youth and foster parents', *Childhood*, 17:2, pp 197–211

Luster T., Saltarelli A., Rana M., Qin D., Bates L., Burdick K. and Baird D. (2009) 'The experiences of Sudanese unaccompanied minors in foster care', *Journal of Family Psychology*, 23:3, pp 386–95

Macdonald G. and Turner W. (2005) 'An experiment in helping foster carers manage challenging behaviour', *British Journal of Social Work*, 35:18, pp 1265–82

Macey M. (1995) 'Same race adoption policy: anti-racism or racism?', *Journal of Social Policy*, 24:4, pp 473–91

Mankekar P. (2005) '"India shopping": Indian grocery stores and transnational configurations of belonging', in Watson J. L. and Caldwell M. L.

(eds), *The Cultural Politics of Food and Eating: A Reader*, Oxford: Blackwell, pp 197–214

Mann G. and Tolfree D. (2003) *Children's Participation in Research: Reflections from the Care and Protection of Separated Children in Emergencies Project*, Stockholm: Save the Children

Marriot K. (2001) *Living in Limbo: Young separated refugees in the West Midlands*, West Midlands: Save the Children

Mason J. and Tipper B. (2008) 'Being related: how children define and create kinship', *Childhood*, 15:4, pp 441–60

Masten A. S. and Powell J. L. (2003) 'A resilience framework for research, policy and practice', in Luther S. S. (ed), *Resilience and Vulnerability: Adaptation in the context of childhood adversities*, New York, NY: Cambridge University Press

McCann J., James A., Wilson S. and Dunn G. (1996) 'Prevalence of psychiatric disorders in young people in the care system', *British Medical Journal*, 313, pp 1529–30

McMillen J. C., Zima B. T., Scott L. D., Auslander W. F., Munson M. R., Ollie M. T. and Spitznagel E. L. (2005) 'Prevalence of psychiatric disorders among older youths in the foster care system', *Journal of the American Academy of Child and Adolescent Psychiatry*, 44:1, pp 88–95

Meltzer H. (2003) *The Mental Health of Young People Looked After By Local Authorities in England*, London: HMSO

Minority Rights Group International (ed) (1998) *Forging New Identities: Young refugee and minority students tell their stories*, London: Minority Rights Group

Mitchell F. (2003) 'The social services response to unaccompanied children in England', *Child and Family Social Work*, 8:3, pp 179–89

Mitchell F. (2007) 'Assessment practice with unaccompanied children: exploring perceptions to the problem', in Kohli R. K. S. and Mitchell F. (eds), *Working with Unaccompanied Asylum Seeking Children*, Basingstoke: Palgrave Macmillan

Mitchell M., Kucynski L., Tubbs C. and Ross C. (2010) 'We care about care: advice by children in care for children in care, foster parents and child welfare workers about the transition into foster care', *Child & Family Social Work*, 15:2, pp 176–85

Modood T. (2007) *Mulitculturalism: A civic idea*, Cambridge: Polity Press

Morgan D. H. J. (1996) *Family Connections*, Cambridge: Polity Press

Mosselson J. (2007) 'Masks of achievement: an experiential study of Bosnian female refugees in New York city schools', *Comparative Education Review*, 51:1, pp 95–115

Munro E., Maskell-Graham D., Ward H. and National Care Advisory Service (2010) *Evaluation of the Staying Put 18+ Family Placement Pilot Programme, Interim Report, Overview of Emerging Themes and Issues*, London: Department of Education

Munro E. R. (2011) *The Munro Review of Child Protection: Final report – a child centred system*, London: The Stationery Office

Munro E. R., Lushey C., Ward H. and National Care Advisory Service (2011) *Evaluation of the Right2BCared4 Pilots: Research brief*, London: Department of Education

Murray L., Tarren-Sweeney M. and France K. (2011) 'Foster carer perceptions of support and training in the context of high burden of care', *Child and Family Social Work*, 16, pp 149–58

Nandy L. (2007) *Going it Alone: Children in the asylum process*, London: The Children's Society

National Institute for Health and Clinical Excellence (2010) 'Promoting the quality of life of looked-after children and young people', *NICE public health guidance 28*, London: NICE

Ni Raghallaigh M. (2011) 'Religion in the lives of unaccompanied minors: an available and compelling coping resource', *British Journal of Social Work*, 41, pp 529–56

Ni Raghallaigh M. and Gilligan R. (2010) 'Active survival in the lives of unaccompanied minors: coping strategies, resilience, and the relevance of religion', *Child and Family Social Work*, 15:2, pp 226–37

Ofsted (2003) *Ofsted: Education of Asylum Seeker Pupils*, Norwich: Ofsted Publications Centre

Portes A. (1998) 'Social capital: its origins and applications in modern sociology', *Annual Review of Sociology*, 24, pp 1–24

Portes A. and Borocz J. (1989) 'Contemporary immigration: theoretical perspectives on its determinants and modes of incorporation', *International Migration Review*, 23:3, pp 606–30

Putnam R. (1993) 'The prosperous community: social capital and public life', *American Prospect*, 13, pp 35–42

Quinton D., Rushton A., Dance C. and Mayes D. (1998) *Joining New Families: A study of adoption and fostering in middle childhood*, Chichester: Wiley

Radley A., Hodgetts D. and Cullen A. (2005) 'Visualising homelessness: a study in photography and estrangement', *Journal of Community and Applied Psychology*, 15:4, pp 273–95

Rees A., Holland S. and Pithouse A. (2010) 'Food in foster families: care, communication and conflict', *Children and Society*, doi: 10.1111/j.1099-0860.2010.00332.x.

Rees A. and Pithouse A. (2008) 'The intimate world of strangers – embodying the child in foster care', *Child & Family Social Work*, 13, pp 338–47

Refugee Action (2003) *Young Lives in Liverpool: Experiences and hope of young asylum seekers and refugees*, Liverpool: Refugee Action

Refugee Council (2006) *Unaccompanied Children and the Dublin II Regulation*, London: Refugee Council

Refugee Council (2010) *Recent Developments Relating to the Plans to Return Unaccompanied Children to Afghanistan*, Refugee Council Briefing, August, London: The Refugee Council

Remsbury N. (2003) *The Education of Refugee Children*, London: National Children's Bureau

Ressler E. M., Boothby N. and Steinbock D. J. (1988) *Unaccompanied Children: Care and protection in wars, natural disasters and refugee movements*, Oxford: Oxford University Press

Richman N. (1998) *In the Midst of the Whirlwind: A manual for helping refugee children*, London: Save the Children

Robinson D., Reeve K. and Casey R. (2007) *The Housing Pathways of New Immigrants*, York: Joseph Rowntree Foundation

Robinson V. and Segrott J. (2002) *Understanding the Decision Making of Asylum Seekers*, London: Home Office

Rousseau C., Said T. M., Gagne M. J. and Bibeau G. (1998) 'Resilience in unaccompanied minors from the north of Somalia', *Psychoanalytic Review*, 85, pp 615–37

Russell S. (1999) *Most Vulnerable of All: The treatment of unaccompanied refugee children in the UK*, London: Amnesty International

Rutter M. (1999) 'Resilience concepts and findings: implications for family therapy', *Journal of Family Therapy*, 21, pp 119–44

Rutter J. (2003a) *Supporting Refugee Children in 21st Century Britain: A compendium of essential information*, Stoke-on-Trent: Trentham Books

Rutter J. (2003b) *Working with Refugee Children*, York: Joseph Rowntree Foundation

Rutter J. (2004) *Aiming Higher: Guidance on supporting the education of asylum seeking and refugee children. A Guide to Good Practice*, London: Department for Education and Skills

Rutter J. (2006) *Refugee Children in the UK*, Maidenhead: Open University Press

Rutter J., Cooley L., Reynolds S. and Sheldon R. (2007) *From Refugee to Citizen: 'Standing On My Own Two Feet'*, London: IPPR

Rutter J. and Jones C. (eds) (1998) *Refugee Education: Mapping the field*, Stoke-on-Trent: Trentham Books

Ruuk N. D. (2002) *The Pharos School Prevention Programme Manual*, Canterbury: University of Kent

Save the Children (2003) *Young Refugees: A guide to the rights and entitlements of separated refugee children*, London: Save the Children

Schofield G. and Beek M. (2005) 'Risk and resilience in long-term foster-care', *British Journal of Social Work*, 35:8, pp 1283–1301

Schofield G. and Beek M. (2006) *Attachment Handbook for Foster Care and Adoption*, London: BAAF

Schofield G., Ward E., Warman A., Simmonds J. and Butler J. (2008) *Permanence in Foster Care: A study of care planning and practice in England and Wales*, London: BAAF

Sellick C. (2006) 'From famine to feast: a review of the foster care research literature', *Children and Society*, 20, pp 67–74

Selwyn J., Quinton D., Harris P., Wijedasaa D., Nawaz S. and Wood M. (2010) *Pathways to Permanence for Black, Asian and Mixed Ethnicity Children*, London: BAAF

Selwyn J., Saunders H. and Farmer E. (2010) 'The views of children and young people on being cared for by an independent foster-care provider', *British Journal of Social Work*, 40, pp 696–713

Separated Children in Europe Programme (2004) *Statement of Good Practice* (3rd edn), Copenhagen: International Save the Children Alliance in Europe/ UNHCR

Simon A. (2008) 'Early access and use of housing: care leavers and other young people in difficulty', *Child and Family Social Work*, 13:1, pp 91–100

Sinclair I. (1971) *Hostels for Probationers*, London: HMSO

Sinclair I. (2005) *Fostering Now: Messages from research*, London: Jessica Kingsley Publishers

Sinclair I., Baker C., Lee J. and Gibbs I. (2007) *The Pursuit of Permanence: A study of the English care system*, London: Jessica Kingsley Publishers

Sinclair I., Baker C., Wilson K. and Gibbs I. (2005a) *Foster Children: Where they go and how they get on*, London: Jessica Kingsley Publishers

Sinclair I. and Gibbs I. (1998) *Children's Homes: A study in diversity*, Chichester: Wiley

Sinclair I., Gibbs I. and Wilson K. (2004) *Foster Carers: Why they stay and why they leave*, London: Jessica Kingsley Publishers

Sinclair I., Wilson K. and Gibbs I. (2005b) *Foster Placements: Why they succeed and why they fail*, London: Jessica Kingsley Publishers

Sinha S. and Uppal S. (2009) 'Lesser youth? Particular universalisms and young separated migrants in East London', *Journal of Youth Studies*, 12:3, pp 257–73

Sirriyeh A. (2008)' Young asylum seekers' conceptions of "home" at a time of transition to adulthood', *International Journal of Migration, Health and Social Care*, 4:1, pp 12–27

Sirriyeh A. (2010a) 'Home journeys: im/mobilities in young refugee and asylum-seeking women's negotiations of home', *Childhood*, 17:2, pp 197–211

Sirriyeh A. (2010b) *Inhabiting the Borders: A study of 16-25 year old refugee women's narratives of home*, Leeds: University of Leeds

Sirriyeh A. (forthcoming) 'Hosting strangers: hospitality and family practices in foster care for unaccompanied refugee young people in the UK', *Journal of Refugee Studies*

Spicer N. (2008) 'Places of exclusion and inclusion: asylum-seeker and refugee experiences of neighbourhoods in the UK', *Journal of Ethnic and Migration Studies*, 34:3, pp 491–510

Stanley K. (2001) *Cold Comfort: Young separated refugees in England*, London: Save the Children

Stein M. (2004) *What Works for Young People Leaving Care?*, Barkingside: Barnardo's

Stein M. (2009) *Increasing the number of care leavers in "settled, safe accommodation"*, London: The Centre for Excellence and Outcomes in Children and Young People's Services (C4EO)

Stein M. (2010) *Increasing the Number of Care Leavers in 'Settled, Safe Accommodation'*, Knowledge Review 3, London: Centre for Excellence and Outcomes in Children and Young People's Services (C4EO)

Steinbock D. J. (1996) 'Unaccompanied refugee children in host country foster families', *International Journal of Refugee Law*, 8:1(2), pp 6–48

Stone R. (2000) *Children First and Foremost: Meeting the needs of unaccompanied asylum seeking children*, Barkingside: Barnardo's

Summerfield D. (1998) 'The social experience of war and some issues for the humanitarian field', in Bracken P. J. and Petty C. (eds), *Rethinking the Trauma of War*, London: Save the Children, pp 9–37

The Children's Legal Centre (2003) *Mapping the Provision of Education and Social Services for Refugee and Asylum Seeker Children: Lessons from the Eastern Region*, Colchester: The Children's Legal Centre, University of Essex

Thomas S., Thomas S., Nafees B. and Bhugra D. (2004) '"I was running away from death" – the pre-flight experiences of unaccompanied asylum seeking children in the UK', *Child: Care, Health and Development*, 30:2, pp 113–22

Tizard B. and Phoenix A. (1993) *Black, White or Mixed Race?*, London: Routledge

Tolfree D. K. (2003) *Community Based Care for Separated Children*, Stockholm: Save the Children

Tolfree D. K. (2004) *Whose Children? Separated children's protection and participation in emergencies*, Stockholm: Save the Children

Triseliotis J., Borland M. and Hill M. (2000) *Delivering Foster Care*, London: BAAF

United Nations High Commissioner for Refugees (UNHCR) (1994) *Working With Unaccompanied Minors in the Community: A family based approach*, Geneva: UNHCR

United Nations High Commissioner for Refugees (UNHCR) (2009) *2008 Global Trends: Refugees, asylum-seekers, returnees, internally displaced and stateless persons*, Geneva: UNHCR

Van Hear N. (1998) *New Diasporas: The mass exodus, dispersal and regrouping of migrant communities*, London: UCL Press

Van Hear N. (2006) 'I went as far as my money would take me', in Crepeau F., Nakache D. and Collyer M. (eds), *Forced Migration and Global Processes*, Maryland: Lexington Books

Van Horst H. (2004) 'Living in a reception centre: the search for home in an institutional setting', *Housing, Theory and Society*, 21:1, pp 36–46

Wade J. (2006) 'Support for young people leaving care in the UK', in McAuley C., Pecora P. and Rose W. (eds) *Enhancing the Well-Being of Children and Families Through Effective Interventions – UK and USA Evidence for Practice*, London: Jessica Kingsley Publishers, pp 228–39

Wade J. (2008) 'The ties that bind: support from birth families and substitute families for young people leaving care', *British Journal of Social Work*, 38, pp 39–54

Wade J. (2009) 'Placement for unaccompanied asylum-seeking children', in Schofield G. and Simmonds J. (eds), *The Child Placement Handbook: Research, policy and practice*, London: BAAF, pp 382–400

Wade J. (2011) 'Preparation and transition planning for unaccompanied asylum-seeking and refugee young people: a review of evidence in England', *Children and Youth Services Review*, 33:12, pp 2424–30

Wade J., Biehal N., Farrelly N. and Sinclair I. (2011) *Caring for Abused and Neglected Children: Making the right decisions for reunification or long-term care*, London: Jessica Kingsley Publishers

Wade J. and Dixon J. (2006) 'Making a home, finding a job: investigating early housing and employment outcomes for young people leaving care', *Child and Family Social Work*, 11:3, pp 199–208

Wade J., Mitchell F. and Baylis G. (2005) *Unaccompanied Asylum Seeking Children: The response of social work services*, London: BAAF

Walker S. (2011) *Something to Smile About: Promoting and supporting the educational and recreational needs of refugee children*, London: Refugee Council

Watson S. and Austerberry H. (1986) *Housing and Homelessness: A feminist perspective*, London: Routledge

Watters C. (2008) *Refugee Children: Towards the next horizon*, London: Routledge

Whenan R., Oxlad M. and Lushington K. (2009) 'Factors associated with foster carer well-being, satisfaction and intention to continue providing out-of-home care', *Children and Youth Services Review*, 31, pp 752–60

Williamson L., Rutter J. and Jones C. (1998) 'Unaccompanied – but not unsupported', in Rutter J. and Jones C. (eds), *Refugee Education: Mapping the field*, Stoke-on-Trent: Trentham Books, pp 49–74

Wilson K., Sinclair I., Taylor C., Pithouse A. and Sellick C. (2004) 'Fostering success: an exploration of the research literature in foster care', *Knowledge Review 5*, Bristol: The Policy Press

Wilson K., Sinclair I., Taylor C., Pithouse A. and Sellick C. (2005) *Fostering Success: An exploration of the research literature in foster care*, London: Social Care Institute for Excellence

Yaya B. (1998) 'Finding substitute carers for unaccompanied refugee children: the European dimension', *Social Work in Europe*, 3:3, pp 49–51

Index